Concrete Leprechaun

Bronx Boy Does Life

By Stephen Walsh

For information regarding permission, please write to:
info@barringerpublishing.com
Barringer Publishing, Naples, Florida
www.barringerpublishing.com

Design and Layout by Linda S. Duider
Cape Coral, Florida

Cover by Tara Walsh

ISBN: 978-1-954396-76-0
Library of Congress Cataloging-in-Publication Data
Concrete Leprechaun / Stephen Walsh

Printed in U.S.A.

CONTENTS

THE BRONX

There's no 'the' Brooklyn, or 'the' Queens, or 'the' Manhattan, or 'the' Staten Island (assuming that's even a real place). But you bet your ass there's a 'The' Bronx! It begs to reason why you can't be 'the' man unless you get your mail in a Zip Code that starts with 104.

If the man refuses to be a boy, but the boy is not yet a man, and the two are really one, can the boy be a man when necessary? Further, does the man have the imperative to retreat back into the boy when that is equally needful? What if the line that separates the two is so fine as to make the distinction nearly impossible, given the moment in time when the separation occurs? If the gray area exists, it is so fleeting that it never is, in theory, real at all. Life does not merely unfold, it is thrust upon you. To a sixteen-year-old male whose world thus far has been limited to a small region of the great, big universe, things may occur that he never planned for, and sometimes those things can even be tragic. But whether within his power or not, such matters must be dealt with. The decision to confront, or to retreat, will determine his fabric. He can stand up and be the man, but when that responsibility becomes overwhelming, so much so that it depletes him to the point of ruin, becoming the boy again may be his only savior.

And other soupy, philosophical bullshit emanating from the concrete beneath our feet.

I'm your all-American boy—stout and brave, a heart of gold, and a body of steel. Brains and guile I have in abundance. I'm hung like a donkey, and am an accomplished swordsman. The blood of the two most dominant civilizations known to mankind, that indistinguishably being of the Irish and of the Americans, courses through my veins. Of all my infinite virtues, perhaps the greatest gift that the Almighty has bestowed upon me is my devilishly magnificent good looks. In other words, I, Jack McGee, am the fucking cat's meow.

THE BRONX

"Hey Al, you ever love someone so much it hurts?"

"Yeah man, everywhere but my wooden leg."

"If you really loved her, it would even hurt there, it'd hurt everywhere."

"Shit man, who dis beauty queen got you all wrapped up in desire?"

"Ain't just desire, my brother, it's 10,000 other emotions as well—problem is, she's way outta my league—won't have nothing to do with my poor Irish ass."

"Sound like you be aimin' you little Irish gun at the wrong target."

"Yeah, I guess that's so. Don't make it any easier knowing though. Hey, you fat Jamaican fuck—I need to open the gas station in like three fuckin' hours. If I leave now, I can still get an hour or two of sleep. What say we light up this cannabis cigarette before I depart, help both of us sleep."

"Save your white boy, windowsill-grown, impostor weed yo. We gonna smoke some shit from the motherfucking cradle of civilization—that being the land of my origin and the most bee-u-ti-ful fuckin' place on god's earth—that being Ja-may-ka! Knock your white ass the fuck out."

"Get it goin' and done, my man. I need to go beddy-by."

CHAPTER 1

Sweet, Sweet Summertime
in the Land of Strength
and Struggle—The Bronx, NY

That summer they dropped like flies—on ludes and barbs and heroin and booze and knives and baseball bats. The Grim Reaper never seemed to take a day off. Spanky was the first to go—90 degrees and the middle of the day, before the beach chairs came out on the sidewalk, and before Jack the ice cream man rang his bell. Couldn't have been much later than two or three o'clock; the sun and humidity suffocating the air out of all us, trying as we might to pay it no mind. So there he was, a junkie being administered to by other junkies—a kind of junkie honor system.

Spanky, barely aware of his being, was crossing Creston Avenue while being held from collapsing by Chico, the Albanian, and Mikey King, former badass stud and heart slayer, now reduced to scrawny nothingness.

Spanky was a collage of colors: blue-ish skin, green vomit, and crimson nose blood. People were coming to attention; the heads of neighborhood women popping out of just opened windows—everyone sensing that something was wrong.

"Call an ambulance; someone get the police; someone run and get his mother, or his brothers."

Spanky, one of six, was never much of a problem; never one of those kids you'd ever expect to do something this horrific. Got his nickname from his baby face, the child-aged likeness to the Little Rascal. Things were not looking good—one of my friend's fathers, an off-duty cop, taking things over—harshly dismissing the good Samaritan junk heads—orchestrating control. Spanky sliding into the abyss, his eyeballs pushing high up inside his skull, the skin a ghastly white/gray now, his limbs atremble, fluids erupting from his mouth and now more ominously, from his nose and ears. An ambulance finally arrives. Spanky's brother, sister, and mother now at his side; the sister letting out a sickly, terrified moan, his brother begging him to survive, his mother knowing, as mothers tend to know, that all was now lost between her and her little boy. The boy she gave birth to; the boy she never stopped loving.

THE BRONX

Spanky died, of course. We all knew he would. He was the first that summer, but he was far from the last. Within weeks, his buddy, Chico, was dead, eerily in almost the exact manner, at almost the same time of day, with the same blistering hot weather, and in the same nondescript place. And then there was Sandy, Robert the Jew's sister, and Phil Magnum, another lady killer and future all-American boy, choking to death on his own vomit. And, of course, those lesser-known junkies, the ones we'd all waited on to die anyway, making us soothsayers when they passed their last breath and floated into oblivion.

Then Johnnie Boy Jones perished under the el trains on Jerome Avenue, inside a cardboard box. Sheila, Johnny Boy's punching bag girlfriend, apparently too distraught to go on, pulled off the same trick barely a week later. Even in the depths of hell, love has no conqueror. All around us, the junk heads fell like autumn leaves. Even the glue sniffers and whip cream can inhalers, who try to scrounge up enough coins to get themselves a handful of ludes, find big enough handfuls to send themselves to early graves.

But Father Death has many venues, and a vast repertoire of peril he did wield. Larry Mullin, a nineteen-year-old who never wore anything but black, more Lucifer than western outlaw, hacked his aging parents to death in the hallway outside their apartment on 199th Street. The excitement of the news trucks and crime scene tape being more than us kids could stand—celebrity, either light or dark, is still celebrity. Imagine a double murder in your very own backyard? Stuff to tell the grandkids. Maybe get me on *Eyewitness News*.

Then there was Tommy Stack, forlorn and broken-hearted, young father of three, who caught his wife in the sack with his best friend and beat her to death with a baseball bat while his best bud grabbed his pants and ran. His children orphaned not too long after when Tommy hung himself in his Rikers Island cell.

And the miscellaneous stabbings and car crashes and assorted misery that come and go in the land of strength and struggle—the Bronx, NY.

THE BRONX

Meanwhile, the likes of me, Jack McGee and his boys, kept on movin' on in pursuit of "The American Dream" in the land of milk and honey.

"Jack get up, it's time for work—get up."

"Waaaa—oh shit, what time is it, Ma?"

"Watch your mouth smart guy—5 minutes to 7."

"Oh shh . . . eesh. I'm late. Oh man, my fu . . . nny head is killing me."

"Don't look to me for sympathy."

"You're a peach, Ma—your empathy knows no bounds—gotta move, I'll see you later."

"By the way, you see your brother around? He hasn't made it home yet."

"Last I saw him was at Harris Field last night. He disappeared with his girlfriend, and as far as I know, it wasn't my turn to watch him."

"Go on, get the hell out of here before I give you a good kick up yer ass."

"Love you too, Ma."

THE BRONX

Seven a.m., turning the keys to the gas station lock, American dream job here I come; it's another day in paradise. The inside of my head mimicks the sensation of an empty soda can in a drying machine. Hollywood, the scraggly German Shepherd and guard dog supreme, comes running over to greet me. Some days she bites at me, but this day, fortunately, she does not. Her grease-matted, mangy coat is repulsive enough; she gets no love from me.

The ritual begins: turning on the pumps, counting inventory, sticking the tanks for measure, and counting out the day's starting cashbox. When I open the bay door, Hollywood scampers out and makes her way across Jerome Avenue on her way to the Greek diner. In about 10 minutes, the Greek will be outside screaming across at me to come fetch my dog, after Hollywood has terrorized the place, climbing up on a random table to steal someone's eggs. As is apt to happen, if history repeats itself, things will go downhill from there.

I want to come alive to the morning dew, baste in the joy of existence, but my hangover is too fierce for any of that, and slime and grease don't provide much of a pastoral setting.

Hollywood tied up safely inside, I started to get my first customers. Mostly straightforward, one after the other, five dollars worth here, ten dollars worth there, hustling to wash windshields and check oil and tranny fluid to scrounge extra cash from tips. The whole time I'm doing two or three things at once, but always staying completely aware of my surroundings.

The majority of the customers are decent and honest but, this being the Bronx, NY, many are not. There's always someone trying to reset the pumps to zero after pumping some gas, and pretty much everything on the property is in danger of being stolen, no matter how useless it will be to the thief. I once chased some crazy fucker three blocks to retrieve an oil filter he stole, maybe to match it to a car he hadn't yet stole. I'm guessing he was hoping that when the time came, they'd match. I must have rules—cash upfront and nobody pumps their own gas—and fuck it if I hurt your feelings.

I also needed to be strategic and prepared on top of being alert. Murphy's law doesn't apply when you expect the worst, all of the time. I made sure I was never more than a few steps from where I had weapons stashed, a tire iron here, a mallet or an ax there. Ready to grab and swing, damage and sting. Try to skip without paying and get a smashed-in car window. If you're planning to rob the place, be sure to bring a gun.

It wasn't much more than an hour after I opened, my hangover waning, that life again was seeping into my veins. A guy comes in, pretty normal looking. Clean shirt and pants, shoes not sneakers. Hair combed neatly and held in place by some Vitalis.

"Here to pick up my car . . . Green Dodge."

So, I pull the work receipt and slap it on the table in front of him—brake job and a new battery. "That'll be $260," I say.

"$260?" says he.

"Yup. In cash and she's all yours."

"Bob told me $180! This is bullshit! Listen kid, I know it ain't your doin', I'll take it up with Bob tomorrow. Take the 180 and I'll pay the rest after I talk to Bob."

"Can't help you, man," says I. "Bob says I don't turn over any keys unless I get full payment in cash."

And thus, his tone changes: "Are you shittin' me? Listen you little fuckin' punk, give me the keys or I'm going to light this fuckin' place on fire."

"Suit yourself. But bonfire or no bonfire I ain't letting the car go without full payment."

So now the guy is agitated beyond belief and muttering all kinds of threats about fire, dynamite, broken windows, and even a bazooka. Storms away across Jerome Avenue, cursing and screaming the whole time. Sounds like idle boasts but who knows? Keys safely in my pocket, his car still on the lot, I sauntered over to help a customer. The lady wants to know what just transpired and I dismiss it as the rantings of a lunatic. I gas her up, take the money, and wish her a fine day. Same thing goes for the next three or four customers, and a half hour passes without further incident. Then I hear the screeching of tires coming down Bedford Park Road and my instincts tell me that they somehow have something to do with me.

Mister '80 dollars shy' apparently went and borrowed someone's car, and before he could get a wrap around his emotions, decided he'd run over the one person (me) he hated most at the moment. A customer had just pulled out, leaving me standing exposed out in the open. The screeching tires were nearly upon me. The car's engine raged, but not to the extent as its driver. I ducked between pumps just as the car skidded past me, feeling the force of the metal in the small distance between us. I was not only still alive and unscathed, but I was also very much alive, and eager to turn the tides.

The homicidal vehicle swung in a U-ey, headed back in the direction it came from, and was forced into a violent stop by a car waiting out a red light in front of it. The number of lunatics involved had increased by one, and I was the lunatic in charge now.

I grabbed the aforementioned tire iron and closed in on 'Eighty-short' as he sat stymied, unable to move his car, and equally unable to activate his thoughts. From diesel to weasel you might say and praying for a hole to scamper into. With little thought given to mode of execution, I sprung on the scene like a rat shot from a cannon. First, I smashed in the driver's side window, sending shattered glass into the car's chamber, and then, as he was pulling away, I took a swipe at the rear window but barely made contact.

Despite coming up somewhat short on my second swing, I think my intended assailant comfortably got my point. As he raced away, I stood out in the middle of Jerome Avenue, tire-iron in hand, spewing invectives at the fleeing vehicle. In a strange way, I felt pretty damn well-pleased with myself, as my victorious champion's posture might suggest. The excitement didn't go unnoticed, and a peripheral crowd of onlookers had assembled. The looks on their faces ranged from surprise to amusement to horror. It was then that I noticed her, the girl from the neighborhood, the new face on the block—the beauty in the land of eyesores. She was staring directly at me, mouth agape, a hand held up as if to stifle a scream. When our eyes met, she composed herself briefly, and then rushed off as if fleeing the lava from a volcano.

THE BRONX

"Hey, McGee, what's up? You hear that racket last night? Old man Moran must have tied one on tight and decided to terrorize his family again. You fuckin' micks are all a bunch of drunks and wife beaters."

"Listen you fuckin' swarthy greaseball, keep your trap shut before I make you swallow your teeth like a bunch of little macaroni. That family is going through some tough times and no one, especially a dumbass guinea like yourself needs to remind them. Mind your own goddamn business."

"Hey, don't get so friggin' testy, McGee. I was just sayin', you know, that some shit went on last night and everyone and their friggin' mother knows about it."

"I hear ya, Sal. Just breaks my heart with that kid of theirs being sick and the stress that family is going through. Whatta you feel like doing today? The fuckin' walls of this neighborhood are closing in on me."

"How bout we take a train ride? Everyone else can ride inside, we'll ride outside."

"Deal."

THE BRONX

First day at the new school and 'how to make friends and influence people' is the operating mantra for the day. Saint Joseph's Prep, a boner of a misnomer if ever one existed. Not sure what is intended with the 'prep' but I doubt if it has anything to do with preparing me to be an outstanding man of the future, unless that man has designs on being a petty criminal, drunk, drug addict or an all-star miscreant. Located in the bucolic 'park' section of the Bronx, nestled between the Grand Concourse and River Avenue, with unmatched views of Yankee Stadium and the Bronx County courthouse, St. Joe's continues to churn out eventual college dropouts at an alarming rate. Most pathetically, it is all male, a cold, cold shower after two years at a coed high school, where plaid skirts with knee-high socks awaited me in every classroom.

St. Joe's is, essentially, the school you go to when all the other Catholic schools won't have you. If you're a disciplinary nightmare, or say mildly retarded, it is the institution of higher learning for you. Fortunately, I am of the former category, and with many classmates of the latter category abounding, I am the one-eyed king in the land of the blind. These kids will actually pay me to help them with their third-grade level math problems. Though it is a poor choice for educational enlightenment, it is a far better option than the public schools. The public high schools of the Bronx are 'schools' in name and theory only. Halfway houses and holding pens are more apt descriptions. If you're a white boy attending a school that is 10% white and 'other,' with the 'other' being white-hating, non-whites, then education takes a distant back seat to self-preservation.

Nothing of substance happens in a math class but math is not an overlooked concentration—everyone knows at least a little math—"1 for 2, 3 for 5," says the cannabis merchant. "My cousin's doing a 15 stretch with a chance of parole after 10 and could be out in five with good behavior, but that's a million to one chance with that crazy ass motherfucker," says the odds maker. "I count to 10 your white ass bess be five miles the fuck away or I'm gonna cut you open like a mango," says the diplomat. If you're a white boy at DeWitt Clinton or Roosevelt H.S., you may never learn any of the names of those historic early Americans who signed the Declaration of Independence, but you will know how to curse fluently in Spanish, and how to flash the Black Panthers salute. You will also learn never to turn your back or let your guard down, not for one fucking second.

St. Joe's, in contrast to public (non) education, has the societal norms of the public schools contorted. The negroes and portable-Ricans are more earnest in their educational pursuits; they're there because they want to be there, unlike the whites who would rather be somewhere else. The white kids wear long hair because this is the rare Catholic school that has no hair length restrictions. We're not going for the hippie look, more the caucasian Comanche look.

We're the misfits who couldn't get into the more demanding Catholic schools. The inmates run the asylum here, and the darker persuasions fear us, not us them. It's an aspiration to be a badass, albeit a necessary character trait. It was upon this platform that I received my first invitation to make new friends, on my very first day of the new school year.

"We're fightin' the niggers after school," said Doheny, the prototype, large-headed mick. "You in or out?"

I was in, of course. What choice did I have? I could not appear to be a coward, nor could I pretend not to hate niggers and spics the way any properly exposed Irish kid from the Bronx should.

It's 2:45 in Mullally Park, directly across from the front entrance to St. Joe's, and the shit has shown no hesitation to hit the fan. I'm standing close to the front of the pack, making sure everyone can see me, and conclude that I'm no pussy. The 'whites' have been more successful in their community organizing and consequently outnumber the 'non-whites' by at least a 2 to 1 margin. No coin need be flipped nor does any judge caution the combatants to fight fair.

We pounce with the intention to maim. Mike Doyle is swinging a car antenna at every natty head of hair within reach, and Brendan Burns has some guy by the back of the neck and is attempting to smash his head on a park bench. Fists fly and kicks flail amid screams of 'honkie,' 'nigger,' and 'spic.' Good Catholic boys emanating hate from every blessed pore. Some black dude is in a kung-fu stance challenging someone to try him, a strategy that does not serve him well as he gets knocked forcefully on his black ass by a well-placed, pale cement fist.

Amidst the chaos comes the desperate voice of reason— Brother Kearns, our esteemed principal, has arrived on the scene, his high-pitched voice demanding an end to the violence. He pulls the car antennae from Doyle and then catches a punch to the head trying to break up a pair of combatants. His face registers horror, his voice dismay. He has dedicated his life to these boys, to their education, to their moral conditioning; he cannot believe what he is witnessing. No doubt, he has lots of doubt concerning his career choice.

The collateral damage was limited: loose teeth, lacerations, and a black eye or two. Order has been restored by Brother Kearns and some of the other high school personnel, none too soon. The local residents, brought to fury at the sight of their ethnic brethren under siege, were moving aggressively towards the park amid the landscape of violence, with the promise of a much greater collision threatening to unravel. As if sent by Jesus Christ himself, we now hear cherry tops whirring and with cops jumping out of patrol cars, tensions at once abate and the good little schoolboys head back to their lessons. For my part, I got some blood along the front of my shirt and some kind of stinging wound across my back. I have barely any recollection of who I hit or who hit me. I know I have accounted well for myself with my new group of friends—I at least appeared to not be afraid and to hate sincerely—I could expect to be an accepted member of the pack going forward.

THE BRONX

Waking up, I brush my teeth, and immediately sense that the only thing that's got a chance of changing around here is my underwear. You have no choice, kid, you need to keep rolling with the punches. What happens next has a whole lot less to do with anything than what I do about it. Keep your chin up, lad, and don't bat an eye when fear tries to best you in a staring contest.

Chapter 2

God Created Alcohol to Keep the Irish from Ruling the World

Things are hardly rosy at home. Mom is working crazy hours at night, and we're left to fend for ourselves. Being the lone breadwinner is her reward for a life hard-lived. She was thirty years old with five kids when the old man was gunned down like a dog, working the stick behind the bar he'd saved over a decade to buy. Two lowlifes, from south of Fordham Road, decided his life was worth less than the measly take from the cash register. Shot in the neck and chest, he bled out before the first ambulance arrived.

There were several eyewitnesses, all happy to have escaped alive, and the scumbags were caught within hours; too stupid to take enough precaution, they were caught with the gun and the money, One of them, this Puerto Rican motherfucker named Jiminez, was beaten to death in custody by 'Nutsy' O'Ryan, one of New York's finest and a lifelong friend of my dad, shortly after he was apprehended. He made sure we all knew how Jiminez died, and he recounted his last moments, moments of agony and suffering, so we'd know just how much he loved our dad. It was nearly as satisfying as it would have been to torture and kill the bastard myself.

Nutsy, fingered and accused of manslaughter, spent years and a career to defend himself, eventually trading his badge for a paintbrush and a hammer. A PR (Puerto Rican) in a grave, another behind bars along with a dope fiend coon, five fatherless kids, and a bereaved widow—the game of life with no winners.

We do the best we can to keep our heads above water and do an adequate job of looking out for each other but it's hard getting everyone on the same page. All six of us crammed into a rathole of an apartment, getting on each other's nerves, each of us pushing for space that doesn't exist. Mom waits tables till after midnight most nights and then is up early to get the house in order and then right back at it again and again, climbing the insurmountable, treading water that's thicker than quicksand. There's no quit in the old girl, she shows up for life every day and fights the fight she has little chance of winning. But she is not the type to complain despite hardships that would bring even strong men to their knees. We are stoics, us Irish, and crying is for those who can afford it. So, like mom, we trudge along and keep the emotions inside. Better stuffed deep than out in the open where it can only bring trouble. Whatever you say, say nothing, the micks are apt to say.

THE BRONX

I caught my little sister, Cathy, hanging out in the schoolyard drinking beer and smoking Marlboros like she was some hotshit wannabee hoodlum. It was after 11 p.m and I was sent as a search party to find out where my 14-year-old sister could possibly be. I assumed the worst and was rewarded for my optimism when I turned the corner by the playground to see her blowing circles with her cigarette smoke. Our eyes met instantly, and she mouthed 'Oh shit' as they did. Her friend, Joanie, the daughter of a pair of drunks, long past being intimidated by anyone, ogled me with disdain. The two guys who were with them held their ground, tough guys with hearts of steel, or so they thought. "Get your ass home now," I shouted as I moved upon her and kicked her hard enough up the ass to send her three feet in the air.

One of the males, who I'd never seen before, jumped to his feet with a 'yo' and took a step in my direction as if he planned to intercede. It was just enough stupidity on his part to move me to the next level of rage, the level that can't be wound back, the level that has no relationship with reason, the level that brings out demons you didn't know you had. I left him a bloody mess and was not 100% sure I hadn't killed him.

But the thing that stuck with me after that night was how worried I was when my little sister went AWOL. The tricks my mind played on me by assuming the worst. How my life would be destroyed if anything tragic happened to her, or anyone else in my family. And the ironic thing here was that I was my little sister in spades, time after time not coming home at night, no one knowing where I was. Off on another drunken escapade, I never stopped to think of the terror I was plunging into my mother's heart as she sat up praying I'd be walking in the door in one piece.

THE BRONX

From a distance they look like cotton bunnies, little balls of fur dancing in the haze of sunlight, a kaleidoscope of pastel colors. Me and Bobby, riding in his fire engine red Fury, with the Doors blaring at deafening decibels. I reach over to turn down the volume as we approach the curb and Bobby slaps my hand, but I smile and ask him to trust me. The bright colors are there in front of us now—pink, yellow, baby blue—the girls of Mount Saint Ursula, congregating outside school in their summer uniforms. The music lowered, the cacophony of their voices now a melody.

"*Bonjour mademoiselles,*" I say to a group of five or so that awkwardly approach the car. They giggle amongst themselves, but they are more intrigued than dismissive. "Got a cigarette?" asks the ringleader, a young gal with angular Napoleonic features who had already captured my attention and a small chunk of my heart.

Jim Morrison implores me from the background if 'I love her madly,' and yes, Jim, at this moment I surely do. "Love me two times, babe, love me twice today." Well, Jimmy boy, they say three times is a charm.

Bobby slides a Marlboro from his box and hands it to me. I light it in my mouth, take a nice long pull, and hand it to the fair maiden. She doesn't hesitate and immediately takes the cigarette from my hand and takes a drag, longer and deeper than mine, with a bewitching flare. A highly favorable gesture on her part, and I hope her heart beats for me as mine doth for her.

Before our epic love story can be carved for the ages, a hefty voice, emerging from the backdrop of the pastel collage, commands the young ladies to cease and desist and pretty much get the fuck away from Bobby's Fury. Adorned in the traditional black-and-white, Mother Penguin chases her charges back to the safety of the school's outer walls.

A menacing figure she, no words are necessary for us to get her drift. Now Mick is on the radio telling us we can't get no satisfaction, and I concur for the moment only—to the young and ambitious, satisfaction must be achieved, not expected. The search goes on, the day is young, and the future, like a beautiful woman, makes promises it can't possibly keep.

THE BRONX

Willie the Rogue is an institution for the denizens of Creston Avenue. A World War II veteran who never left the states, his heroism in simple matters has shaped the man. He is a source of endless entertainment; he's a railcar hobo who manages to never wander far. A library of hilarious anecdotes, he is a delightful prince whose kingdom was built from tar and concrete.

This morning, like most mornings of his life, he beckons himself to abstain from all manner of bewitching liquids and honor the professional appointments he's scheduled. The Rogue, you see, is a window washer by trade. Today, he has yet again endeavored to wash the windows in the apartments of the various widowed ladies who look forward to his arrival. They refer to him as William. Rumors of the occasional dalliance follow him through their doors.

Dressed smartly, in his green khaki work pants, accentuated with a gleaming white T-shirt, hair neatly combed, the tools of his trade—rags and a spray bottle— faithfully at his side, he strolls amiably down the street. Black Irish from the roots of his slicked back ebony hair to the darker recesses of his soul. A decent man at heart, his intentions always start honorably. Any imbibing, he again tells himself, will have to wait until the work is done.

But the claws of the liquified monster are powerful. Temptation to a man like Bill is no less acute than what Adam endured in Eden. Offered a cold can of Rheingold, he jumped the starting gun, instantaneously headed to his daily fate of dismal failure. His loss is always our gain as we now have his companionship assured. A day of hilarity awaits all fortunate enough to cross his path.

"A friendly game of Casino fellas? Jackie, my boy, neither gentleman nor scholar," and so on and so on, the joviality spreads with each wisecrack. More than a dozen times he will have just one more beer. "There are windows to be washed, and the damsels await," will be his oft repeated mantra.

There will, of course, be no windows washed today. The women will wait in loneliness, anxious for human contact. The comical stories, ones we've heard a million times, will commence. The one where he's supposedly in front of the army shrink who asks him 'what would you do if you saw a submarine in the desert.' To which the Rogue replies, 'I'd sink it with my battleship!' 'And where exactly would you find a battleship?' retorts the brain doc. 'The same fucking place you found the submarine,' Willie concludes. We laugh sincerely, as the delivery is what makes the joke. Slowly the fire stops to burn and as the sun begins to set, Willie the Rogue falls asleep on the pavement, slumped down against a wall. Some hours later, when no one else is around, he'll gather up his things and make his way home.

THE BRONX

I woke up this morning with a monstrous hangover. It felt like my head was my balls, and my balls were dipped in a boiling cauldron of battery acid. For most of the night, I was drinking vodka and grapefruit juice which explains the acidity sensation, but I seem to recall doing shots of Jack Daniels as well. I also smoked a ton of cigarettes which I bummed all around, being how I don't smoke so have no need to carry around a pack of the ol' cancer sticks. My throat was so parched when I dragged myself from bed that I would have swallowed sewer water if it were within arm's length.

Through the fog of my surviving brain cells, there's a recollection of a conversation with this girl, Laura, who I'm kind of seeing. She said something to the tune of me having a drinking problem and ruining my life. I doubt I responded so hence no memories of a further dialogue.

Get that! A sixteen-year-old with a drinking problem. I'm no expert but there's gotta be an age minimum to be a drunk. It's like denying an adult midget a ride on a roller coaster because he doesn't meet the height requirement. Common sense must be the judge and jury, no? Well, I've ruined many a relationship and this won't be the last. She wasn't my type anyway.

THE BRONX

"McGee, what's an Irish seven-course meal?"

"Gee, Sal, let me think for a second . . . hmmmmm . . . a six-pack and a potato? You told me that lame joke a week ago but you're too fuckin' stupid to remember. But the gloves are off now, and I have a joke or two for you."

"Oh, here we go!"

"Why wasn't Jesus born in Italy?"

"Why ya prick?"

"They couldn't find three wise men and a virgin."

"Oh, man."

"How do you find the bride at an Italian wedding?"

"She's the one that's hot, not like some Irish pig?"

"She's the one with the braided armpits!"

"Awright enough now . . ."

"Listen, you dumb, guinea, dog fucker, an I-talian should never try and match wits with an Irishmen. Lost cause, game over, go choke on a bowl of overcooked spaghetti. We're talking about different stratospheres of intellect here—two different gene pools. Your ancestors are the ones at the rear of Darwin's evolution but you're too stupid to know who Darwin is anyway. You probably think he plays for the Mets, who suck by the way."

"Okay, Jack, why don't you rattle off the names of all the great Irish artists? We got Michaelangelo and all them other guys."

"Like Mussolini?"

"Yeah him, too."

"So, there's no Irish barbers or chefs either—right?"

"The fuckin' micks can't cook, unless it's boiled potatoes."

"Precisely. Know why? Cause the Irish are too masculine for shit like cooking, painting, and cutting other men's hair. And they are busy banging all the Italian broads, the good-looking ones that is."

"Yeah sure . . . with your little Irish peckers."

"That's why they call us donkeys, because we're hung like them. Let's get some beers, It's hard talking to someone like you when I'm sober."

THE BRONX

The key to happiness is surrounding yourself with some funny fuckers. That and a steady supply of your favorite beverage and the occasional piece—maybe throw in a fist fight now and then to keep your spirits up.

Chapter 3

Local Denizens: The Good, The Bad, and The Downright Ugly

The A-rab oil embargo situation did more for race relations in the Bronx than a thousand Nobel Peace Prize winners could ever come close to accomplishing. Me and a few of the boys were on Fordham Road to get the world's best hot dogs at Gorman's, and to see if we could scare up a little excitement. We were crossing the Grand Concourse from the east side to the west when we heard a commotion. It was near the spot where we'd usually harass the Hari Krishnas. A large crowd had gathered around a group of about 10 people, male and female, carrying American flags and various cardboard signs. They were chanting stuff about Americans not being pussies and the need and desire to kill every last Saudi Arabian or any other Arabs within 10,000 miles of there. That last bit was a real crowd pleaser, and every ensuing mention of complete Arab eradication was met with raucous applause.

What made the entire spectacle fascinating was that the crowd was a jumbled mass of the various races mutually rooting against the same thing, Soul brothers who detested honkies who hated Puerto Ricans who in turn loathed them both, were high fiving each other and proclaiming death to all things Saudi Arabia. Damn if us Bronxites are gonna let those goat fuckers jack the price of oil without doing something, whatever that something could possibly be.

It's a strange concept to view collective hate as poignant but this was! People had, at least for the absolute present, forgotten their disdain for each other and were uniting in a common cause. The Bronxites, it seemed, just needed someone to hate. And the object of that hate had miraculously created a common benevolence.

Our crew of comedians was busy entertaining the crowd with verbal depictions of the carnal pleasures of the Saudi man, like fornication with sheep and camels and such. My guess was that many of the bystanders couldn't find Saudi Arabia on a map if you spotted them the continent, a few neighboring countries, and nine of the eleven letters. All they knew, or thought they knew, was that there was a lot of sand and a lot of people with hairy backs.

My game was on, and I rattled off one slanderous anti-Arab joke after another. A hot Puerto Rican chic who I'm sure didn't get half the shit I was spewing laughed along nonetheless and cast googly eyes in my direction. A tall, black dude with a monster afro told me 'you one funny motherfucker white boy'—which I took as touching, though not quite to the level of shedding a tear. But it was yet another beautiful miracle in a day of many when dogs loved cats, and all colors rolled into one. Love is merely the crystallization of hate, I concluded. Raise a beer to the destruction of Saudi Arabia! That beautiful melting pot of humanity—the Bronx, NY!

THE BRONX

I like being up early and being outside before the world gets busy, maybe grab a dash of solitude. Free space and quiet are always in short supply around here. I usually take our dog, Chuck, with me and let him run loose in the vacant lot down the block. Chuck is a little scruffy thing with a Napoleonic complex. My mother found him as a stray a few years back and after feeding and washing him, she didn't have the heart to throw him back to the wolves. He's a mutt on both sides of his family lineage and probably has about ten different breeds of canine coursing through his blood. If I had to try and describe him as it pertains to his characteristics, I'd pretty much simplify it by saying he's like a Puerto Rican—small and scrawny but tough as shit. And he stinks! But in fairness to the Puerto Ricans, I know quite a few small and scrawny Irishmen who smell pretty awful themselves.

As Chuck ran around the lot aimlessly, I took a seat on one of the milk crates that substituted for a park bench. I lit up a cigarette that I'd stolen from my brother, a fucking Parliament no less, as if no one ever told him that it ain't a white man's first choice of tobacco. Get yourself some Marlboro for Christ's sake. Beggar's, of course, cannot be choosy. And thieves less so.

So, there I sat, puffing away, and doing my damndest to look cool even though there was small chance anyone could even see me. I was practicing blowing rings when Kenny Mullers strolled into the lot and grabbed a seat on the milk crate next to mine. He was dressed in some ill-fitting attire that was a poor stab at civilized haberdashery. He kind of looked like what you'd expect a guy to look like who was taken off the streets and dressed by nuns at a Salvation Army so that he'd be respectable on a job interview. In all likelihood, he was wearing the best his family had to offer for such an occasion.

Realizing I was taken aback to see him dressed so elegantly, he took a moment to explain. He was headed down to the courthouse on 161st Street to address a marijuana possession charge. Kenny was several years older than me and I felt a pang of prestige that he was giving me the time of day. But the man needed to talk to someone, and the choices were obviously limited. He was nervous about being sent to Rikers where long-haired white boys tend to be in the distinct minority, and rarely fare well. Many a story has circulated about the horrors inflicted on the white minorities in that 'wonderful institution.' Kenny had little desire to be someone's story. Or worse.

Given his uneasiness, it was little surprise that he would seek a remedy to calm his nerves, but it was quite a revelation to see a man about to face charges of drug possession fire up a doobie an hour or so before he was due before a judge. Out of politeness, I took a few tokes and wished him well. He was fucked, and I surmised that I wouldn't see him for a few months at the earliest, and when I did, he would have the sheepish appearance of one who's been through the fires of hell.

The Mullers family, since I'm on the topic, was an all-star collection of misfits and miscreants. They lived on the fifth floor of their building on Creston Avenue, but the five stories failed to provide enough of a sound buffer to the streets below. When the old man was drunk, and he was gassed more often than not, the symphony of screams and cursing bounced out of their windows and reverberated to the sidewalks below. It was pure encouragement to our group of aspiring hoodlums fifty feet below. As bad as we might have it, they had it worse.

The eldest Muller son, Marty, took the first chance he had at an exodus, but never managed to escape all that far. No Moses he. All of nineteen, he took up with a local divorcee who was at least ten years his senior. Marty was smitten and pledged eternal love for his chunky new love, Dee. Dee, already well past her prime despite being well south of middle-aged, took to Marty and his muscled torso, as if he were a male Lolita.

They moved in together almost immediately to try their hands at bliss; a bliss that proved to be fleeting. The thing was, Dee had an on again off again romance with heroin, and Marty was a heavy drinker with a penchant for rage. Their relationship was a Molotov cocktail with a fuse too short to ever stop an explosion. Dee, who worked late nights as a cocktail server, would often fall prey to her various temptations. Marty would sit on the couch waiting to hear the key turning in the lock of their apartment door. Every minute that passed beyond her expected time of arrival would notch up Marty's despair, and as per his demeanor, his despair turned to blind rage. Mister Hyde he became, one neck hair at a time.

Drunk and drifting towards psychosis, he took to the streets beckoning his beloved. 'Deeeee . . . Deeee . . .' he would call over and over again, as if the surrounding buildings held clues to her whereabouts. The hole in his heart grew deeper and darker with every pained lament. It was not the cherished Dee, however, who strained to listen to his call. Anyone who had witnessed Marty in this state before knew what was likely to ensue, so they kept their ears peeled to the howling outside.

If you were a male head of household, living below the third floor, you would jump from your bed or couch and prepare for the impending onslaught. To soothe his rage, Marty found release in tossing garbage cans through low lying windows. If garbage can hurl was an Olympic event Marty would have his ugly mush plastered on a box of Wheaties. Hence the terror that gripped the neighborhood.

The usual turn of events would unfold as such: before the cops would subdue him, Marty will have managed to successfully toss a couple of full garbage cans through lower floor windows and have fended off at least a few baseball bat swings from the local fathers whose windows he came too close to. Dee would, as always, miraculously appear just as her man was being thrown into the back seat of a patrol car. Later that night, she would bail him out, and with tears streaming down her cheeks, attest her never dying love. Marty would agree to pay for all damage incurred and move on to the next adventure. The story book romance would turn another page though never get to the happily ever after part.

The rest of the Mullers family would continue to take dysfunction to levels thought unachievable by even the worst of the wife-beaters, thieves, con-artists, and the all-around dregs of society. One family's war against normalcy would be a symbolic *Blitzkrieg* meant to annihilate the image of a Norman Rockwell world. Crazy from top to bottom and all shelves in between.

That's not to say they were all taboo in the neighborhood. Little Mikey, maybe the most sinister of them all, could be counted on to have your back in a brawl, or to gamely assist in a crime spree of your choosing. His older sister, the lovely Linda, could only be scorned by a man with poor eyesight and numbness below his belt. Last time I checked, I was no fag, so Linda was all right with me.

THE BRONX

It's never fun to be roused from a stupor with a shotgun barrel six inches from your head.

Thanks to my boy, Squid, that's exactly what happened to me the other Friday night. The evening had begun innocently enough with me and the Squidster enjoying a few beers and pondering an excursion on our motorcycles. We'd just wrapped up our shifts at the gas station and the warm summer night whispered excitement. Squid, who earned his nickname from his too noticeable lisp, mentioned a party his sister was throwing in a house over in the Soundview section of the Bronx. He wasn't from our neighborhood, and I was of the belief that a change of scenery is good for the soul. So, off we went on our two-wheelers, his a beat-up Sportster and mine a barely refurbished 750cc Triumph Trident that I bought for 400 bucks from a local junkie down on his luck.

Both of us, not quite drunk, at least as yet, set off into the budding night on our unlicensed, unregistered machines, sporting plates that we'd borrowed from unaware donors. There's something about being on a motorcycle that can make you feel invincible. The two of us shooting down Bedford Park Boulevard using traffic lights as suggestions and doing our damnedest to be loud and noticeable. Heading east towards the Bronx River Parkway, flashing the bird to groups of non-caucasians as the neighborhoods turned a shade or two darker, maintaining our distance to keep the restless natives at bay. Fuck 'em, fuck 'em all, fuck every last one of the bastards and pray for a full tank and an even throttle.

The sun rotating into a blood orange glow, we cruise side by side in the middle lane headed to Squid's domain, the Soundview section of the Bronx. A car swerves recklessly into our lane just in front of us and almost takes out our bikes. Squid is incensed and guns his motor until he's now alongside the offender. I can barely make out what he's saying but I know my man is swearing profusely, promising bodily harm. The guy driving the car yelling something back when Squid does the improbable and stretches out his right leg in an attempt to kick the prick in his head through the driver's side window, a stunt I'm not sure even Evel Knievel would have the guts to pull. Squid seems to disappear from sight for a second but then miraculously bounces back up steadying himself, another of his nine lives now used up. I am dizzy with amazement. The car and its driver are now far off in the distance. Unable to speak, we communicate with nods and hand signals. Squid, seemingly unperturbed by his near-death experience, flashes me a huge grin.

By now, I've lost all sense of direction, and I have no idea where I am or where I am headed. Soundview is a strange place. We ride alongside the water where bridge lights glimmer in the distance, and I notice small houses that look like shacks. What used to be a summer respite for New Yorkers is now permanent housing for the locals, a mix of shanty Irish, spics, and spades. Where cultures collide with the Enlightenment tools of fists, knives, and tire irons.

Squid pulls up in front of a crowd on a wide boulevard of four lanes, two in each direction. I pulled up next to him and we both shut off our bikes and dismount. My kickstand is slightly mangled, and I feel like an idiot as I lean my cycle against a light pole, Squid now laughing and breaking balls with his motley assortment of friends. His buddy, Skeets, reaches into a brown paper bag and presents us with a couple of cold ones. I am quite gracious, my throat dry and burnt from the ride. I'm introduced all around and my immediate impression is that Soundview doesn't have any dentists. Teeth are overrated anyway and missing some is a steel case sign that these boys are definitely not a pack of sissies. These fellas can turn any night into a carnival.

Squid is physically imposing for a guy who's not quite seventeen, and it's obvious he commands a certain respect from this assemblage, despite most of them being three or four years his senior. The atmosphere on Soundview Avenue is comic book surreal. There's money changing hands between opposing corners with the onset of streetcar races percolating in the imminent future. Amazingly, everyone seems to be getting along despite the range of skin color and assumed predilections. The homeboys and white boys high fiving each other, sharing laughs and even beers. There's one of every ilk here, including a few Albanians leaning against their evening entry—a jacked-up Trans Am that looks like it was painted by a gay, color-blind Puerto Rican. The Albanians are given a wide berth despite being in the distinct minority. Albanians without guns are like albino lobsters, unicorns, and Irish porn stars—rarer than rare.

The entire scene feels like a sci-fi movie where multitudes of meteors shoot within inches of each other without ever colliding into an explosion. My veins pump with adrenaline. Squid taps me on the shoulder and motions to me that this segment of the evening has concluded for us. We're destined for the main event—a party his older sister is throwing. I have serious doubts that Squid, or myself for that matter, are even invited, but that's beside the point. By now, most things are a blur and I'm not captain of my own ship. Squid says his sister has good-looking friends and that's a fine enough reason for me.

His house stands out for its oddity, that oddity being that it's pretty damn nice. It doesn't look like the type of home that would spawn a Squid.

I'm conditioned not to feel comfortable where residences are less than five stories but I'm pleasantly at ease. The outdoor air has sobered me and as we walk towards his sister's party, me and his Squidness make less than successful attempts at tidying our appearance. There's only so much you can do with stained white T-shirts and dirty dungarees. Hopefully, our stunning good looks will render our attire unimportant. Cool before clean. Fuck you and your societal norms. And there we stood, at the foot of the stairs, ready to make our gallant entrance.

The grand gala is in yet another single-family residence, again putting me out of my established realm. Squid walks in like he owns the place. The partygoers, at first blush, look like a bunch of candy-assed preppies. They are visibly aghast at the sight of the most recent arrivals, two sore thumbs in the land of polished nails. Almost immediately, Squid's sister pushes through the crowd and comes to our rescue. Her name is Eileen, and she is beautiful. She addresses her baby brother as Timothy and I realize, for the first time, that he has an actual name. It definitely pokes my funny bone. Squid, or should I say, Timothy, flashes me a mortified glance. Eileen hugs her brother and turns to me. My heart thumps like a Charlie Watts bass drum set. I am smitten, I am paralyzed. 'I've heard so much about you,

Jack,' she tells me. Her voice is like silk. I hope that what she is saying is true. 'You're Timothy's idol, he never shuts up about you,' she muses. My tongue is in a knot, and I respond with something inane like 'Yeah, I bet.' This gal is a penthouse and I'm a basement apartment. If only, I say to myself, if only.

Eileen introduces us to the closest partiers, and I sense that everyone in the room is watching us. My confidence resurfaces and I make small talk with some of the young ladies. They're all several years older than me but what the hey? I have them giggling and the frat boys have their panties in a bunch watching us. What a clump of goofballs! And their outfits are a gas, collared shirts, and khakis. More collars than you'd spot at a priest's convention. The type of douchebags that wear sweaters tied around their necks.

We are among the educated it seems. I'm generally not a fan of college boys, never quite see eye to eye with them. Eileen senses the friction and gently prods Squid and I towards the door, softly suggesting we leave. "These guys are a bunch of assholes," she tells her brother. "Take some beers and go watch the Yankee game with Dad, I'm sure he'd like to meet Jack." Seems fair to me. There's no way I can get back on my bike and ride home; so, I'm sleeping in Soundview, even if it's on someone's lawn.

We're about to depart when Squid overhears one of the college boys make disparaging remarks in regard to our person. Something to do with punks and dirtbags. More than any man worth his honor in piss and vinegar should allow to go unchallenged. Squid is across the room in the wink of an eye, and I follow him into the fray.

These guys are talkers, not fighters, and they are not prepared. They have the numbers, but we have the grit. The melee is short but sufficiently violent. Things break and blood spills. Eileen is screaming now, and her voice is no longer angelic. Her brother bows like a chastened puppy as she grabs him by the ear. My hands are bruised and there's crimson dripping down my face. We invite our adversaries outside to finish things up but hear no footsteps behind us on the way out.

Who's the punks now you bunch of Poindexter faggots? There's more than one variety of higher education.

It's still relatively early, barely ten o'clock, but we've packed a lot into a few short hours and we're both shot. Squid invites me to crash at his abode and I solemnly acquiesce as my options at this point are limited. He leads me the handful of blocks to his family's house, cursing and spitting the whole time, rattling off the ways he's going to trounce his sister's asshole friends. I yes him and yes him some more, too tired to do otherwise.

Home sweet home is a converted garage adjacent to the main house. Squid is living large.

The place has its own TV and a mini refrigerator. He shares the space with his older brother, Johnnie, whom I'm told is staying at his girl's house for the night. Squid pulls off his boots and lies down in his bed fully clothed. He is unconscious almost immediately. I mosey over to an unmade bed in the corner and pass out on contact.

Sometime in the middle of the night there's a violent commotion. Someone kicked in the door and has entered the room. Visibility is extremely limited and it's difficult for me to tell what in the fuck is happening. All I know is that it can't be good. Then, as if in an apparition, there's an adult male, a very, very angry adult male, pointing a rifle in my face. Now he's screaming something about 'his money' and how I'd better fucking find it right now or he'll splatter my brains across the wall. Somewhere in the diatribe he uses the word, Timmy. I cowardly, but sensibly, pointed across the room to my boy, Squid. I like my friend a lot but not to the level of taking a bullet for him. A discord of stuttering and lisping emanates from the corner amid promises to make whole on every last penny of debt owed to this fine gentleman with the menacing rifle.

When the dust clears and I'm 100% positive that I'm still alive, I ask Squid what the hell just happened. Thankfully, the antagonist has departed. Thus begins a yarn about buying some motorcycle parts on credit from this guy who is in some motorcycle gang, maybe even the Angels, and somehow neglecting to pay him. My man, Squid, is nothing if not a severe fucking idiot. My heart is racing like a motherfucker and going back to sleep will be impossible. I say my goodbyes and hop on my bike. This will be my last ever pajama party with Squid, of that, I am sure.

THE BRONX

It's hard not to get philosophical, if not downright depressed, when I consider my options. I've been tossed from one high school and I'm finishing out my four-year commitment in a place that's more like a half-way house than an academic institution. So, essentially, I'm on a path, if I get lucky, to be a cop, fireman, or construction worker. My mom is always telling me I'm selling myself short but that's what Moms are supposed to say. For my entire life, teachers have described me as smarter than I let on and not working to my potential. My Uncle Joe says I need to just show up for life and things will take care of themselves.

Easier said than done when you don't know exactly where to show up or for what reason.

A social worker had me seeing a shrink after my Pops died and he told me I had internal conflicts that I wasn't addressing. He had nose hair issues that he wasn't addressing, and I had a hard time listening to most of what he said. When he asked me if I was angry with the lowlifes who killed my dad, I thought it was a trick question. Yes, Sigmund fucking Freud, of course I'm angry. Do they pay you to ask these jackass questions? I was angrier after the sessions than before. Main point being I have no idea what I'm doing with my life. If I can avoid jail, nuthouses, and the grave, I'll just continue to dust myself off and take another run at another day. *C'est la vie*, as the frogs say. Guess that one year of French I took wasn't a total waste.

You can learn a thing or two in school but getting to three is a stretch. I have the attention span of a schizophrenic squirrel so the teachers are talking straight at my third dimension. At the end of the school day, I actually feel dumber and more afraid for my future. But I'm an educated kid nonetheless; when that school bell rings at three o'clock, assuming I'm still there to hear it, the real education begins and my outlook on the future improves by the can. But, shit man, I miss my dad. It's like no matter what happens that can be described as good, the flip side always has the greater power.

Chapter 4

Characters of Various Talents and Even a Puerto Rican Friend

I have a Puerto Rican friend named Vinny. No relation to Vinny the Ginny (and half spic) from Villa Avenue. We worked together at the Associated Supermarket in Kingsbridge and Jerome. Ordinarily, I'm not supposed to admit I have a non-white friend, or I might get tossed from the 'hate 'em if their different' social club, but Vinny is hard not to like. And he is a funny fucker. He has a chubby, Irish girlfriend and he tells me that Irish guys should be thankful that the Puerto Ricans are willing to take the fat Irish chicks off their hands. I call him Sanchez because he has this ridiculous Mexican-style mustache that looks like he stuck a finger up his ass and painted his upper lip. He calls me Donkey Boy and adds a braying noise that sounds like Ricky Ricardo summoning Lucy.

Vinny is an industrious fellow and he's always spinning some arcane business idea. Lately, it's some scheme about selling beer in Central Park when they have those free concerts. The way he'd approach it is he'd drive his Puerto Rican chariot, complete with the "Ass, Grass, or Gas Nobody

Rides For Free" sticker that every Rican seems to have on his rear bumper, down to the West Side of Manhattan loaded with cases of *cerveza* on ice, and we'd sell them to the freak concert goers.

We'd wait until the concert had been going on for an hour or more and the bastards would all be thirsty as hell and desperate, begging us to sell them a can or two or five. Doing basic math, we'd get 48 bucks a case for our five-dollar investment. I'm helping him with the figures now, something that comes easy to me, and I tell him we'd clear $430 on 10 cases, not including the cost of the ice which would be less than ten bucks.

"What about my expenses, you dirty, Irish, mick cocksucker?" he asks.

"They can't add up to much," I counter.

"Fuck you, man. What about gas and wear and tear on my wheels? And tolls."

"There are no tolls, you dumb, spic motherfucker."

We're arguing over something that will probably never happen, but I have to concede it's intriguing. For two born hustlers, it should be something we can pull off, though we have ignored most of the logistics like where we're going to park and how we're going to lug 10 cases of beer and ice a half mile or more into the park. Necessity is the mother of invention, and we are two needy boys. One way or another we'll figure it out should it come to that.

Besides, me and Vinny already have a history in the beer distribution business from our days together at Associated Grocery. One of my first tasks when they hired me was to break down the empty cardboard boxes in the storage room and put the flattened boxes in stacks. I was pretty good at it because I treated it like a workout, and I challenged myself to keep a certain rhythm. Plus, there was a violent aspect to tearing things up that juiced me.

My prowess in deconstructing boxes was favorably recognized by management and it became a regular part of any shift I worked. Being an after-school job, I usually worked until closing. I was alone in the storage area with boxes, empty and full. The solitude was nice but so also was the unfettered access to the inventory. It was easy enough to snake a bottle of Heineken, albeit a warm one, or some kind of snack. The key was to leave no trail. The simple-minded might stop there but a man with ingenuity, a man of enterprise like myself, will uncover further opportunities.

After some moderate research, it became quite clear to me that I should be able to stash cases of beer under the cardboard stacks when I brought them outside to be carted away. Then I would wait a little bit after closing, when all was clear, and retrieve my bounty. When I told Vinny, who usually worked the same time slots as me, he was beside himself with excitement. At the time, he was too young to drive but he said he had a friend with a car who could throw the beer in his trunk.

We'd meet beforehand, pull up to the store and load the shit into his boy's car. I told Vinny that at this point in my life, he was the only Puerto Rican I trusted so how did I know his amigo was on the up and up? "Because I said so, and because he's kinda like my cousin and shit," was his response. *Cousin? I'm thinking to myself. Are the Ricans like the ginzos where countless generations of inbreeding have left pretty much everyone a relative by default? Yeah, I think to myself, don't go down that road, because the Micks probably don't have a leg to stand on in that category.* "Good enough for me, chico. But it's 50/50 down the middle and save me all the bullshit about gas and wear and tear on the car. The fucking thing is probably stolen anyway."

I told him I'd be bringing my boy, Downtown Brown, to even up the sides aiding and abetting. But I told him firmly that any of that spic beer was off the table. We'd aim for the top of the shelf.

Heineken or the like. Vinny told me his favorite beer was Guinness Stout, and that he never drank any of the Latin piss brands. The boy has class, mostly low, but he has class. Actually, I was getting pretty nervous thinking that Vinny was more like me than I realized, and God forbid, could the Irish just be a lighter shade of Puerto Rican? Both ethnicities like to drink, fight, dance, and sing. And multiply! Scary stuff, yes indeed.

The scheme worked like a charm for several months. Vinny and his man, Paco, took their share to their own parties, and me and Brown took ours back to the neighborhood. I knew management was onto the thefts and sensed they were planning a trap, so I told Vinny, and we backed off. Without the added benefits, the job wasn't worth it. Shitty pay and slave work. I quit soon thereafter with a clear conscience. My personal code of honor told me stealing from bigger stores and companies was fair game. But I'd never take so much as a peanut from any of the smaller local stores, or anyone on my home team. The Associated was run by a bunch of rich Jews who drove sweet cars and lived in fancy houses. Sticking it to them was a pleasure.

Every game has its rules. Who writes the rules is what matters most. My game, my rules, I win, you lose. Works nicely for the home team. Bob and weave, shuck, and jive, land the first punch. When their legs go wobbly, move in for the kill. Notch the stick and keep the count going. Never quit, never show fear and always, always watch your back. Kinda like the Constitution Bronx style. The Founding Fathers would have their hands full if they jumped ahead a couple of centuries and found themselves hanging out on a corner. The wigs would have to go, that's for fuck sure.

THE BRONX

It's getting a little too cold for it to be another "Long Hot Summer of 1967" but the mercury isn't the only thing that can raise the heat. "Kill the Pigs" is still a popular refrain but more so from the Africans than the long hairs. The city is a war zone, and the papers are six pages in before you read about anything other than murder and mayhem. Riding the subway at night, by yourself, is the easiest way to get killed. There's always rumors about the great uprising where the Black Panthers, the Mow Mows, the Black Spades, and every other nigger tribe, will march north on the Grand Concourse wreaking havoc of biblical proportions, burning buildings and killing every white person they encounter.

Our neighborhood, like most majority white areas, is arming itself for what they believe is inevitable. There are stores of baseball bats, billy clubs, and the ingredients for Molotov cocktails for when, not if, the day comes. 'Kill the niggers; send them back to Africa; let 'em pick cotton,' and on and on go the mantras. If the words are incendiary, the actions will likely be as well. I've taken to carrying a knife with an eight-inch blade that snaps open with the flick of a wrist. Most of my boys carry knives as well. Some of us have wrist rockets with metal balls that can crack a skull depending on the velocity. The occasional household has a rifle or a handgun. To the rest of the world, there was bewilderment and dismay at watching buildings burn in the background of the World Series. For us, it was another day at the beach. 1977 and Howard Cosell, who all of us hate for being an Ali fan and Jewish to boot, has interrupted the live game to utter, "Ladies and Gentlemen, the Bronx is burning." Howard makes no mention of marshmallows. Welcome to primetime, motherfuckers, but it's been burning long before tonight.

Beirut, the poster child for the destruction of mankind, has no leg up on us. For burnt out buildings and indiscriminate violence, the Bronx is the reigning, fucking, heavyweight champion. The gates of hell have opened and there's a Lucifer on every corner, in every alley and subway car. Looting and wilding are now sporting events. It gets so that you're never at ease; there's always some type of tension rattling your existence. Staying on your toes and watching your back become feral instincts versus cliché suggestions. Keeping the strut and looking tough are a shield whenever you venture from your home turf.

To the uninformed, being from the Bronx means you have some type of connection with weapons and crime. The good and decent, the greater majority, are obscured by the headlines of a smoldering borough. Being part of it, you tend to default to what you believe in—the beliefs imposed on you by those around you. The niggers and spics are your enemies. We are not meant to live together in peace and never will be. We're in the northern end; they occupy the south.

You put one foot in front of the other, one day at a time, and pray that someday you get to leave. Live somewhere where there's grass and trees. Where you don't have to lock your doors and bar your windows. Where your personal property is safe and untouched by anyone other than yourself. No incessant car alarms or sirens. No screaming voices of anger and desperation. No junkies trying to rip you off. None of all that insane bullshit that presently feels inescapable.

THE BRONX

When deciding on play dates, I get to make various choices. My best friends, the guys I've known since first grade, will always be my first choice. But time changes people and sometimes those people are no longer walking on the same roads you're walking on. Basically, the good kids do things like attend school on a regular basis and do homework and such. They may hang out on the corner on Friday night but will generally go home at a decent hour and avoid getting too drunk or stoned. They'll even take time now and then to consider what path to success they'd like to pursue in life. My basic default of "if it feels good do it" doesn't apply to them. Their type of fun is clean and mostly harmless. I love these guys and would go to war for them but sometimes they just don't scratch my itch.

Then there's that other type. The kids that are pretty much up for anything. Their needs are always immediate—how do I get a beer or a joint? How can I get laid? These kids are not big on academics and will never go to college. Most will barely get their GEDs. Almost to a man, they have wild heads of long hair though the image they pursue is way more Conan the Barbarian than Jerry Garcia. Often, they come from messed up families but not always.

There's just a breeze in the streets that either draws you in or it doesn't. When you're younger maybe you see a bunch of guys (and girls) hanging out in the schoolyard, looking tough and projecting cool, and you want it. You imagine yourself being in the mix, a badass and a rebel. You take the first chance you get to impress them. Something stupid like jumping out of a third-floor window and getting right back up on your feet. Or riding on the back of a bus using just one hand to hold on. Cutting yourself with a knife or a razor and showing no reaction.

Jumping across roofs six stories up or hanging over them smoking a cigarette. Real, real moron stuff that gets you noticed. "The kid's got balls," they'll say. And you'll ease your way into their good graces. One foolish act after another and your rep grows.

Soon enough, you're on the inside looking out. The trick is staying within the circle for the long haul. At some point, you'll have to move past the low-level thuggery to more advanced forms of criminal activity, like stealing cars or setting fires or chasing niggers with baseball bats. The comfort zone shrinks quickly. If you decide to stick around, it's all in or all the way out.

THE BRONX

Cliff the ironworker was there and then he wasn't. He happened upon us one day when we were all hanging out on the corner. This goofy guy comes ambling over to a bunch of us standing around drinking beer and asks if he can tell us a joke. We're like what the fuck do we have here? None of us had ever laid eyes on this clown in our lives. Cliff had a goofy smile on his face, and he was clearly fearless. Nothing about us made him uneasy. I forget what the joke was but Cliff was a welcome addition to our boy's club from that day on.

What he told us was that he was from some podunk-hillbilly-sleep-with-your-sister-one-horse-town upstate.

Said he was part Cherokee and part Irish, so you didn't need Perry Mason to tell you the lad had a drinking problem. He was a high-wire ironworker, and the jobs were in the big city, so he stayed in Mrs. R's boarding house across the street and trained it into Manhattan. He left his wife back home in their small town and I doubt either of them complained about the arrangement. Mrs. R, an Armenian shrew, had warned Cliff about the bad kids who stayed up all hours of the night causing trouble. She also strictly enforced the no 'girls' and no booze rules with the efficiency of a firing squad chief, which left Cliff with no choice but to seek his pleasures on the streets of our neighborhood and beyond.

So, Cliff would spend his days tightrope walking on iron beams hundreds of feet above the streets of New York, and his evenings drinking beer on the corner with us, reaching now and then for the silver flask in his back pocket, for a sharper twist of fire water. No matter what the weather, Cliff was without hat, coat, or gloves. He was as immune to the elements below as he was from those above. When he wasn't in his room or on the corner with us, he might be found in the warm embrace of Big Black Bertha, who he may or may not have known to be a lady of the night.

Bertha was the beloved daughter of Big Ernie Coombs, who was the super of 201 Creston Avenue, and one of the few black men held in esteem in our local parts. On her way to visit her father, Bertha would amble down Creston Avenue, swinging what had to one of the biggest asses any of us had ever seen, cooing some Ella Fitzgerald song. She'd always give us a sweet hello and say something like "my ain't you the handsomest fellas," and she said it with such a smooth rasp that it would make us almost believe it. Cliff had met Bertha via Johnnie Griffin, yet another Black man to ingratiate himself to our corner. Johnnie worked at Key Food up the block and commuted north from Harlem. He proudly wore a scar along his cheek from a knife fight he claims to have won. Johnnie smoked Kools and drank Miller High Life, graciously confirming our stereotypes.

We were never quite sure if Cliff knew Bertha was a hooker or just didn't care. He shelled out a twenty on each date night and professed eternal love. No one ever asked him, and then we never got the chance. After being noticeably absent from his corner visits for several days, we just figured he'd gone back home upstate. It wasn't until Dumb Danny, who we were surprised could read after all, spotted the 'Iron Worker Plunges to His Death' article in the *Daily News*, that we discovered Cliff's fate. In retrospect, none of us was shocked. Walking narrow beams with a silver flask in your back pocket is a well-known health hazard. Cliff died as he lived, a touch too fearless, and a touch too numb.

On any given day, you can meet someone fascinating on the corner. It might be Estelle Maron Marie on her way to the laundromat to use the payphone, where she will attempt to call the FBI to report various threats to her well-being. The alleged perpetrators vary from her very own *mamasita*, to extraterrestrials, to the local police. Estelle is a soft spoken delusional, and actually quite attractive, which can cause the occasional idiot to try and engage her in conversation. Though there are moments of lucidity there can never be any real back and forth with her, she's too far gone. Everybody likes Estelle and we do our best to keep the predators away.

There is of course, the aforementioned Willie the Rogue, a true legendary figure, but the list is a long one. Some are seriously psychotic, but most are just your run-of-the-mill troubled individuals. There's Smokey, who lost most of his family to a house fire, something he never recovered from, which is quite understandable. He lives with his aunt these days and spends most of his time indoors. The guy is a wizard on sports trivia and seems to know every at bat Mickey Mantle ever took. He'll come around every now and then and smoke a few cigarettes and drink a beer or two. I'd guess the guy is in his early twenties but looks older. Fortunately, none of the cruel bastards around here break his balls. His aunt clearly takes care of him because his hair is always combed, and he's got clean, neat clothes on. There he'll be stunning everyone with his sports knowledge and then, out of nowhere, he'll mention his little brother who died in the fire and your heart will rip into pieces and you'll feel tears welling up in your sockets. The poor son of a bitch. You gotta just hang with him and let him spill his piece, and somehow pray that you're easing the guy's burden.

Then there's the occasional visit from TJ, the bum who doesn't seem to be on any schedule or pattern, but just shows up out of nowhere. TJ is authentic, as Skid Row of a wino as can be found, a first ballot entry into the Bum's Hall Of Fame. Upon seeing him, in all his wretched beauty, the first thing that crosses your mind is amazement that the guy still walks the earth.

Different stories have circulated as to his former life, from circus performer to ex-con who did decades in the pokey for homicide. Whatever the circumstances, he's just a harmless bum now, using up the last bits of his borrowed time.

His filthy mouth coupled with his sharp wit makes him a real keeper for an hour or two of genuine entertainment. We'll usually take up a collection to get him a bottle of the finest gutter wine, Wild Irish Rose and the like. Then we'll let him go to town singing raunchy diddies and offending women of all ages as they walk by. Stuff like 'I love ya, honey but ya got no tits.' The local gals, most of them anyway, don't take offense and get a few giggles for themselves.

They treat him like a vaudeville act and have pretty thick skin to boot. After a final swig of the donkey piss, TJ will be on his way to another neighborhood and another bottle of swill. Nobody knows when we'll see him again, or if we even will, but your instincts tell you he'll be passing through at some later date.

John O'Grady is a former prize fighter and construction worker who was disowned by his wife and kids for being a hopeless drunk. He lives a few blocks south in a boarding house and has found our corner using the same radar system the other misfits seem to use. We kid about hanging a sign on the light pole that says "all crazies welcome." By now he's been coming around enough to know a bunch of us by name and can be counted on to politely bum smokes and beer. He can't be more than five-six and a buck thirty-five. Even at his advanced age of fifty-five or thereabouts, you'd be a fool to underestimate him. Wiry and coiled, he's not one to fuck with. For laughs, and to prove his might, he'll offer to shake your hand. No matter what your size, he'll have you on one knee grimacing and begging him to stop. Claims he was supposed to fight Sugar Ray Robinson one time but got drunk and never showed. Sugar Ray in his prime couldn't come close to administering the beatdown John Barleycorn has brought down on John O'Grady. He's on the ropes fending off punches every minute of his existence.

John the Bat's moniker has nothing to do with Batman or baseball. He is so named because he's bat shit crazy. He fell off the back of a bus when he was fourteen years old, and it scrambled his marbles something fierce. He was in a coma for a few weeks and presumed to be a goner but emerged from the rabbit hole physically whole but mentally disabled. The guy has ceaseless energy and is constantly doing push-ups and chin-ups. Doesn't seem to have a mean bone in his body but you want him on your side should the shit hit the fan.

One night when I was working in the gas station he stopped by and took a seat in the pig sty that substituted for the office. First thing he says to me, without so much as a hello, is "If I had a hundred million dollars, I'd buy a helicopter." I replied with "Yeah, that'd be nice, John" but what I'm really thinking is *where in the holy fuck did that come from?* What I did know, being my parents are not first cousins, is that it wasn't worth trying to find out. I could think of lots of things I'd buy with a hundred million dollars, and none of them would be a helicopter, but every man has a right to his dreams. I went out to pump some gas for a customer while the Bat did chin-ups on a door frame, using just his fingertips. By the time I got back, he was gone. I never got the chance to give him the name of a good helicopter salesman.

THE BRONX

Perhaps the figure of greatest intrigue would be someone living squarely in the neighborhood, but without the wherewithal to make it down to the corner. Little is known of Zulu, but rumors abound. On most days, even the coldest, she can be found on the roof of our building on Minerva Place, walking endlessly in circles around the tar, and chain-smoking cigarettes. She's the adult daughter of the Kennedys, an elderly couple that live on the 6th floor.

Her unkempt black hair and burnt red skin give her the aura
of a Cherokee squaw, though not the peace pipe smoking
kind, the scalping kind.

Somewhere in her past, she had been severely
traumatized and had gradually shrunk from society. Some
of the older people in the neighborhood remembered her
as a beautiful, engaging young woman, and her parents
as doting and highly affectionate. That's where things get
murky, and the legend takes hold. They ranged from her
being kidnapped and raped, to her killing her fiancé with
an axe. Some say she has superhuman strength and once
lifted a car to free a young boy stuck underneath. Though
nothing has neither been proven, nor will it ever be, even
the toughest kids keep their distance.

No one went on the roof if they thought she might
be there. That is unless you don't count me and my dear
mom. She knew the elder Kennedys and felt terribly sad for
them. Every couple of weeks, she'd go upstairs to check on
them and see if they needed anything. She wasn't the least
bit afraid and told me I was a jackass for spreading stupid
rumors. Our recent discussion on the matter went like this:

"Ma, ain't ya afraid Zulu will kill you? Throw you across
her shoulder and toss you off the roof?

"She has a name, birdbrain; it's Mary, and no, I'm not
concerned that she'll toss me off the roof."

"Did she really chop up her boyfriend with an ax?"

"Yes, of course, and then she ate him."

"Stop it, Ma, I'm serious."

"Is that what you call it, serious? You are seriously a
knucklehead. The poor people. Mary is as harmless as a
lamb. Her family has been through so much and you and

your idiot friends make it worse by passing around these baseless stories. You know what?"

"What?"

"Next time I go up to see the Kennedys, you're coming with me."

"You just don't want to get murdered by yourself so you're selfishly going to risk my life as well? And I thought I was your favorite, Ma."

"If you're going to get murdered, I'll do it myself. I won't need Mary to help."

The list goes on and on, and you can safely wager that every type of kook or miscreant has found their way to our friendly corner of paradise at some time or another. For fifty cents or less the entertainment is better than anything you'll see on Broadway, though I wouldn't mind getting a closer look at some of those Rockettes.

THE BRONX

Word to the wise, watch your ass in Alexander's basement; my mom is going shopping. Alexander's, on the corner of Fordham Road and the Grand Concourse, is the only discounted department store within walking distance for hordes of people east, west, north, and south. It offers all manner of goods at what it advertises as 'bargain basement' prices. Consistent with its pitch, it has a bonafide basement area where the real steals (for those paying money that is—I focus my real steals in the pricier departments upstairs) can be had. Merchandise is strewn out atop cabinets in heaps with even more stuff jammed in the drawers below.

For women with families on a tight budget, this is where *Roller Derby* meets *Ozzie and Harriet*. For pure combativeness and the fury of the Tasmanian Devil, the smart money goes on my own personal, beloved mom. When the doors open at 9 a.m., you might see mom descending the stairs dragging behind her a couple of my younger siblings, a look of fierce determination etched across her face. If you're foolish enough to get in her way, she will take you out Bronco Nagurski style. She has already mapped out a strategy in her head and is now proceeding wholly on adrenaline. Once she has found the right display counter, be it shoes or pajamas, she will box out an area better than Wes Unseld. To the shopping arena, mom brings sharp elbows and an even sharper belief that people's hunting and hoarding tendencies can be traced directly to their ethnic origins.

For instance, she expects to see her fellow Irish women heading directly for the lower drawers as if digging up potatoes, unconcerned about getting down in the dirt. She doesn't anticipate much competition from the Italian women who she considers to be *prima donnas* and useless outside of a kitchen. The Negroes and Spanish, as she refers to them, have different tastes and agendas that will keep them occupied fighting with each other over stuff she has no interest in. The Polacks and the like, in her mind, are too dumb to do on the spot math, so pose no immediate threat. Her greatest concern, and it outweighs all the others combined, is the Jews.

As mom tells it, those gals can spot a bargain from the other side of nowhere. Besides, she'll tell you, they get insider tips from other Jewish women who somehow or another know someone who knows someone who is a relative of the people who own the store. So, when you watch mom, you'll see her scoping out some lady with a beehive hairdo out of the corner of her eye, convinced the scheming bastard has an angle on some prized stash. Then mom, pretending nonchalance, will slink up beside her, fully prepared to beat her at her own game. And if push comes to shove, Mom will be both pusher and shover. So, if there's a moral to this story, it's simply this—do not fuck with my mom in Alexander's basement.

Colorful characters abound in the Bronx; some even have different colored skin; some are slightly crazy; and some have taken the express train to Fruit Cake City. I promise you this boys and girls, hang around with Jack McGee and his assorted collection of acquaintances and you sure as shit won't be bored. You may be scratching your head quite a bit but that'll keep at least one of your hands away from your balls for a few minutes. Being tough is a necessity—being as tough as my mom is a gift.

CHAPTER 5

The Education of Wee Jack McGee—with the Assistance of a Pretty Smart Irish *Fecker*

My esteemed high school, St. Joe's, advertises itself as a 'shaper of men.' Something along the lines of 'shape 'em up and ship 'em out' I guess. From my vantage point, there seems to be very little shaping up of any kind, and the school produces mostly dumb motherfuckers with no aim in life. I have kids waiting for me in the park across from the school in the morning to copy my math homework, which is so basic as to be an offense to the intellect. As I've noted before, you don't go to Joe's unless you're borderline retarded, or you've been tossed from some other Catholic school, like I was. The interesting thing is that the bros and the Chicanos are actually the better students. The white kids are just looking to get the diploma and expend as little energy and effort in the process.

Brother Brian, who is new to the school, and also my American history teacher, pulled me to the side one day a few weeks back and asked if I could come to his office. The guy looked regular enough to me, but you can never be sure with these types. Needless to say, I've come across more than a few diddlers in my Catholic education days. The brothers, as opposed to the priests, seem to be swinging from the same side of the plate as me. Or they're just leaving the bat on their shoulder and taking the third strike looking. They're not required to take any horseshit vows of celibacy. Personally, I don't think anyone's numb down there despite divine intervention, cold showers, or limited access to *Hustler* magazine. This cat was definitely cooler than the average man in cloth and I trusted him. Still, I was surprised he expressed any interest in me whatsoever; I felt like he barely knew me.

When I arrived at his office, which was really no office at all, just a tiny room without a window, he got up and firmly shook my hand. Right off the bat, he told me I could call him Brian. He told me he had done a little research on me and knew that my old man had been murdered. Then he went on to tell me how his pops had died at the age of thirty when he was just a wee lad of five back in the Emerald Isle.

Before I could intervene, he assured me that his experience did not compare to mine, that murder is infinitely different than sickness, but that he could still relate on some level. The more he spoke, the more I liked him. He told me he had all kinds of fallibilities, and he wasn't here to judge me, simply to lend an ear or advice if I chose to take it. I pretty much told him to shoot, lay it on me, and man did he ever. That brogue of his somehow added a certain wisdom to everything he said.

It was like the guy was looking right into me. He said that it was useless to hide my anger because it was dripping all over me. He said he bet that I hated Puerto Ricans and thought constantly about avenging my father's murder. He said that I was way smarter than I let on and that it was a shame I wasn't using it in a constructive manner. He said I had a masculinity problem, that my need to project bravado would just eat up my insides and backfire. He read me up, down, backwards, forward, left, and right. Talked about mistakes he's made in his own life and how it pained him to see young men, like me, squander opportunities. Any college, any college on earth, would take a cleaner version of myself he implored. We talked about boxing and booze and girls. I told him stuff that I never told anyone, and I knew implicitly that it would never leave that room.

During one of our sessions, Brother B asked me if I'd read *Red Badge of Courage* by Stephen Crane. I told him sure, but that I'd read it in one sitting the night before a book report was due the next day. So essentially no.

"Well, Jack, the kid, or should I say young man in the novel, was not unlike yourself.

Sixteen or seventeen years of age, and life has dealt him certain circumstances that he'd never bargained for. He ultimately is forced to choose between cowardice and death. So, he does choose inevitably, and he earns his red badge so to speak, and gets to celebrate it in a freshly dug grave.

"You told me the last time we spoke that the reason you've avoided competing in the Golden Gloves is that you're deathly afraid of losing. You'd rather die than lose, so to speak. You're afraid to be a coward or any other form of a lesser man. You would have chosen the same fate as the boy in the story, of that I have no doubts. If you continue to engage this side of yourself and try to prove to the world that you're some kind of fearless macho man, the internal conflict will mar every single instance of your life. It will stand in the way of accomplishments; it will damage your relationships, and it will destroy any hopes of a contented life.

"And I emphasize contented versus happy, because happiness will come with the contentment, but in a much purer form. You spend your days trying to impress your buddies, when the only one you need to impress is yourself. Despite beliefs to the contrary, the better man doesn't walk away from a fight—he stays in it. I'm of the opinion that a fistfight is sometimes necessary and unavoidable. But do it for the right reasons, maybe to defend your mother's honor, but never for some idiotic concept of manhood. There's lots of folks out there that are in need of a good ass-kicking, it would actually improve them. Choose your battles wisely and you'll never be a coward."

The whole time he spoke I was thinking to myself . . . *man, this guy is the real live version of the Chinese master in* Kung Fu, *and I'm Grasshopper. Oh man, he'd given me a lot to chew on. He wanted me to look inside myself, understand my motivations, and make peace with my demons. A little introspection never hurts anyone—helps, in fact,* he told me. *Yeah,* I'm thinking, *good fucking luck with that one.*

"Yeah, I guess most of that is accurate, Brother, but it's probably, at this point in my life, too tall of an order. I can't see myself stop hating the motherfuckers who killed my father (he was cool with me cursing) and looking at every Puerto Rican like they had something to do with it, the whole race of them. It's too late for college. It's already too late for most things."

"Stop right there, Jack, I won't sit here and humor that bullshit. Too late? I'm sorry to change the temperature here, lad, but you're feeling sorry for yourself. It's not too feckin late for anything. Are you saying you're going to quit, give up, throw in the bloody towel? Tis just a load of nonsense. I told you, choose your battles wisely! The corner and your silly notions of bravery, or a future that your father in heaven can be proud of? He's with you every step of the way whether you realize it or not. What do you think he'd choose for you? You know that answer better than anyone."

I left that room feeling more angry than enlightened. Feeling sorry for myself? Man, that pissed me off. Made me out to be some kind of whiner when I never complain to anyone about anything. He pretty much called me a bitch. My last two classes were a joke, so I just kept on walking down the corridor in the direction of the exit.

Barely the afternoon and here I was, grabbing a brewski at the local *bodega*, swaddled in a paper bag so I could consume it in public, and waiting on the platform for the D train on the uptown track, the lone cracker, getting eyeballed up and down. Doing the white boy shuffle, avoiding the kerfuffle. Lots of time to kill before my 5-10 shift at the gas station, my radar taking me back to that corner on Creston Avenue, where no doubt there'd be some misfit or unemployed loser waiting for someone like me to come along to tip some cans and share some weed.

There I'd hang, fretting my future for an hour or two or three, until I'd show up at the Gulf station wearing at least a strong buzz. Pumping gas and praying that some junkie doesn't have a mind to stick a gun in my face and rob the place. It's the cold dark nights that do it the most, conjuring up all manner of frightening possibilities. Wouldn't that be something going out the same way as my pops.

THE BRONX

I hit the fuckin' jackpot landing a gig behind the stick at the Alibi bar. The owner knows I just turned seventeen and he doesn't give a shit. He told me I had personality and would draw a mixed age crowd, liven the dump up a little. Plus, he figures I can handle myself with the mitts and thus the rougher blend of patrons. The biggest plus from his standpoint was that I wouldn't dip my hand into the register. He knew I lived by the honest thief's code to only take from those who can afford it. Neighborhood bar, neighborhood owner, neighborhood manners. Jimmy Gleason was right to trust me, I'd never take a nickel that I didn't earn fair and square.

Not only did I land this highly prized and sought-for position, I got the Friday night shift. On a busy night with a generous crowd, I could haul in 200 to 250 clams. With minimum wage statewide not even two-fifty an hour and 35 hours a week at the Gulf station barely cracking 140 a week with tips, this was like going from a tin hut to the Taj Mahal. Don't think for a minute that I didn't have jitters at the irony of being in the very setting that took my father's life. But man, we're talking 200 large here. I'd fight Ernie Shavers and his shaved bean for 200 dollars. I'd even let him load his gloves. Plus, I'd know just about everyone in the joint. With the area changing colors like an autumn landscape, the Alibi never sheds its leaves, and all of those leaves are white, except the occasional outlier who has the prudent sense to 'act like a white man.'

Working the stick at the Alibi gives me a celebrity glow that doesn't require lying down on the casting couch. Amid a drinking world, I was the sentry that you needed to pass to get to the well. The bar was what we all aspired to. The day you become a bar drinker is like a passage into another realm. No matter the filthy bathrooms or the multitude of Department of Health violations, if you can make it here you can make it anywhere. Sorry Sinatra for stealing that line but you're from fuckin' New Jersey anyway. Who's some guinea crooner to be the spokesman for all things New York? Bet the chickenshit peddler never set foot in the Bronx.

The night shift starts at 6 p.m. and theoretically ends at 4 a.m., the legal closing hour, but it's a flimsy guideline at best. You might think that nothing good ever happens after 4 a.m. but the good things stop happening well before that. In fact, sometimes the good things are barely in the door before they start going south.

The happy times are way earlier in the evening and things get increasingly darker from there. I've determined that there are four stages of every drunkard's journey into oblivion. The first stage is after the first couple of drinks when you're feeling light and smooth, not a care in the world. The second stage is when the liquor has really taken hold, and you become giddy and reflective. At this stage, you pretty much love everyone and you tell them such. You hoot and howl, hug, and kiss. You might even sing a song or dance a jig. The warm fuzzy is gone but this is even better. The right song or a cute girl can deliver you damn close to ecstasy. Life is fucking perfect, and you are the king!

Ecstasy, like orgasms, is a fleeting whimsy. It also drains your energy and leaves you spent. Now diminished, you enter stage three. Stage three is the somber stage. Now, you become sad and regretful. You conjure up that girl who left you, the school you flunked out of, the litany of blown opportunities. Maybe, you'll even weep openly. This is where the bartender's storied psychiatric skills come into play. The problem with these situations, at least in this slinger's case, is that even if you give a fuck, and I certainly don't, you're putting out fires elsewhere all around the place.

The poor jackass is looking for a shoulder to cry on and the only body part you care to offer up is your foot. The good news for the crybaby is that quite a few of the other drunks have also entered into stage three and they now have each other to blabber to. Stage three has left coherence in the rearview mirror. All the while, you're thinking that if this clown or the other repeats himself one more time I'm gonna grab him by the nape of his neck and plunge his mug into the nearest unflushed toilet. If you work in the right type of places, the gin mill apples of your eye, no one bothers to flush the toilets anyway.

Stage four is when the wheels come off the wagon. The stage four drunk is angry and spiteful. He'll take a swing at his own mother. He's bitter at the world and trusts no one. The Frankenstein monster has more charm than the inebriate at this point. The good news is that stage four doesn't last long; it's the onset of a black-out and all consciousness will soon evaporate. When you have a front row seat to watch this shit, you can appreciate the skull and crossbones on the booze bottles in the cartoons.

The early crew on a Friday evening is older and just coming from work or places unknown. There's usually some leftovers from the afternoon crowd who by now are slurring and nodding off to sleep. As a rule, they are not a talkative bunch. The ones shuffling in now are energized by the thought of the day's first drink and the onset of the weekend. In an hour or so, half of them will be on their way, and the other half will be frantically waving to me whenever the phone rings, code for 'I'm not here if that's my wife calling.'

Like clockwork, Tony the Horse will have his two shots of Fleishmann's with a beer chaser, then head out, either stiffing me or leaving a nice tip, depending on how his day at OTB went. Frank the Mex, who may or may not be Mexican, will come in nattily attired, too nattily for this dump, and have his Smirnoff and soda. I've seen the Mex do the Sunday puzzle in the New York Times in less than an hour, but unfortunately his smarts never translated into anything resembling commercial success. He is one funny motherfucker though, to which I can sincerely vouch for. When I asked him last week why he always arrives in a gypsy cab, he told me he lost his license years ago. "Why was that?" I asked. To which he replied, "I only know how to use two things on a car—the gas pedal and the horn."

These types of customers provide some steady register receipts but will never be able to put the place over the top. That's where I come in. I'm intended to lure a younger, livelier mix. Ideally, the ones who never sleep (sorry again, Sinatra). A crowd draws a crowd, and the aim is to create a buzz. Make people think they're missing out if they don't at least stop by to check out the vibe.

Getting women in the place is crucial, as is a properly stocked jukebox. Like some folks are hanging out at some other dump a few blocks away and they're bored. You want them to be thinking, *let's check out the Alibi*. They walk in, music is blaring (Stones, Doors, that kind of groove— the Beatles may be the 'greatest ever' but those mopheads put you to sleep), maybe some chick dancing on the bar, and they're Friday nighters for keeps. Then, the problem is not getting people to come, it's what to do with them when they're here. I try to be a steward of love and happiness which hopefully keeps me from being the prison warden.

You have this neighborhood bar where everyone knows each other and all of sudden there's these new strange mugs popping up all around. People get real territorial in a neighborhood joint. The drug dealers are like flies on shit when they sense opportunities, and they come out of the woodwork when the crowds start becoming consistent. Their appearance may or may not piss people off but like everyone else they have to play by the rules. The regulars can handle a little change but only in bits and pieces. My job is to spot the miscreants and then do my best to give them the hint to pack up their bags and get the fuck out. You try the nice way once or twice, but reason doesn't always suffice with a thick-headed scumbag. Then you do what you have to do.

Misery acquaints a man with strange bedfellows as per Willie S, so I try to keep the misery level low and the good cheer flowing. The bad shit is inevitable but a talented man behind the stick can make it less frequent and modify it some. Some guy's girl might have come here with her friends, and without him, and is getting sweet-talked mouth to ear by one of the in-house Romeos, and in walks 'Prince Charming.' Without warning it could get ugly. And trust me, it does. Sometimes. Many nights, I'm like Arther Mercante, breaking clinches and catching a few in the head while I'm doing it. As the wise man says, you take the good with the bad. Like I said before, for the kind of money I'm collecting here, I'd put up with a whole lot fucking worse.

The tensest situations are not when soused off-duty cops are threatening to shoot someone or each other, or when someone drops to the floor unconscious. It's when we get the most dreaded of visitors, unfamiliar explorers of a darker persuasion, who decide to test fate and hang out somewhere that they know they're not welcome.

I was filling in on a Thursday night a couple of weeks back and these three Puerto Rican guys came sauntering in the door—real gritty, bonafide down and dirty South Bronxites, with attitude in abundance. Early twenties and small in stature, like the breed in general, with an arrogant confidence that they are the ones to be feared, not vice versa. The bar was not particularly crowded but there were plenty of people of a certain mindset that could turn up the heat in a flash.

When these fellas walked in, the low rumble of talk and laughter that had filled the room ceased, and an eerie silence took its place. Every neck hair in the bar stood at attention. Every eyeball in the place had daggers. Always the practical man, I immediately leapt into action to defuse the ticking time bomb. The three amigos had staked their position at the corner of the bar nearest the door, which at least separated them somewhat from the house patrons.

When they ordered drinks, I told them it was probably not a sound idea, and that they should be on their way, no sore feelings. Instead of partaking of my wisdom, wisdom dispensed with their well-being in mind, one of the motherfuckers actually walked over to the pool table, slapped his 50 cents down, and called next. They looked at me perplexed that I didn't want to serve them, and I returned my own glare of perplexity that they had not heeded my advice and were still standing in front of me. I suggested we cut a deal. One drink each and one game of pool and then skedaddle. They keep their pride and machismo intact, and

I don't have to mop up any blood. They turned out to be individuals of poor reason.

The thing to remember here is that this trio of desperados were not merely challenging their own sense of machismo, they were simultaneously forcing every other male in the Alibi to confront their very own manhood. While the outsiders were nonchalantly sipping their beer and rum and cokes and analyzing the pool table, there were voices speaking inside the heads of all the rest of us. My voice was praying softly that these mooks would find the wisdom to depart before all hell broke loose. The other voices were not quite so inconspicuous, they said things like, "I'll be damned, if some spic thinks he can just walk into my bar," or "one false move motherfucker, one false move," or something less cerebral like "I hate fucking spics." They say the inside of one's head is a bad neighborhood, but what if that bad neighborhood is surrounded by many other bad neighborhoods, and all those neighborhoods are right on the verge of a large-scale urban riot? It generally means it's too late to do anything.

I felt like I did my best and, hence, withdrew my diplomatic skills from the forum. I'm no Henry Kissinger and Puerto Ricans from the Bronx are no Chinese. So, I shrugged my shoulders, patted myself on the back, and resigned myself to letting the chips fall as they may.

It didn't take long. The Puerto Ricans were now at the pool table, their time had come. Best I could decipher, there were some harsh words over tactics and accusations of dirty pool met by further accusations. Pool sticks and pool balls converted from game equipment to weapons. The three amigos were grossly outnumbered, and the carnage was swift and unforgiving. I managed to force the action outside and actually felt an urgency to protect these guys from more serious harm. I oddly felt sorry for them. Getting the genie back in the bottle would be damn near impossible. Alcohol can get you drunk but it can't touch the high one gets from uncorked anger. It was an ugly scene. Pitiful for sure.

The cherry tops lit the night, and the cops arrived to see the Puerto Ricans in various states of beatdown. Blood was splattered everywhere, and all manner of weapons that had been used in the exercise had been tossed. Though the victims refused medical care, they wanted the cops to arrest someone, anyone. That is, of course, not how things work around here. When it's a white man's bar wielding the sword, the cops will naturally assume that the men of the paler shade were the solution, not the problem. The problem, from their perspective, was the three bloody mutts attending to their wounds.

Chances are that we'd not only know one or two of the cops, but someone in the bar would be related to them. They'd sign off on our version of things, not caring how much, if any, of it was fabricated. Away from the crowd, they'd snicker, even laugh. In their minds, people were expected to stay on their own turf, and the consequences of failing to do that were evidenced right here. Later that night, after they clocked out at midnight, officers Riley and Murphy would stop in for a few beers which, of course, would be on the house. Then we'd all recount the jovial time that transpired before and after the men in blue arrived. A good laugh would be had by all, and the white knight would ride off into the sunset, the evil dragon's carcass in his wake.

The next morning with a clear head to reflect on the previous night's activities, I felt overwhelmed with guilt. There had to have been something I could have done to prevent these guys from getting their heads kicked in. In retrospect, they really hadn't done anything worse than to walk into a bar where they weren't welcome. Taking responsibility has never been my forte. It's much easier to justify my part in things. Hadn't I warned them? Why were they there in the first place? It was easy enough for me to move past this and declare my innocence. The thought that stayed with me was what would happen when the Puerto Ricans came back to even the score. They definitely were the type that would. If and when, I hoped I wouldn't be around. And if I was, they'd remember that I wasn't such a bad guy after all.

THE BRONX

There are certain laws that even the biggest criminals among us must abide by. There's the law of the universe that may leave you without a father or a best friend. There's the law of the land which suggests that all animals stay in their own stockade, and then, of course, there's Murphy's law which will pretty much assure you that all kinds of bad shit will happen if you just give them time. I just can't figure out why I'm so ridden with angst all the goddamned time. I can't help but feel that something's coming that I don't want to come, and Murphy will, as always, have the upper hand.

CHAPTER 6

You Can Find an Oasis Anywhere—
Even Around Here

"Hey Jack, did you read *Catcher in the Rye*?"

"Why Sal, you starting a book club?"

"No man, I need to do a book report that's due tomorrow."

"What kind of high school still has you doing book reports in senior year?"

"The type of high school that I'm not going to graduate from if I don't do this fucking book report."

"Alright greaseball, what's my incentive to help you?"

"Invent what?"

"Forget it moron, what I'm asking is what's in it for me? What do I get for helping your dumb ass finish the book report so that you can graduate, get a job, and raise a family with kids that hopefully will look like their mother?"

"No mother jokes!"

"That wasn't a mother joke, you knucklehead! Oh, forget it, it's not worth explaining. Sal, you may be Italian, but even for an I-tal you're one thick cocksucker. You have paper and pen? I don't have all day, so we're gonna make this quick. The book isn't that long anyway."

"Thanks, Jack! Yeah, I got my notebook right here, it's hardly been used. For an Irish prick, you're not half bad."

"Okay, write this down word for word, don't trust yourself to improvise. Now pay attention . . ."

"Shoot, I'm ready. But go slow please, I'm hard of hearing."

"Most things are hard for you, Sally, my boy. Okay, let's get started. Holden Caulfield is the book's main character and the narrator . . ."

"Wait spell that . . ."

"First name, H-O-L-D-E-N. Last name, C_A_U_L_F_I_E_L_D. Try to remember it like this, you're holding your dick in a cornfield."

"Now we're in a cornfield?"

"Oh, forget it, numbnuts. It's takes place in a school, not a fuckin' farm."

"Got it. Continue . . ."

"He's away at prep school when he gets busted by the dean for dealing coke. He also just found out that his girlfriend, who is the dean's daughter, is pregnant."

"Whoa! I shoulda read this book, it sounds fucking awesome! How come I never read it?"

"I'd take a wild stab at the reason being that you've never read a book cover to cover in your life, on top of your complete disregard for the English language, but that's just me. I told you Sal, I don't have all fucking day so just shut up, listen and write. Holden, his back to the wall, decides to kill the dean . . ."

THE BRONX

Janis Joplin said . . . "freedom's just another name for nothing left to lose," but a good way to get killed is to fuck with someone who has nothing to lose. To me, freedom came with cash in my pocket. I remember hustling on the delivery bikes when I was a mere lad of twelve, with the older kids at Food City, helping them haul bags of groceries up the stairs to people's apartments. They'd split the tips with you, or kinda split the tips, but it was money either way and it added up. I loved the feel of those coins jingling in my dungaree pockets, man, I absolutely fucking adored it. It didn't matter how many flights I had to climb or how many boxes and bags I had in my arms, all that mattered was the tip waiting for us at the end. Most people were pretty generous because they knew if they stiffed you, it'd be a cold day in hell before you ever took their order again. I might have been a twelve-year-old, snot-nosed punk but now I was a snot-nosed punk with money.

I remember heading towards home one Saturday, after a long, exhausting day on the bike. It had been busy as hell and for seven or eight hours all I'd eaten all day was some Fig Newtons that Chuck, the guy I was working with, had stolen from the store. Working with Chuck was lucrative because he was lazier than shit and would gladly split the tips 50/50 if you did the lion's share of the work, which was not a problem for me. So, here I was feeling both pretty damn rich and pretty damn hungry.

Normally, I'd just head for home to see what there was to eat. With the five of us kids, food generally didn't last too long, and the menu was always take it or leave it. Mom wasn't about to start taking individual orders. Then it occurred to me that I had another option. I walked straight to Frank's pizza shop and ordered myself a deuce of piping hot slices with sausage and extra cheese. Basically, top shelf stuff. I threw in a crisp, cold bottle of Coca-Cola to facilitate my digestion, and there I was.

Sitting there amidst my culinary jackpot, I was thinking that somewhere in the world, at that very exact moment, be it Paris, Rome, or New York City, there was some guy sitting in a fancy pants restaurant ordering some shit I couldn't even pronounce, and thinking to himself that he has the world by the balls. Well, if I had the chance to talk to that fellow I'd tell him, guess what pal, we're even! Or maybe I even got you beat, because there's no way in hell that at this very minute you're enjoying your meal more than I'm enjoying this feast right here, right now. So, whatever you're eating, good for you, I'm happy for you. But I'm also pretty damn delighted for myself.

You see, sir, I have money in my goddamned pocket— yes siree, motherfucker! So yeah, Janis, feeling good is good enough for me too, but freedom's just another word for money. Good enough for me, me and my Jackie McGee.

THE BRONX

Money became a theme in my life early on. You always want what you don't have, and there were lots of things I didn't have. Don't get me wrong, my mom made sure I had everything I needed and then some, but life's desires extend past the necessities. If I couldn't buy it, I'd find some other way to get it. Over the years, I've stolen a lot of shit, from sneakers to jackets to food to whatever I was tempted to palm at any given instance in my life. I've stolen cases of soda off of trucks, cakes from the bakery, cans of tuna fish, and even the occasional steak, which left me with bloody underwear.

When I've brought the stuff home, my mom gets on my case about the source of the merchandise but generally chooses to turn a blind eye. She was pretty damn happy when we had people over to the house and I pulled three cases of soda from under my bed. She'll act like she's still angry, but I can sweet talk her to no end, and even leave her feeling sorry for me because I had to lug the cases a long way to get them here for her party.

Old ma was a hundred times happier, in fact, on a different occasion when I slid a basket of cheer, still smartly wrapped, from underneath the bed. Any disgust at the origin of my bounty was quickly replaced with her curiosity as to the basket's contents. There was some nasty good shit in there, Johnnie Walker and the like. I had stumbled upon said basket underneath one of the tents at the school bazaar, Catholics have an affinity with booze, I imagine it gets you closer to heaven. If you greet Saint Peter at the gates with a shiny bottle of Beefeater's gin, I'll wager donuts to dollars that it's gonna greatly increase your chance of getting in.

The problem with all this theft is I know it's wrong. Yes, I have a conscience. Brother Brian, who I've confessed to about my thieving history, which is more past than present, didn't condemn me but asked me some theoretical questions.

"How do you think your dad would feel about your stealing?"

"Do you ever stop and think about the person, or people, that you're stealing from?"

"Wouldn't you enjoy it more if you'd earned it as opposed to stealing it?"

The problem with that guy is he makes too goddamn much sense. His questions hang at the back of my mind now whenever I'm in a situation where I'm tempted to slip back into that behavior. As usual, he's got me figured out.

No doubt I still covet things. Moses, it seems, had me pegged as well. The silver lining nowadays is that I have other ways to acquire things, mainly through hard work. I am not afraid of getting my hands dirty busting my ass. Maybe it's the mick in me. My roots trace back to the hills of Tyrone where the land is hard and the work harder. I'll always be more comfortable with a shovel in my hand, standing on my feet, versus a pen in my hand sitting on my fat keister. The thing is this, I don't know how the hell I'm gonna do it but one way or another I'm going to be rich. Maybe, it means I'll have to work 15 hours a day, seven days a week, and never take a vacation. Get my hands on some real estate, open a business, invent something.

I'll buy my mom a big ol' house in the suburbs and throw massive parties for all my friends and relatives. There will be people I've never met who will know my name. I'll drive a sweet car and a tricked-out Harley, and the girls will fight each other to get at me. My brothers and sisters will have new bikes and fancy clothes. We'll all eat like kings and queens. I'll have to rent a U-Haul to deliver my Christmas presents. As the saying goes, "you can take the boy out of the Bronx, but you can't take the Bronx out of the boy." I'll be loaded but I won't be some candy-assed pussy like these rich types I see. My accent is staying, and so is my attitude. I'll never soften up or pretend to be anything other than I am. I won't bend or break or quit or back down. I will never forget my friends or forsake my family. Truth.

Some days, I believe all that shit. It's like I have no choice but to believe it. I need to keep playing Side A because Side B plays a completely different song, like some old Hank Williams tune where nothing ever works out and you're left wallowing in a misery that swallows you whole. I can't be that Side B guy, I simply cannot. No sir, no fucking way.

THE BRONX

These days, on Thanksgiving, we head out to Rockaway Beach to my aunt and uncle's house. After years of scrimping, living in a low rent apartment on 166th street and Walton Avenue, where they were one of only two white families for blocks on end, my Aunt Joan and my Uncle Joe bought a house in the Rockaways, fulfilling a lifelong dream. Now, it's a dream of sorts for my family as well. Aunt Joan and my mom have been going to Rockaway Beach pretty much their entire lives, doing it the same way each time out. Packing up all kinds of supplies, including enough food for two meals for eight kids, and enduring the two-hour, three different train trips from the Bronx. I'd say we did it all with just one subway token a head, but the math isn't quite that straight.

You see, the 108th Street Rockaway station is the only station I've ever known in all of New York where they actually charge you to EXIT. And not just one token, but two! Which for two ladies on a short budget is a conundrum indeed. Though I'm pretty certain, neither my mom or my Aunt Joan would ever abandon their kids, they did manage to disown the eight of us for the twenty seconds or thereabouts that it took us, large and small, to scoot under the turnstiles, managing to keep the one token per head ratio intact. So, one plus two isn't always three as I have just proven.

Fortunately, the two-hour ordeals on the MTA system are a thing of the past. Our family trips to Rockaway are now in my older brother Mickey's new wheels, a used Plymouth Duster, that the six of us manage to squeeze into. The car is a strange orangish color, and it rattles like a motherfucker, but it's lightyears better than riding in that Fun House they call the New York City subway system where, it seems, another person gets murdered every day. So given the choice between rats, bums, muggers, the stench of urine, and the occasional murderer, or an old jalopy with my squabbling family, jammed in like sardines, I'll take the latter. As an added bonus, the radio works, and Mickey likes the same music that I do, so I sit prepared to slap away any hand that approaches the dials.

Before I get into the spectacular Thanksgivings we spend at my aunt and uncle's house, let me digress a bit on that wonderland they call the Irish Riviera. Real live ocean, real live waves, real live times. I feel like I've never spent a bad minute in Rockaway, though my memory tends to be selective. From the earliest days when my father was still alive, when we'd rent a bungalow for two weeks, it'd be a blast. Fourteen days of no shoes and showers outside. The nights are a gentle blur of Irish music and laughter. Cousins, aunts, uncles, friends everywhere.

I'd fall asleep as late as possible and rise in the morning at daybreak, always worried that somehow, I'd miss out on something.

Days at the beach were pure ecstasy even with the inevitable sunburn that every pasty white Irishman is cursed to endure. The ones after big storms, the best of all, when the waves are powerful enough to toss you and spit you out, where only those with an iron pair of nuts dare to challenge them. Staying north of 102nd street with the other Irish, maintaining the divide, a healthy distance from the black and tan day trippers who like to congregate near Playland, you feel safe, the men, a sturdy bunch, who are not inclined to take shit from anyone. The women are equally tough, fearless and staunchly protective of their broods. That beach and the one next to it and the one next to that one and so on up until 112th street, all the same. Our people, our world. Things couldn't possibly get any better.

The fourth Thursday of November and here we are in an actual private home, one owned by a blood relative no less. There will be food enough to feed a small country, and booze enough to get them drunk. My Aunt Joan is a killer cook, somehow dodging the ineptitude that has characterized Irish cuisine since the start of time. My cousins, still dumbfounded that they've left their Bronx apartment, feeling damn near royalty in their new abode. My uncle Joe sliding a beer my way, telling my aunt and my mother that if they disapprove, he's taking me a few blocks over to the Irish Circle where the two of us can drink in peace. My older bro, Mickey, already a beer or two ahead of me, being reminded that he needed to drive us home. All traditions are in full swing. The March of the Wooden Soldiers and the boogeymen vanquished for another year, the Macy's Day Parade faded from the TV screen, and the bunch of us eating and drinking like we're slated for the electric chair. I find myself drifting into melancholy, my chest tightening with sadness, despite all these wonderful people in my midst. It's only one day, I think to myself, and it'll be over too soon. Then I'll go back to that other existence, the one where life can't be dreamed. The clock will be reset to zero and the race, which seems to be all uphill, will start again.

I'm going to drift into a warm weather theme here despite the lower mercury outside.

Rockaway Beach has a way of supercharging my memory. It was, still is in fact, my number one option for a cool respite in the summer heat. The other options are not quite as glamorous. The go-to as a kid was the fire hydrant, or johnnie-pump to the more erudite, because it was pretty much right outside your door.

The NYPD and NYDS would come around and install sprinkler caps on the hydrants, but within minutes of their departure, the local hoodlums, me included, would figure out a way to get them off. Someone always had the right type of wrench to turn the pump on and then, poof, water would gush out like a motherfucker, sometimes blasting some little kid across the asphalt and igniting a chorus of laughs all around. A little soft cruelty never hurt anyone.

Then there's the budding engineer who brings the hollowed-out metal coffee can to the party, enabling the operator to redirect plumes of water in every direction, high and low, and into the occasional car or second floor window. If you happen upon the scene dressed for church, be you male or female, you're essentially fucked. Dogs don't get a pass either and sometimes even one of the neighborhood moms gets a soaking. A splendid time is had by all, or should I say most.

The next closest option, one that comes with older age, is the local reservoir behind Harris Field. Here you'll find all manner of delinquents: junkies, perverts, drunks, felons and wife beaters. Old, abandoned cement blocks, ten feet long and five feet wide, meant for a construction project that never got started, are stacked across the abutting lot, allowing for convenient coverage. Within the confines and crevices of these urban mountains there will be drug taking and drinking, inevitably followed by puking and passing out. The love birds try their luck with various forms of amorous entanglements, including the harder to achieve basic fornication.

Given the looks of some of these folks, on both ends of gender and in between, a solid case could be made for bestiality. The place gets to be like a mini-Woodstock but with a lower class of clientele. Then some daring moron, the likes of me, will suggest a refreshing dip in the reservoir. If there's girls to impress, that person will strip to his undies, climb the fence, and launch himself into your drinking water. If some of the ladies can be coerced to do likewise, in the same state of attire, the picnic begins. But a word of caution to would be bathers: once you're in, the only way out is to use the climbing rope strung from the handrail. If the water is too shallow, and you can't reach the rope, your swimming days are over. Seems to happen every year. How often does the average drunk or pill head pause to consider consequences before acting?

About as often as an Irishmen gets the starring role in a high budget porn film. Look before you leap as they say and pray to God you can reach the rope.

Then, of course, there's Orchard Beach. A little slice of paradise with a legitimate Bronx address. Not too far by car but a bitch of a trip by bus, where you need to make two transfers, the last being a cattle car with no air-conditioning where beachgoers are crammed in like sardines. By the time you make it to the beach, you're more overheated than the radiator on an AMC Pacer. The only thing on your mind is getting to the water and diving in for a refreshing dip. Then you suddenly remember where you are. Yeah, Orchard fucking Beach, the cesspool of Long Island Sound. Forget for a second that sewage and garbage invade the shores—those are commercial infestations. That pales in comparison to what the daily swimmers deposit in the water, be it urine, feces, or various other bacteria. It's even possible that the shanty Irish, with the dirt behind their ears and unwashed nether areas, are among the tidiest humans here. A young biologist could make a name for himself discovering a strain of bacteria previously unknown to science. Still, when it's a thousand friggin degrees out, getting into the briny becomes a matter of survival, all other elements be damned.

Orchard Beach is also a study in social science. A true-life melting pot, it manages to define segregation as a necessary way to be able to listen to your own type of music. I'll explain. As you look at the shore from the promenade, you'll notice that the entire beach is separated by groups, all tuned into their radio station of choice, all synced with a blaring stereo effect.

To the left, at the furthermost end are the brothers. You can tell by the afros sticking up above the crowd. No umbrellas needed for this crowd. They are menacing enough that little white boys like me are sure to provide them space though not enough to make them think they scare me. The music will of course be loud, and every boombox on this section of beach will be echoing with Sly and the Family Stone or the ilk. The sisters and brothers will be gyrating, shaking their hips, and clapping their hands in harmony. They will yell anti-white shit loud enough for you to hear if you walk by, like "look at Casper the honky ghost" or something equally clever. The drink of choice will be Colt 45.

Next to them will be the Italians, soaked in Crisco oil and trying to become just as dark as their nearest neighbors. There will also be lots of jewelry and body hair, and the chicks will be a slim garment or two from nudity. They will rarely enter the water for fear of messing up their hair, and the males will continuously puff their chests and look around to see if they're being noticed. There will also be a lot of rearranging of the family jewels in the tight-fitting bathing suits. You will also see something that no self-respecting Puerto Rican would dare to sport, that being white bathing suits, such as banana hammocks and bikinis. The type of attire no Irishman would chance due to the given fear of front and back stainage. Every radio will be tuned into the BeeGees or some other disco crap. There will be way more pot smoking than alcohol consumption. Each person will refer to any other person within arms length as 'cuz,' be they related or not. I suspect this dates back to the Roman era when family members were the first choice for marriage and procreation.

The next beach over is where the Latinos congregate. It'll be mostly Puerto Ricans but there will be a healthy sprinkling of Dominicans, and even a few Mexicanos. The *señoritas* here make the Italian girls appear overly clad. The *samba* music can likely be heard on the northern tip of Long Island and everyone, even the grannies and niños, will be dancing. There will also be, despite the heat, open fires that roast various species of mammal. Every time the wind blows, some will grasp their shoulders cross-armed and go brrrrr. When they go in the water, the boys and girls will playfully tear each other's clothes off. The radios, though synchronized akin to the other beaches, will be accompanied by a slew of other instruments of sound. Bongo drums, tambourines, harmonicas, and the shrill, throaty 'ariba, aribas' that are not unlike a mating call. If there ever was 'a day at the beach,' it is right here. These people know how to enjoy themselves, that is for shit sure.

Last, but not least, is the beach at the end alongside the jetty, where those of the palest shade congregate. Mostly micks but with the Irish being the most democratic of races, the crowd will include all types, many who have no ethnic identity whatsoever. There will be individuals in long pants and shirts, heat be damned, to avoid nasty sunburns. That also means that they'll head into the brine close to being fully dressed and be doomed for discomfort for the remainder of their stay, being too thick-headed to think they might have needed to bring a change of clothes. The water will be most crowded here because these people actually came to the beach to go swimming.

Every radio will be on the same rock station trying to drown out all other sounds emanating from enemy territory. The Doors, the Stones, Zeppelin etc., i.e. real music. The drinking will be beyond excessive as will the weed intake. Fool around slap fights and wrestling matches will turn real. Blood will spill. Intermediaries will step in to make sure nobody breaks up the fights. Good cultural sense dictates that fights are necessary and allow you to vent. Long before the sun sets most of this crowd will realize that, despite their efforts, they're sunburnt to hell. They will wish that their skin had more repellent from the sun, and they will envy, at least in the short run, their darker skinned brethren. Still, no sunburn could ever be bad enough for them to want to be anything other than white.

The parks department employees and the NYPD's finest will hope and pray that the various ethnicities stay in their own lane, and that they don't all leave at the same time, with the funnel effect hyper infused by the alcohol intake and the natural cross-culture hostilities. Even more so, they pray that it rains every day until September.

I admit I've exaggerated a bit here but it's not that far from the truth. Really, what it comes down to is a bunch of working class, and even poverty level people, with few options to beat the heat. Most of the memories of Orchard Beach, mine included, will actually be sweeter rather than bitter.

Look hard enough and you'll find a lot of good in your life—look harder still and you can even get to the point where you might admit you don't have it so fucking bad after all.

Chapter 7

Wanting to be the White Joe Frazier

Saturday, my one day off, and I'm enjoying the company of my comrades, sipping a few while freezing my ass off, when this spade approaches me out of nowhere. Pretty ballsy move for him to come strutting right into our circle, seemingly without any hesitation whatsoever. There I am with my sweet, blue, leather jacket, my fingerless gloves wrapped around a twelve-ounce Bud, every bit the badass. At first, I have no clue as to what exactly is happening, but then realize that this negro fella, who is about my size, is addressing me alone, ignoring everyone else, babbling some silliness about how I disrespected his little sister, and how he has no choice but to avenge her honor and engage me in a fistfight.

He is neither someone I've ever seen before, nor do I have any idea who his sister is or what the hell he is talking about. And he's talking like he lives in the neighborhood, which is equally, if not more, confusing. What I do know is that I have but one choice, and that is to let him know that if it's a fight he wants, it will be a fight he gets. To appear even mildly reluctant or, God forbid, intimidated, would be a severe violation of the man I profess to be, and who my boys expect me to be.

Street fights will make or break you. People will remember the one you won, or the one you lost, for eternity. You get your ass whipped on a street corner, in front of a crowd, and your life changes forever. It is, to me, one of the worst, if not the worst, possible thing that could ever happen to me. Most fights happen on the spur of the moment, but others are prearranged. A free-for-all between groups is light-years different from a one-on-one.

I had an agreed upon fight one time with a guy who I'd never met when I was 14 years old. An argument had started between my older brother and this other guy who wasn't from our neighborhood but was visiting his aunt, who lived in a building just around the corner from us. I was never told how it actually came about; all I remember is a bunch of kids knocking on our apartment door all excited. I was reading MAD magazine on my bed, and I was half dozing off.

My mother yelled into my bedroom which, given the size of our living quarters, felt like she was screaming in my ear. I looked towards the door and saw the eager faces of my friends, coaxing me outside.

"Hurry up," one of them said, "You have to fight Tommy Gibson's cousin!"

I was like, 'what the fuck? I don't even know his cousin. Why do I have to fight him?'

"Your brother set it up."

Gibson's cousin, who's half spic, half Irish, was bragging about how tough his younger brother was. Mickey bet him that you could kick his ass. "C'mon, everyone's waiting."

I'm sure this would strike most people as odd, but I didn't question the logic, or rather the lack of logic, which placed me in this position at this time. I viewed it as an obligation, one that I couldn't avoid. So here I was, walking out of my building into a waiting crowd. A circle already formed, like it was the Roman fucking Colosseum. I quickly scanned the landscape to figure out which guy I was fighting, I barely had time to be nervous, but I also had practically no chance to limber up. Things got blurry with all the clamor that surrounded me, but then there he was, this kid a full head taller than me.

Don't ask me why but I remember being drawn to his carefully combed black hair. It gave me confidence because I immediately thought that anyone that spends that much time on his hair must be somewhat of a pussy. The other thing that stood out was Tommy Gibson's mother, Grace, a woman I'd known my entire life, who was rooting for her nephew and, by default, against me. When I look back it was the one thing that upset me the most. Thankfully, just as the fur was about to fly, my mom pushed her way into the audience and yelled, "Kick his ass, Jack!" And that is exactly what I did.

As I said, this guy was a lot bigger than me. At fourteen, I was small for my age. He began by stalking me, walking to his right, stopping to see how he should attack, then walking and stalking some more. I held my ground then sprung towards his lower body, got under him, grabbed his legs, and then flipped him on his back. His head hit the pavement hard, and I knew I had him. "Is there concrete all around or is it just in your head," as Mott the Hoople might say. I jumped on his chest, pinned his arms under my knees, and bashed his nose in. He gave up immediately, proving to be the pussy I pegged him out to be.

The one voice I heard through all the others, was good old ma hooting and hollering like a banshee cheering for her baby boy. Kind of like she does when her horse comes in at Yonkers Raceway. Grace Gibson, who was her friend at the beginning of the day, shot her a nasty look.

Mom took it in stride and just kept on gloating.

Winning a fistfight is in direct opposition to losing emotion wise, pure adrenaline ripping through your veins. Like a New York Yankee player in the clubhouse after winning the World Series. Like waving the American flag with a gold medal around your neck in a boxing ring at the Olympics.

Some street fights become epic classics, just like Ali vs. Frazier. Battles between evenly matched combatants, stretch across 10 or 20, or even 45 or more minutes. Neither side is willing to concede, pulling on every last bit of oxygen, every last ounce of strength. The type of fight that will be etched in the memory of everyone who witnessed it. I still remember fights from when I was barely five years old, who won, where they happened, why they happened.

Witnessing some of these street fights provides me with the same sensation I got the night I snuck into the Loews Paradise on the Grand Concourse just south of Fordham Road, to watch the Ali/Frazier rematch from Madison Square Garden. My mother never even knew that I'd sneaked out of the house to go. Barely thirteen and freezing my ass off as I walked that frigid January night down the dark streets for a fight that wouldn't start until after 11 p.m., I was so excited that I would have walked twice as far at half the temperature to be there.

The feeling of relief that I had when I scaled the fire escape behind the Paradise and found the back door unlocked. Grateful that some older guys, black and white, shielded me from the ushers, and pretended that I had a seat. Standing in the side aisle, shadow boxing as I rooted for Joe Frazier, in his green trunks, to beat Ali senseless. I was so damn electrified that I never went to sleep that night, recounting every bob and weave, every punch landed as I lay in my bed staring at the upper bunk where my brother lay snoring. Absolutely ecstatic that Frazier prevailed, beating the Black man's choice, the demon we all despised. I can still see that closed circuit screen as clearly today as I did then. Like any great fight you're lucky enough to witness, it stays with you like a warm hug from your mother.

The guy I fought was named Ricky, I found out. To show some class we shook hands. It was easier for me to be cordial than it was for him, but I stayed wary that he could be a sore loser and try to jab me as we got close. He didn't, and we actually became friends from that point on. Whenever he'd visit his aunt, we'd pal around.

Back to the corner where I told this joker I never said shit to his sister, but if he thought I did, and wouldn't be convinced otherwise, then let's get this over with. He told me he'd be back. A few minutes later, he came back with his sister who said that I wasn't the guy who harassed her. The brother actually apologized to me and walked away. I'd accomplished what I needed to, proving to all my buds that I wasn't afraid. In their minds, with this encounter bearing significantly more weight given that the would-be challenger was a nigger, I had passed the test. Bobby, always the voice of reason, told me I should have fucked him up. In his eyes at least, I had fallen short by letting it die.

I have always been impressed, maybe a little bit too much, with guys who have the rep of being supreme ass-kickers, the ultimate badasses. If I had to choose between being the richest guy in the Bronx, or the baddest, I'd probably take the latter. I hear about legendary tough guys from different areas, and I seek them out just to be in their company, see them with my own eyes. I'm not unlike a celebrity stalker. Mesmerized, that's how I'd put it. I like to think that someday I could be in that group, and when I walk down the street, my reputation would precede me. No one crazy enough to fuck with me, everyone eager to please me. My closest friends would brag about me, knowing I'd always have their backs.

In the meantime, I'll have to be content with the notion that people know I can scrap, that I can 'handle' myself, that I'm not a punk or a pussy. In any tussle, once they spot fear in your eyes they own you. I prefer to retain ownership of myself. My old man told me once that he'd rather see me get tossed out of school for fighting, than hear I let myself get pushed around.

The man I plan to be is the man who can defend his family, stand back-to-back with his friends, and fight for what he believes, no matter the consequences.

THE BRONX

"My man, Jamaica Al, king of the tropics! What's up, you lady killin' black ass son of a bitch?"

"Little Jackie foo-foo, prince of the emerald isle, what goin' on baby boy?"

"Hey Al, you are way too smart to be Jamaican, you should check the family tree to see if maybe some Irishman was seduced by one of your great, great grannies. Women all over the globe lust for Irishmen, so it 's not a stretch."

"Please, bro, please. You ever see what the average Jamaican is carrying down there between his thighs? It's like, swing low sweet chariot. Follow that pendulum side to side for a minute and you fuckin' hypnotized muthafucka!"

"You know why they call the Irish donkeys, Al? Because we're hung like 'em, that's why. Now what you got in that magic bag of yours?"

"Thai ganja sweetness, even better than what Bob Marley he-self smokes. One toke and you sittin' on a throne next to Jesus. Sun always shinin' and the birds always be singin' when you light up with Uncle Al, that a promise yo."

"Hit me, my man. Hey Al, one more thing before I go. I'm curious but never wanted to intrude on your privacy. How'd you end up with that wooden leg? Sometimes I almost expect to see a parrot on your shoulder, I swear I do."

"Well, little Jackie, I like you so much I ain't even gonna tell you. Too fuckin' gruesome for your precious ears. Let's just leave it at that. Let me ask you a question, my man, now that we playin that. Why you always so uptight, lady killa? Who you at war with? Peace is the solution, bro. Peace inside and out. You need to give it a try; stop fightin' wit you own self."

"Hey, I'm sorry, my man, I shoulda never asked. You know, life has a way of twistin' you around, that's all. I'm good, just need to take care of some things. Pleasure doing business, as always Al, you are a fine representation of fair and equitable commerce."

"Same same, little Jack. Hope you got some pretty missus to share that magic dust with. Be well worth your while, and hers too. Be cool, my man."

THE BRONX

Though I dabble in weed and the occasional need for speed, Black Beauties, and the like, I'm essentially an alcohol man. I view drugs, even cocaine, as a way to get mellow, which translates to yellow, because it puts you in some realm that you completely escape into. So, you're basically incapacitated and unprepared for the unexpected. I do not like to let my guard down.

Admittedly, that philosophy becomes ass backwards when I'm legless drunk, and incapable of standing up straight, never mind doing something that requires substantially more coordination. By my way of thinking, booze is the manlier option, and heavy drugs are for pussies and pacifists, my least favorite animal breeds. I grew up in a drinking world where it's a rite of passage, like making your First Communion. You get dressed up, walk to the fountain, and say ah. Then the Holy Spirit, in solid or liquid form, enters your being and fills your soul.

Then you're in. You get your membership card, and you go about fulfilling the requirements and honing your skills. It's a lifelong endeavor with the eventual goal of becoming one with the spirit, or spirits.

My first drunk was three months after my twelfth birthday, on Saint Patrick's Day.

Incidentally, I was born nine months and a day after Saint Paddy's. I'll let the scientists and mathematicians out there figure out when I was likely conceived, and what my parents might have been up to.

Catholic schools are closed on St. Pat's, an obvious bias that is nonetheless warranted given to how the Irish have taken the world on their backs and rescued civilization. So, what better way to celebrate your heritage than with some solid underaged intoxication?

The plan was to get oiled-up and then train it down to the parade. I headed toward Jerome Avenue under the el train, my boys, Mahoney, Reilly, and Murphy in tow, the oldest of us a ripe thirteen, I secured my half-pint of Seagram's 7 from inside my coat pocket, twisted off the cap, and took a slug of the devil's poison. It tasted absolutely fucking horrific and I barely kept it down, trying my damndest to act like it went down smooth, me being the he-man and all.

To cut to the chase, I never made it to the parade. In fact, I never made it to 9 a.m. I remember the world spinning and wishing I was home in my bed. When I did get home, courtesy of being carried by the police, I was covered in puke and blood. My boys had scattered when the man arrived on the scene. The next day, I was even sicker, and my beloved ma was completely lacking in empathy. So, it wasn't a smashing success, my cherry breaker. One would have thought that it would sideline my drinking career indefinitely, but stupidity, when it comes to alcohol, is a personal trademark.

Our neighborhood is a little weird with how the various age groups have different tendencies when it comes to alcohol and drugs. Of the groups that hang out on the corner or on the Rocks, or in the general vicinity, those in their early twenties, let's call them refugees from the Flower Power days, are all-in druggies. If they drink at all, it's usually some fruity dog piss wine, and they'll pass the bottles around like they would a joint, poor adherence to basic hygiene. These types, of course, tend towards the tie-dyed and bell bottoms look, and they fight off bathing like it's the plague. Their music of choice runs along the lines of God-awful shit like the Grateful Dead. If these fuckers could spend the rest of their days high and idle, they most certainly would. The best thing about them, maybe the only thing, is that the gals are none too concerned about shielding their titties. Overall, they are a pretty harmless bunch.

Then there's the crew my age, and maybe two to three years older. We are tried and true drinkers. The emphasis is on excessive consumption and the ability to ingest it gracefully.

Everything we seem to do, even involving sports, is centered around alcohol. But, hey, the War on Drugs makes no mention of alcohol, and we are all American flag waving patriots. We don't like draft dodgers, who are almost always drug users, and we respect the cops. To most of us, commies, pinkos, spics, niggers, Jews, etc. are anti-establishment and an affront to all things truly American. I like to think of myself as a little more open-minded but, as the adage goes, when in Rome . . .

Behind us, let's call them the youngsters, the fifteen and sixteen-year-olds, who flip-flop back to drug use. It's almost like they wanted their own identity and are too young to remember the hippies. They are not as laid back as previous drug cultures, and they are not afraid to get drunk in the absence of accessibility to drugs. Many a time, I have seen more than one of these dumb motherfuckers blow their entire week's pay from some minimum wage job on an ounce of blow, which they will work through in a matter of hours, forget days. So, twenty or thirty hours of toil gets washed down the toilet in just a few hours. Then they start the cycles anew, a week of work to pay for some shit to shove up your nose. If this is the future of our great country, we are truly and miserably fucked.

What it all boils down to, from my perch in the sky, is that everyone has their own hustle, and every hustle is different. But what's the same for each of us, is the need to manipulate the background scenery in the production that is our lives. Change the colors, change the roles, just change something. Pretty up the picture, smooth the road, clean up the atmosphere. Then put one foot in front of the other and do the best you can.

THE BRONX

My brother, Mickey, broke off the engagement with his girl. The dumb fuck is too young to get married anyway. So, from my perspective, that's good news for my big brother. The dilemma is that his never-to-be-betrothed decided she wanted to keep the engagement ring, which my poor sucker of a sibling had dropped close to a grand on. Speculation was that she was messin' around with the manager of the shithole restaurant she was working at. So, we needed a plan, and I came up with one. You can call me General George Patton II. The assault on our enemy needed to be swift and decisive. It needed to ensure that the other side raised the white flag and begged for mercy. This is how it went down.

We stopped by the gas station and loaded that filthy mongrel, Hollywood, into the backseat of Mickey's car. Hollywood was a little skittish at first, but we gave him a couple of Slim Jims to calm his nerves. This kind of drove my brother mad because he's a stickler for keeping his wheels spic and span, and now his seat covers were a fucking mess. Me and Lukie sat in the rear with the dog between us. Mickey drove and Bobby rode shotgun. Then we headed north to Yonkers to execute the plan and reclaim the ring.

On arrival, Mickey pulled the car into the backlot of the restaurant. It was one of those Sizzler chains where you get cheap steaks and get what you pay for. My brother had driven his girl here numerous times, so he knew his way around. He spotted the manager's car, and we gave the cheating bastard four flat tires as an appetizer. Lukie pissed in his gas tank but from the looks of it, didn't aim too well. I got into my costume: a pair of sunglasses and a rope for Hollywood and approached the front entrance. Hollywood picked up the scent of red meat and willingly came along. The idea was that I was blind, and he was my seeing eye dog.

Lukie, who I was sure didn't wash his hands post-potty, held the door open for me, as my brother and Bobby watched from a short distance in the background. As soon as I opened the door, the young lady who was hostessing, gasped, and then her jaw dropped. In all the excitement, I lost hold of the rope that was serving as a leash for Hollywood, and he ran straight to the salad bar and propped himself up. Once there, the reeking mutt commenced to tear into whatever food was closest to his snout. Ever the discerning diner, Hollywood quickly realized that his preferred meal of choice rested on the tables around him, and he aptly picked up the scent of carnivorous desire.

The place by now was a disaster with the salad bar mess just a small part of what now had the appearance of a five-year-old's finger-painting project. On seeing my companion, most of the diners had jumped from their seats and bolted towards the door, upending tables, chairs, and food as they did. One black gentleman stood up, saw Hollywood at work, and yelled to his wife ". . . holy shit it's a dog, and it's a big muthafuckin dog," then grabbed her arm and sashayed to the door. My brother's ex, who will remain unnamed, came from the kitchen, espied myself and Lukie, and let out a blood-curdling scream.

Realizing, having been positively identified, that we were about to have some serious problems, I picked Hollywood up into my arms, a piece of steak hanging from his mouth, and ran as fast as possible to the exit. My brother's running car waited outside and I tossed Hollywood through the open window into the backseat and then crawled through behind him. Mickey took off before we realized that Lukie wasn't with us. "Fuck him, leave him here," bellowed the stoic and always empathetic Bobby. My brother fortunately ignored him and waited for Lukie to catch up and hop in the car.

As we sped away, we could hear the former affection of my brother's heart cursing and threatening revenge. The last thing I heard her say as we disappeared into the distance was "I will fucking kill you, Mickey, I swear to fucking God. I hate yooooouu, you bastard, you fucking baaaastard!" The nerve of her to threaten my brother with that filthy mouth of hers.

Mickey did get the ring back, but I'm not sure it was my master plan that did it. Being how we were spotted and identified at the scene of the crime, even though the real crime was that girl's theft of the aforementioned jewelry, we had some explaining to do.

Our ma fielded a call from Yonkers finest who wanted to know if she was of the same residence as Mickey and Jack McGee. Ma, ever the wise ass, assured the officer that she was, but not necessarily by choice. Ma was told that her sons were believed to be the perpetrators in an incident that resulted in damage done to the inside of a Sizzlers restaurant, and to a car in the parking lot of that very same venue. Now, I know my beloved mom knew in her heart that what the police officer was saying was in all likelihood accurate, but she was also pretty furious that her daughter-in-law-not-to-be had tried to make off with Mickey's ring.

I'm of the impression that Ma did not like the young lady, having referred to her as 'that little bitch' on more than one occasion. So, when queried, she went on the offensive. She asked the fellow on the other end when the supposed incident had occurred and when informed of such, she told him that we'd been home at the time for our younger sister's birthday party. She then told the man in blue that if he had concrete evidence to the contrary, he would need to produce it. Keeping the caller with no chance to get a word in edgewise, she proceeded to remind him that she was a single mother of five children and her life, including at that very moment, was extremely busy. The cop was no match for our dear mother and the query ended with her curtailing the phone conversation with something along the lines of "now if you don't mind, I have a family to tend to." So, we got off scot-free which was a huge relief, but the ring in question remained in the hands of the enemy.

The prized jewel was returned in a couple of days, delivered by the hand of a mutual friend of both families, who cautioned the young woman that she was dealing with unstable people, and keeping the ring would just create misery for her. The delivery woman and my mom had a good chuckle over that, and a beer and a smoke. My mother's little angels had tested her patience, but she sure had a difficult time keeping a straight face when we regaled her with the details of our quest for the holy grail. In fact, I am of the opinion that she was damn proud of her boys.

Now, all we needed to do was to keep my knucklehead brother from ever getting the notion of marriage into that thick, and oddly squarish, head of his.

Ask yourself every day that single question of the utmost importance—*would I die for my family?* If the answer is 'no,' get a new family. Not only would I die for my mom and my brothers and sisters, but I might even kill for them. You can never say for sure until you're in a situation at a specific moment of time but I'm pretty sure I'd get there. More than pretty sure actually.

Chapter 8

An Irish Rose Blooms Brightest

I'm pretty sure I'm in love with this girl named Mary, a blue-eyed blond of Emerald Isle stock. The torture, for me, is that she barely knows I exist. She lives a few blocks away on the other side of the Grand Concourse and I've only met her a few times. I kind of know her brother but he knows me a little too well, which means he would likely go to any lengths to keep me away from his little sister.

The last time I saw Mary was on a Sunday at the gas station. She was in the backseat of a car driven by her sister's boyfriend, and her sister was in the front passenger seat. Her sister's boyfriend is this guy named Timmy who I know from here and there, so we started shooting the shit and engaging in the usual ball breaking, I noticed Mary as I was leaning on the side of the car, all cool like, slumped down a bit to talk with Timmy through the open window.

Timmy is a stud athlete and a good egg all around and he wasn't fooled by my nonchalance towards the beauty in the rear of his vehicle. The more I tried to act suave-a-cool-a, the more I stumbled on my own stupidity. When Timmy asked me if I knew Mary, I tried to say something that would come out intellectually sound, but all I managed was a "yeah, sure." What I wanted to say was something to the tune of 'of course I do, beauty never goes unnoticed,' or to impress her with a quote from Shakespeare, but there I stood mute, stunned into inaction like a deer in the headlights.

Mary did, however, surprise me by saying, ". . . sure I know, Jack, who doesn't?" That illustrious coo relaxed me enough to look towards her and mutter, "always nice to see you, Mary, hope all is well on your end." She returned the gesture and even flashed me a smile that was an arrow straight into my heart. We all said our goodbyes and then Timmy drove off, leaving me to juggle the wave of emotions that had just hit me like a tsunami.

Mary is as smart as she is beautiful. From what I hear, she's on her way to college on a scholarship to study pre-med. Summed up neatly, she's way out of my league. A sensible man would accept his fate and move on, but nothing about me has ever been sensible. I'm already obsessing about her constantly. I dream of being stuck at the top of the Ferris wheel with her. I imagine us married, in a nice house somewhere, with cute little kids with traditional Irish names.

I find myself driving past her building on my motorcycle hoping for a simple glimpse. Then I flip the channel and see her with some smart doctor type, a preppy douchebag, a ticket out of the Bronx. She'll forget who I am; she'll never have a need to even recall me. Yet, I hold onto that sliver of a chance that she feels something towards me, anything. Maybe, what she saw the other day was not some loser without a future, but this handsome, muscular guy with the

STEPHEN WALSH

long hair and an air of confidence, braving the cold in just a T-shirt, destined to rule the world.

Someone who would always protect her, do anything to make her happy. Someone who has the pick of the litter but chooses her over every other woman on earth. Yeah, whatever kid, keep fucking dreaming.

THE BRONX

My Uncle Joe says that if you take a chisel to an Irishman's head, you'll get three inches of sawdust before you hit stone. It kinda pissed me off when he said that because he's Scottish, and that's like the frying pan calling the kettle black. That's not to say I disagree, just that us micks have a lot of company. Have you ever seen an Albanian's head? Picture a metal balloon with a Hitler mustache. In fairness to Uncle Joe, he married my aunt, and our side of the family is certainly a thick-headed bunch. I'm pretty sure he's yet to convince my Aunt Joan of anything, and they've been married for twenty years.

What gets me on the topic of hard knobs is this new stunt I've been performing to an adoring throng of fans in the Alibi on Sundays, after our football games. The Alibi sponsors a team in the local touch tackle league, and the loser is obligated to go to the winner's bar and buy a keg of brew. We win a lot more than we lose and so we get to drink free beer. Depending on when the game ends the beer can often substitute as a late breakfast.

Touch tackle football, Bronx style, has a very violent nature. You might score three touchdowns but if it'll be a hit you laid on someone—that will get the greater press. One week, a game scheduled for 9 a.m. at Ferry Point Park was delayed for over an hour while the cops removed a murdered body from the fifty-yard line. It's a good thing the cops got there first because we wouldn't have let a corpse delay the game. A couple of us would have grabbed a leg each and pulled the stiff at least ten yards from the nearest sideline, and then lined up for the opening kickoff.

Word was that this cat was on the wrong end of a drug deal gone bad. None of the cops I saw appeared to be too shaken up about the passing of a human life. In fact, they were indignant that this unfortunate fellow had somehow deliberately got himself killed on their beat, where not only did they have to freeze their asses off unwinding a crime scene, but there was plenty of paperwork waiting for them back at the precinct house. So, we all stood around shivering until the body was removed, and then erupted in a loud cheer when the body bag was finally tossed in the wagon, signaling the imminent departure of the recently deceased.

The team we were playing, some sissy boys from Queens, with the ridiculous name the Queen's Destroyers, stood by pensively as we hooted and howled. I'm pretty sure it dawned on them at that moment that they were in over their heads. While waiting for the game to start, their coaches put them through a regiment of calisthenics with accompanying team chants.

Bobby, taking a long pull from his Marlboro, shook his thumb in a side to side motion in the direction of our opponents and exclaimed, "Check out these fucking clowns." If it was meant to be intimidating, it failed miserably—the consensus on our end was that they were merely a bunch of goofballs.

Our pregame routine was considerably less organized. Terry, our mastermind of a coach, drew some indecipherable X's and O's on a slab of cardboard, pausing now and then to sneak a nip from his flask for mind and body comfort. None of his strategies would in the slightest way be employed. Terry is a lovable guy but he's no Vince Lombardi. No 'win one for the Gipper' speeches from his bloated lips.

On our sideline, we psyched ourselves up in unison, with an assortment of rituals. Some peeled off their shirts and did push-ups or sit-ups, others threw a ball around. Then there were the less stable of us who partook in friendly bouts of headbutting with the intention of drawing blood. Still others maintained their composure with their last sip of beer or drag of a cigarette before the kickoff whistle blew.

So, when the Queens Destroyers ventured a glimpse at the opposing sideline, the images they saw were wholly disconcerting. There were shirtless men in 25-degree weather, some with blood dripping down their faces. There were crumpled beer cans and the haze of tobacco.

There was laughing, cursing, and threatening chants, what there wasn't, was any semblance of organized team unity, just a poorly contained mishmash of chaos metastasizing. So, as the coroner's van disappeared in the distance, and the refs prepared to flip a coin, the boys from the Bronx stood brazenly ready to engage. The confidence that the boys from Queens had displayed earlier, was notably wilted. We kicked their asses silly, and yours truly had two picks, one that I would have returned for a touchdown had I not tripped over some yellow tape left from the crime scene that got tangled in my cleats. Dead men may not tell lies but it seems they can still play defense in a pinch.

Let's return to Uncle Joe's image of the Irish noggin, and my latest display of ultimate manliness. Sunday afternoon, right around noon, and the bar is packed. The men of the gridiron and their adoring fans are assembled for revelry.

Hassett, the bartender, is preparing the keg. I stand in the back area of the bar and wait for the crowd to part, like Moses waiting for the Red Sea. My green cloth bomber's cap firmly secured; I move towards the tap as the chant 'Jackie Jackie Jackie . . .' resounds throughout the tavern. I stand on a rail directly in front of the bar, reigning over the official opening of the taps, a symbolic popping of the cork. An empty pitcher is placed beneath the two unopened taps.

The deafening chants intensify as I raise my head above the concealed coils. With all eyes now intently on me, and people desperately jockeying for a closer look, I lurch my head back and then violently slam it down on the bar, landing it with a fierce thud at a space between the two taps. Instantly beer pours from each vessel, and the cheers erupt. The conquering heroes have returned, and the greatest among them has shown his immense savagery for all to witness, The party has begun! There wasn't a dry pair of undershorts left in the house—the men's a result of fear, the women's a direct byproduct of lust. Thus, we were beckoned back to the days when men were men and sheep were scared, and the thick heads of the Irish ruled the five boroughs and beyond.

THE BRONX

"Hey mister, can you tell me where a man might find a bed. He just grinned and shook my hand; no is what he said."

There are few levels of despair that exceed the horrible sensation of being legless drunk and an impossible distance between you and your bed. And miles to go before I sleep, miles to go . . .

I have a disturbing pattern of collapsing into uncon-sciousness when I've come within fighting distance of my warm abode, more than once sleeping right outside our apartment door and then discovered by the first one out the following morning. I've slept at bus stops, under stairwells, and even in an alleyway. Each time, I have not been that far from home.

It's like I have an instinctual recognition, despite being in a drunken stupor, of having crossed over enemy lines into a safe zone. Like a homing pigeon diving into its nest. I've slept in snowbanks, rainstorms, and sweltering heat. One night, had the cops not found me, I might have frozen to death outside a warehouse on Webster Avenue. You'd think waking up covered in dirt and piss would teach me a lesson. Blackout drinking does not seem to agree with me. Instead of heeding the warning signs, I tend to write it off as part of a game, and even take a foolish pride in my knack for survival. Rolling the dice will eventually come up snake eyes, but time and time again, I'll spit in my hand and shake the cubes and see if I can spin another seven. The dice don't lie, they say, and they do plenty of talking. Let's hope that when they do talk, they whisper sweet nothings of peace and prosperity.

It's hard to keep your footing when you keep stepping into potholes but there are paths that lead to magnificent things. Is there a better feeling than being in love? Or a scarier one? Mary, Mary quite contrary where will you be five years from now?

Chapter 9

Christmas in the Bronx

Life has a way of surprising us, both good and bad. Now I know that's not an original phrase, nor am I proposing that I'm some kind of deep-thinking philosopher, but it seems to be the best lead into this story.

Christmas Eve at the gas station and I'm feeling no pain. There's been no shortage of booze circling around since the station party started early in the afternoon, including some of the good stuff that the ginzo, wannabee Mafiosi brought over from their social club on the other side of Jerome Avenue, in gratitude for letting them park their Cadillacs on the premises year round. They're actually a decent bunch, darn good tippers and funny motherfuckers to boot. The club doesn't allow females, even goomahs, and the rule is strictly enforced. I always admire the principles of those with few principles. They also sport enough cologne to neutralize the stench from the garbage dump I call my workplace.

The station owners, always solid candidates to fall into Ebenezer Scrooge mode, had given me the green light to close the dump early, even compensating me for a full shift.

'Twas a fine holiday glow I presented. By now, everyone had split to other parties, bars or to their homes, so I was on my lonesome to start the process of locking up the place.

I had just shut down the pumps and was walking inside when a car pulled up and a man jumped out. Normally, I'd be startled but as I said, I was two sheets of the three sheets to the wind. The guy that exited from the car was an Indian, not the Sitting Bull type of Indian, but the Hadji from *Johnny Quest* kind. He asked me if I remembered him, and I drew a blank. He proceeded to tell me that I had given him 75 cents to get on the train one afternoon several months back, after he'd somehow managed to get lost while attempting to visit a friend via bus in the northern Bronx. It was then that I recalled him and the day in question.

Something about him had led me to fork over the three quarters even though I would have generally dismissed him as a scamster. Nine times out of ten, I would have told him to fuck off and beat it, but I had actually believed him. He reached out his hand to shake and I accepted. He was carrying a bag with straps in his other hand and after we disengaged, he reached into the bag and came up with a bottle. In my palm, he pressed the three quarters that made us even. But he wasn't content with even, so he handed me the bottle as well.

It had a beautiful red bow on it and I almost fainted when I saw it was Johnnie Walker Red. With tears in his eyes, he explained how I had rescued him from what to him had been a serious dilemma. Tough guy me was actually choking back a lump in my throat as I told him it was nothing really and that he was being overly generous. He told me that I had proven that the world is full of kind people. We shook hands once more and then he got into his car and drove away, apparently all the way back to Queens.

I hate to admit it but I'm pretty sure I was crying. Christmas Eve and here I was a real live Jimmy Stewart in *It's a Wonderful Life*. I wanted to scream Merry Christmas from the top of my lungs and run and buy the prize turkey for Tiny Tim and the Cratchits. He was right, the wonderful man whose name I didn't even know, the world is full of kind people. I took an oath to myself that evening that I'd be one of them. A promise that will always be hard for me to keep.

THE BRONX

Christmas in the McGee house is nothing short of spectacular. Somehow, my mother manages to stock the bottom of the tree with loads of presents for everyone, and even more so for the youngest. My mom didn't grow up in a home where there was money enough for Christmas gifts. All available funds went for necessities.

My grandma, my mom's mom, died delivering her sixth kid and the family was split up, with the two youngest going to relatives, and mom, at the ripe old age of sixteen, becoming the family matriarch. She ended up running the household because her father, my grandfather, distraught over the loss of his beloved, disappeared for long stretches, usually to the Bowery, and often enough on Christmas day. Gone was his longshoreman's salary and any chance for mom to finish high school. For the record, she's the smartest high school dropout in the whole goddamn world. There isn't even a close second. Throw in my Pop's passing and you can see where she gets the motivation to make Christmas the bonanza it is for the McGees.

No kids of my mom are gonna come up empty on Christmas, you can take that to the bank. The big boys, me and Mickey, get big boy things, as does my sister, Cathy, who is, at least in her mind, a young lady of society. The twins, Danny and Eileen, are past the little kids distinction but still get little kid items, toys mostly. Mom seems to want to keep them young for eternity. But just in case Danny starts getting the idea that he's special, I'll grab him in a headlock and scrape a dent in his noggin with my knuckles.

Want to hear something crazy? She tried to do it discreetly, but I heard Ma had actually given a hundred bucks to a family in need that she had heard about from church. Barely a pot to piss in herself, getting by month to month, and the gal pulls a rabbit out of her hat. Knowing my mother as I do, the thought of kids at Christmas without presents, any kids, pulled her heartstrings tight. I found out through the grapevine that it was actually a black family who had recently experienced a tragedy. My mother never ceases to amaze me.

There's lots of jokes about Christmas in the Bronx. Like how Santa would be beaten to death with a baseball bat if he was caught sneaking around someone's apartment. Given the absence of chimneys, he'd need to come through the front door and that door, of course, would be at least triple locked, on top of having a metal pole jammed behind it. So, he'd have to knock and when asked, "who is it?" he'd be required to loudly shout his name, which would wake up the neighbors who would then open their doors and shout to him to "shut the fuck up," and then slam their doors behind them.

As for landing his sled on the roof, good luck with that, Santa. Anything left unattended for longer than three minutes in the Bronx is likely to be gone upon your return. People will take it whether they need it or not, or even if they don't know what they're stealing. The toys on the sled will be decimated like a liquor store during a blackout. As for the reindeer, there'll be more than chestnuts roasting on an open fire.

The sled itself will be gutted, with everything from the radio to the plush, satin, red interior ripped from the frame. To make matters worse, when he returns to where he last saw his sled and trusted herd of reindeer, someone will be waiting to relieve him of that fine red and white jumpsuit he gallivants around in. Days later, some Puerto Rican will be seen sashaying down Creston Avenue with a jumpsuit of amazingly similar colors, and a familiar looking wide, black leather belt. When Santa stops by the local precinct house to report the crime, the cops on duty will be laughing their asses off. Santa will be on the phone with God the very next day, tendering his resignation.

Christmas Day and the first one up, wakes up the whole house. Everybody's a kid on Christmas, not the least of all mom. Despite being bone tired and begging for more sleep, she sits in the armchair with the biggest smile imaginable, and a twinkle in each of her green eyes. Wrapping paper flies in all directions and the oohs and aahs and screams of delight echo off the plaster walls of our tiny living room. We have, of course, been gifted to our hearts desire. Same as last year and the year before that. But the great anticipation suddenly shifts course, and now points squarely at the armchair where mom sits. As terrific as all the presents are, what matters most to each of us right this moment, and probably has this entire Christmas morning, is how happy our mother will be with the presents we'll give her. To see the glow on her pretty Celtic face is the most rewarding gift of all. It's hard to feel sorry for yourself on Christmas, and sometimes it's even harder to stop and thank your lucky stars. I'm doing a nice job at the moment staying on that lucky side, but when the glow of Christmas begins to ebb, things can get surprisingly sad.

THE BRONX

One of the most delightful annual rituals that transpire in our little neck of the woods occurs each year about a week to ten days after Christmas. What makes it even more gratifying is that the people that would like to prevent it, the local authorities, municipalities and such, know it's coming but are at the mercy of our superior wits and, thus incapable of smoting the beast before it digs in its claws. It's basically a giant art project of a sinister nature, which is flaming genius in both form and execution. It combines the altogether devious with the lesser devious and the barely devious, the fun seekers with the thrill seekers, and the budding neophytes with the masters of their craft. Word spreads like wildfire, so to speak, and before you know it the baby arsonists, snot-nosed kids between ages of nine and fifteen or thereabouts, have spread out like an attacking army to find and retrieve tossed Christmas trees, which at this point in their evolution are perfectly dry and combustible.

Instructions have been given to the scavengers to accumulate and return as many trees as possible as quickly as possible. In the meantime, the older kids, let's say the sixteen to twenty-one crowd, will be readying an area alongside 'the Rocks,' that stone anomaly in the middle of everything, for the stacking and formation of what will become our burning bush.

Interestingly, even a couple of the local fathers will be on hand to help, having promised their kids a spectacular fiery spectacle. Those fathers will be in a distinct minority to the more sensible neighborhood adults who would like to keep Mrs. O'Leary's cow safely in the barn.

Sensing imminent disaster, they will fail once again, to alert the police and fire department before the first match is struck. Each having done his part, we'll all retreat to a safe distance for viewing, knowing we have come together successfully, to complete this magnificent event. For the Bronx, this will be a rare fire not started by a landlord. Within seconds, it would seem, the flames will tower as high as a five-story building, and the air will transform from frigid to a summer bluster as if by magic. As the sirens sound in the distance, we'll all raise a toast to a job well done and bask in the fire's glow. Community planning *non-pareil*, as any competent social scientist is sure to agree.

Santa gets his ass quickly out of Dodge (or the Bronx if you prefer accuracy) but stops by, nonetheless. Why can't every day be Christmas they ask—that's just not how life works around here. You spend 364 days just to get to that one single day; and you spend that single day in constant trepidation that the day is disappearing way too fucking fast.

CHAPTER 10

Dumb Knuckerfuckers

A nickname like 'Knuckles' might lead you to assume that the so-titled individual was a gifted lad with the mitts, the type whose big, gnarled hands strike fear in the average heart. Alas, this Knuckles, aka Sean Malone, got his moniker courtesy of a fist print to the middle of his forehead, etched ungraciously by no less than his very own older brother. Given his moon-sized bean and ultra pasty skin, the impression left quite an impression, so to speak. Thus, that single punch would christen him for all eternity, to those who know him best, as Knuckles, or Knucks for short. He was also somewhat of a mental midget so his being an all-around knucklehead made the tag that much easier to digest. Conversations with Sean, much like they are with my pal, Sal, are predictably painful.

Sal: "Yo, Knuckles, I heard your mother is pregnant again; how many is that now, like twenty?"

Knucks: "I don't have a mother, Sal, me and my father use yours."

Sal: "Watch it with the mother jokes, motherfucker."

Me: "I believe you initiated the mother assault, Sal, and then added more poison to the well with your final word, that being the pejorative, motherfucker, which translates to mean that even a motherfucker can find a mother to participate in fornication, which is an insult to mother's everywhere, including yours."

Knucks: "That's tellin' him, Jack. So, Sal, don't be using that perjury shit when you bring up my mother. If she don't kick your ass, I will—you motherfucker."

Sal: "You're gonna kick my ass? Please Knucks! I'd rather fight you than your mother, I heard she can bench press 200 pounds of potatoes. And you're the motherfucker, not me."

Me: "I can't tell which of you mooks is dumber; it's a genuine quagmire, or let's just say it's a real motherfucking puzzle."

Knucks: "I aint no queermire. You ever see me in a dress with lipstick on?"

Sal: "You're making me puke, Knucks. Why don't you go find a fist to bounce off of your head?"

Me: "I don't think either of you is in danger of damaging the exterior of your head, it's the inside that you've failed to protect. To put it mildly, you're a pair of dumbass motherfuckers."

What's left to be said?

CHAPTER 11

God Forbid, Are Puerto Ricans
Just Irish People with Tans?

Cutting out of school a little early each day doesn't feel like much of a crime to me, but it does put me in a sorry state of mind. It's not like the free time that fills the void creates time well spent doing other things. School is a joke, way too easy to require any effort, and my brain feels like it's in a state of atrophy. Had I not been tossed from my previous high school, where I actually had a chance at an education, I might be looking at college, or something with promise. Now, my life feels like it's in decline and I'll never amount to anything.

Doesn't seem like Hollywood will come calling, and pipe dreams of becoming Middleweight Champ of the World, or something equally impressive are, just that, stupid delusions. Another year has passed when I missed the deadline to sign up for the Gloves, and I hate myself for my cowardice. Each day, I promise myself that today is the day I do something to alter the course, and each day is a repeat of the previous, and nothing changes.

Brother Brian told me that nothing changes, if nothing changes. He's obviously telling me that the onus is on me to force the issue, but he hasn't told me how. The promising thing that I have going for me is that I'm not afraid of hard work. If I become a cop or fireman, I won't be angling for three-quarters with some bullshit injury like a lot of these frauds. I need to figure this shit out. I can't go down a loser.

THE BRONX

Mark O'Toole walks into a bar. Let's call it the Alibi. It's probably not much past 9 p.m. but he's already got quite the load on. The guy has superhuman strength, to a level where he can pull parking meters out of the concrete and toss around a manhole cover like it's a frisbee. So, in he comes, not bothering to stop and address anyone, and walks straight over to the pay phone on the wall and starts shaking it. Keep in mind, the apparatus he is disturbing is surrounded by plexiglass and drilled into the wall. Not much more than a minute elapses before the phone materials are hanging in the air, held on by wires alone. Mark then walks up to the bar, and in a low and polite voice, looks me in the eyes and says, "Excuse me, mister, but your phone doesn't seem to be working."

I say, "Sorry for the inconvenience, Mark, can I get you anything to drink?"

What was I to do? It's not like I was in a position to scold him for tearing the phone out of the wall, or to ask him his motivation for doing so. When Mark gets drunk like this there's nobody home between his ears, as displayed by his eerily blank glare, and it's best to let this sleeping beast lie. I pour him about four ounces of vodka in a short glass, which he gulps down in one concise burst. He leaves me a tenner as a tip, thanks me for my kind service, and disappears into the night.

When Gleason, the owner, called me the next day (not from the bar pay phone) to ask me what in god's name happened to the goddamned call box, I feigned ignorance. To pretend that you didn't see a phone disappear from its foundation, while being in extremely close proximity, requires the guile of a mastermind. I am proud to say, a man of that genius resides within me.

THE BRONX

Vinny, my Puerto Rican alter ego, took me down to his old stomping ground on 175th street and Walton Avenue, for a taste of Latin culture. Somehow, he managed to wedge his boat of a car perfectly between two vehicles. When it comes down to a game of inches, the Puerto Ricans could be considered the world's foremost drivers. I once saw this *bandito* do 50 down a side street without slowing down for a microsecond, and sail by a double-parked car at such a close distance without hitting anything though I swore to myself that I heard the scrape of metal. A psychologist would describe it as auditory impulse association. I'd describe it as 'holy shit, did that lunatic Rican just do what I think he did?' Mario Andretti, if he saw what I saw, would hand over his Indy 500 trophy and concede his title. We got out of the car, and I immediately sensed that my whiteness was stinging the eyeballs of any and all onlookers. Outside of cops, Caucasians are not frequent visitors to this locality. To be frank, that I was there at all gave me a surge of excitement, like swimming in water that you know contains sharks. In warmer weather, there'd be people hanging out everywhere. On stoops, beach chairs, milk crates or the hoods of cars. There'd be dice and dominoes games being played on flattened out cardboard, and people old and young would be dancing to a Latin beat. The *cerveza* would flow and the *bodega* would be buzzing, the *barrio* would be on full throttle.

Winter is another matter altogether. Cold weather is a curse to people with Caribbean roots. Though not quite full hibernation, these fuckers can pretty much disappear from sight from November to March. The streets will often seem uninhabited, but inside the tenements, the need for basic human interaction will continue unabated. The Puerto Ricans, like the Irish, are prodigious procreators. When that first warm day of spring arrives in April, there will be bodies, old and new, coming out of the woodwork.

On this particular day, there's mostly just young people around. The unemployed and the high school drop-outs, the black marketers, and the desperate. You can handle only so much time indoors in a tiny apartment with too many occupants, so the choice between freezing your ass off or losing your fucking mind becomes easy.

Vinny and I walk up to a *bodega* where there's a handful of sinister looking young hoodlum types passing idle time. It's a virtual guarantee that this is also the center of illicit commerce. One of them, a dude named Hector, sees Vinny coming and moves to embrace him. They're long-time pals from growing up in this neighborhood together. A couple of the others know Vinny as well and they exchange the characteristic handshakes that always conclude with a kiss on your hand and a bump on your chest where your heart is supposed to be. The ones that don't know Vinny act like they don't give a shit who he is, and it's likely not an act. But everyone else there, outside of me and my traveling companion, surely wants to know who this skinny, white motherfucker is who has the audacity to come strolling nonchalantly into their world.

Vinny not only sensed the static, but he also predicted it. Told me that his boys would want to cut me open like a papaya, so I should just keep my cool and let him do the talking. I just wanted him to set things straight as rapidly as possible, before anyone got any inclinations to address the perceived affront, and deal with the brazen honkie. Within a couple of minutes, I was greeting my new friends with my own contorted version of their handshake. Any friend of Vinny's, even a white motherfucker like me, was a friend of theirs. Well, not quite a friend in the true sense, but someone they would refrain from killing out of respect for their *compadre*.

Interestingly enough, I wasn't the only white person to make their acquaintance recently. Hector whistled up to a slightly ajar second floor window and two female heads appeared. He asked them to throw him down a pair of gloves. Turns out these two chicks from somewhere in Westchester had run away from home and found their way here. Like the yellow brick road that bypasses Oz and leads you straight to *Dante's Inferno*. Little girls in BMWs generally don't prosper in places like 175th and Walton. I didn't ask any questions because I didn't want any answers. To each his own, to each his own. These young ladies were probably only ten miles or so from home sweet home, but they had a nasty obstacle course in-between.

So went the first leg of our experiment. I left unscathed and with my pride intact. My mind is a strange thing and by the time we left I had convinced myself that one on one I could have taken any of them. Something I needed to square with myself for some crazy fucking reason I'll never be able to define. The next leg would be me bringing Vinny to my corner of spic hating civilization.

Then we'd figure out who hated who more. I have to admit, the cockfights in that Walton Avenue basement would be hard to top. I knew it was a good time to leave when the master of ceremonies, an older fucker, one of the many who went by the name of Papi, spotted me in the crowd and, while dangling the deceased carcass of a rooster, shouted across the room, "Who the fuck invited the gringo? Get your fucking ass outta here before you be bleedin' like this fucking *pollo maricon*." He struck me as a man of his word, so I hastily obliged. I tugged Vinny's shirt and told him we needed to *vamos* with expediency. We left with him cursing the chicken that cost him five bucks.

THE BRONX

It's late Sunday morning in the gas station and I'm sitting in the office during one of the rare lulls in business, taking a mental inventory of everything I drank the previous night. I know I started the night out drinking vodka and grapefruit, and then segued into Jack and Coke, but the math gets super fuzzy when I attempt to tally the endless stream of peppermint schnapps.

Someone started buying shots and then it turned into a free-for-all and I'm sure that if anyone checked the ingredients on a bottle of that piss, turpentine would be one of them. So, between the acid in the grapefruit juice, the concentrated sugar in the Jack Daniels, and the artificial peppermint or whatever else is in the schnapps, my stomach is begging my head to put a bullet in it. Normally, I'd be sipping a cup of coffee and rattling off another set of push-ups but just lifting my head and keeping my eyes open is workout enough.

So, as I'm pleading with God to kill me peacefully, some 'jamoke' has pulled up to the pumps and is beeping his horn, a gesture, at least in his mind, to get some service. I have a very simple rule: if you can't wait patiently, you will wait endlessly, or at least until you learn some manners. The longer the standoff continues, the more incensed the man becomes, until he finally gets out of his car and screams in my direction in an accent I can't quite make out. What I can decipher is that no matter what the dialect, the message is clear, he is very, very angry with me.

Needless to say, I am rather displeased with him, and I gesture my sentiments using my middle finger and a 'go fuck yourself' as the cherry on top.

The guy is approaching me when a snappy, silver Lincoln pulls up and Marko, the house mechanic, hops out. His timing, I would later learn, was fortuitous. Marko knows the man in the car, so they commence talking. For a car mechanic, the guy is pretty amazing when it comes to languages. He can speak Spanish, Italian, Yugoslavian, Albanian and some German, plus the curse words in a slew of other languages, most of which I'm hoping to learn. Currently, he and his pal are conversing in what I'm pretty sure is either Yugo or Albo. Marko's friend, a man in an ill-fitting suit with a mustache, is gesturing towards me in an uncomplimentary fashion.

Marko turns his back on me and walks with the man to his car. As I wait in the distance, Marko gases the guy's car. They shake hands and then my nemesis drives off. Marko walks back and hands me the gas money.

He then informs me that the recently departed gentleman, an Albanian, was genuinely planning to shoot me. Marko educated me on the fashions and habits of the average Albanian male. First and foremost, he scolded me, don't ever insult an Albanian in public. The scorned Albanian will then, pursuant to some ancient code, feel bound to defend his honor, most notably by killing the offender. I tell Marko my side of the story which he dismisses as having zero relevance. The only variable of note from his perspective is that if you fuck with an Albanian, you get what you get.

Albanians are an interesting bunch. Often, they masquerade as Yugoslavians or Italians, for reasons that are unclear to me, nor do I ever expect a valid explanation. Their national flag is in the comfort colors of red and black, with a two-headed bird not meant for a cage. I assumed that it is not designed to lure tourists. When in public, the women, dressed fashionably in all black, walk behind the men. The younger generation makes the disco loving Italians appear conservatively attired in their white pants and designer jeans. They are a comical combination of eurotrash and ghetto chic. The violent culture they were supposed to leave behind has followed them like a storm cloud. Their timing, being in the Bronx in the here and now, is impeccable. Oh, to be in America.

As the Bronx began its process of burning to the ground, Albanians became the buyers of last resort for any landlord looking to get out. As the exodus from South to North gained steam, with gutted tenements going up in smoke in the background, they bought up building after building. The two-headed bird rising from the ashes. The dread of integration in the white neighborhoods became reality. Spics and niggers, niggers and spics, because, because, because, because, because, because of the horrible things they do. For the white folk that didn't want to leave, or couldn't afford it, the Albos made it a Godfather moment. You could refuse to leave, but staying will be a nightmare. By getting rid of you they could jack the rent and get guaranteed checks from welfare. Thus began the systematic torture. No heat or hot water in the dead of winter, no garbage pick-up. Complain or fight, the Black Hand warning would be left outside your door.

The Bronx was never meant to be a melting pot. The pot is cold iron, incapable of melting anything. The sides are meant to hold, for the neighborhoods to keep from spilling one into the other. You stay there, and we stay here. That's the deal, so please abide. Integration will only bring bleeding, and the colors will never blend. If and when the cultures clash, it'll be an atomic explosion. For me, and those who live in my world, hate becomes an aphrodisiac; it gets you excited. All the things that have been drilled into my head tell me to resist the influx, drive the fuckers back. Keep the borders, defend the turf. Do what it takes, whatever it takes.

I'm trying, man, but how long can I swim against the tide? This shit can get really hard. It's like Atlas pulled a bait and switch on me and left me holding the bag. My knees are shakin', the earth's a-quakin' and I'm rubbing the crud out of the eyes in the back of my head so that nothing or nobody sneaks up on me. That's hardly a philosophy for a meaningful life.

Chapter 12

Good Craic

Brother Brian pulled me in for another session. The first thing he mentioned was that he knew I was cutting out of school early most days. He said that it was common knowledge, that I wasn't fooling anyone.

"Look Jack, I could really give a shit. You're too smart for this shithole of a school anyway. You're not exactly being educated in any real sense. But there are things you can learn here. Look at the kids you're in school with. Most of them will end up living bitter, unsatisfying lives. I hate to even say that but it's true. They'll have pissed away any chance at a real education. As it is, they're living their days biding their time for a future that will never come. When I was their age, your age, I thought drinking and using drugs was cool as well. And it can be cool, but not forever. Then it becomes a crutch, and then a wheelchair. You can't make it from one place to another without the push of a substance. And the place you're going to is no place at all. Have you ever heard of a chap named Thoreau?"

"Defenseman on the Rangers?"

"Good one there! Not quite, Jack. He's a philosopher, and he said something along the lines of men living their lives in quiet desperation. I know that to be true, Jack; I'm one of them. After my Pa passed, I went into a long period of self-pity, I didn't see it as that, but it was. It gave me an excuse to drink to bury my sorrows. Sorrows I allowed to fester that I watered everyday with that self-pity. It kept me from taking chances, from moving forward with my life. It drained my ambitions. It got to the point where all that I could be was a martyr. That's what I'm doing here at this school, or at least I thought it was, to save kids I perceived to be me. What a load of happy horseshit! I'm imploring you, Jack, don't go down the same fucking rabbit hole I retreated into.

"You're too damn smart and too damned good. The others here don't have the gifts you have. Don't take those gifts for granted, don't be the coward I was. Don't use your father's death as an excuse."

Wow, Thoreau. Afterwards I looked him up in an encyclopedia. Weird fucker, not someone I'd care to spend much time with. So, Brother Brian is hitting me with that self-pity crap again. He thinks I spend my life feeling sorry for myself. Self-pity, as I see it, is for pussies and I am no fucking pussy. I mean, I like the guy, and I know he means well, but I never had any intention of ducking into any rabbit hole. Better a red badge of courage than the taint of yellow stamped across my heart. It may take me time to figure things out but figure them out I will.

THE BRONX

There's a donkey bar further down Jerome Avenue called the Archway, right across the street from the Kingsbridge

Armory. The place can be a real hoot. The clientele is Irish from the other side, newly printed Americans. Giant sized bar with a massive dance floor. These micks are oblivious to the dangerous confines of the location. There's strength in numbers but if any of these drunken goofballs change the math by wandering off a block or two off the beaten path, they're playing with fire. For the locals, a drunken Irishman by himself is easy pickings. Like taking candy from a baby. When the fallen mick wakes up in the hospital he'll be aching for dear old Donegal, or whichever county spawned him. The good news for the victims is that legless drunks are easy to roll and make lousy witnesses, so there's no incentive to kill them.

It came as a surprise to me that the first time I ever walked into a place that the band was playing country music. I was expecting rebel songs or Irish ballads but what I heard upon entry was an Irish accent cooing Kenny Rogers "Lucille." Four hungry children and a crop in the field, and a couple of hundred howling Irish eating up this fan favorite, acting like they were in the hills of western Kentucky. Though I never really considered Ireland to be part of Europe, just like I don't consider Riverdale to be part of the Bronx, these greenhorns were doing their damndest to prove me wrong. Fat-assed Irishman should not be wearing Jordache jeans, under any circumstances. Assimilation takes time but for the sake of my heritage, I hope it's sooner than later.

Me, Mickey, Bobby, and Luke settled in at a corner of this huge u-shaped bar. There were plenty of women and they weren't all fat ankles and broad-shouldered. Actually, there were quite a few pretty ones. I chatted up this one dark-haired, green-eyed beauty who initially took to me like lice. After a few minutes though, I had her giggling, and she opened up a bit. She was from the northwest of Ireland, still in the Republic, from a town I can't remember.

When the latest hillbilly tune ended, she was joined by a few of her girlfriends, and I motioned my pals over to make it a party.

The lass, whose name was Eileen, told me, 'Yous yanks' were known to be on the 'quick like.' 'Wham bam, thank you ma'am and all that,' is how she put it. Then she told me she was no 'Yankee slut' and I should look elsewhere if 'that's what yer after.' 'Jaysus, no,' I said in my best Irish accent, 'I'm in search of true, everlasting love. I've taken a vow of celibacy until my wedding night. I hope you're as excited with anticipation as I am. We'll make gorgeous babies.'

She giggled again, even laughed. Time for the full court press.

Life was feeling pretty all right and the bunch of us were having what the Irish girls referred to as 'craic.' Not the smoking kind or the indent the plumbers are known for, just a Gaelic term for fun. There's a lightness that floats your veins when you're in a euphoric state, especially when there's a highly attractive lady involved, and even more especially when she's at least a couple of years older than you. Things were feeling too good to be true, and the truth would have its reckoning.

The band unexpectedly swung into a rock song, "Maggie May" by Rod Stewart. Rod Stewart songs have the same effect on Luke as Pavlov's bell did to his dog. The second the first note is struck, Luke is gyrating and gesticulating all over the fucking place. To see him is to love him. Some of his moves, most of them in fact, are pure genius. He'll spin wildly, stop and pause like a statue, and then go whirling to all corners of the dance floor, his limbs akimbo, his head like a dashboard canine.

It won't be long before he has everyone's attention and people are ceasing their own dance steps to watch him. For every person that finds it exhilarating, there's another that thinks it disturbing. Either way you're bound to be raptured. Luke's manic frenzy was picking up momentum as he made his way back to our area. I screamed aloud to egg him on, and he took my cue to ramp up what was already a manic pace, then engaged in a wild spin that was completely out of control. So out of control that his elbow, like a runaway train, came accidentally crashing down on Eileen's head, knocking her unconscious.

I never got Eileen's phone number. I did try to come to her aid but then quickly understood my assistance would be unwelcome. It was like, for the first time that night, our group of four was suddenly noticed for what it was—a quartet of outsiders. It was time to take our leave but that would not come without effort.

Eileen's brother, a strapping farm boy of a man, had been keeping a wary eye on his sister and her would be suitors the whole time, and when she hit the floor, he hit the roof. He stormed across the bar on a beeline towards Luke. Poor Luke, who had surely meant no harm, stood perplexed and shaken at his unintended handiwork. Eileen's friends were down on all fours trying to revive her. Her brother by now had thrown Luke to the floor and had his big meaty hands around Luke's neck. Bobby then jumped on the brother's back to pull him off our boy. Mickey, ever the peacekeeper, was trying to explain it all away as a freak accident.

I noticed Eileen had come to and wondered if I should try one last time to get her phone number; then thinking the better of it, joined the fray. Fortunately, the extraordinarily large bouncers broke things up before we got completely obliterated, and gently tossed us out. There was no fight in me to speak of. It's hard to throw punches back at people who have a valid reason to punch you. If some flailing madman knocked my sister out, I'd be as eager for revenge as the next fella. The notion that stuck in my head, when we were safely outside, wasn't so much losing love before it had even been gained, but that the four of us all had on white T-shirts, and all our T-shirts had spots of blood that, to the keen eye, appeared as art.

It doesn't take donkey blood to make an ass of yourself but it sure as shit doesn't hurt the cause.

Chapter 13

I Have a Few Questions for God but I'm Not Expecting Answers Anytime Soon

They killed my old pal, Jimmy Welsh—the niggers did. Me and Jimmy were locker mates before we both got tossed from school. We were in most of the same classes and were constantly in trouble. It was near impossible not to laugh when you were with him, he was such a lunatic. The antics he pulled could fill a book, and some of the shit he pulled is proof that life can be stranger than fiction. Nothing, nor no one, could shake the guy. He was scarily fearless—death wish fearless. I was unceremoniously dismissed midway through sophomore year, and he managed to hang on until the year was finished before catching the ejection seat. He was from way over near West Kingsbridge, so we lost touch for the most part.

But we would occasionally run into one another, and the laughs were as if they never left off. I heard he'd gone to a public high school, and was going through the motions to get his paper degree before enlisting in the Marine Corps. Jimmy had no ambitions outside of the Marines; it was all the crazy bastard cared about. And man, he was in insane shape. A life of one-armed pushups, fingertip pull-ups, and all sorts of other exercises, including serious weights, had transformed him into a physical force, one badass motherfucker. He had muscles on top of muscles and not an ounce of fat. When we would fuck around slap fighting and I'd get the better of him, he'd get apeshit enraged. There was no play in play fighting with him. We agreed to avoid it. It was a wise choice for me.

The story I heard was that a group of these black-ass motherfuckers had been harassing him. In the public schools, the white kids are a distinct minority and get fucked with all the time. The smart ones take the shit and move on in the name of preservation. Jimmy was incapable of taking shit from anyone. If there had been a hundred of them, he would have done the exact same thing, which was to walk into the crowd of taunters and start swinging. Knowing my boy as I do, he'd have been fine if there was just one or two, better than fine. By the time the melee ended, Jimmy was face first on the sidewalk, bleeding to death from head trauma and stab wounds. The poor fuck was just seventeen.

They're talking about revenge, his friends are. Putting together a mob to attack the school buses that are filled with the enemy; the niggers and spics who pass through the white neighborhoods on their way to destinies unknown. Bats, clubs, and knives accompany Molotov cocktails. Light the buses on fire and everyone in them. No need to separate the evildoers from the innocent when they're one and the same. The whole world feels angry to me, like it's going to explode into a nightmarish riot, and nothing will ever be the same. I'm not feeling that anger so much.

I'm just numb, and really, really sad. I had so much fun with that guy. I loved that kid.

With the weather warming up, more of the crew is venturing back out to hang on the corner. I'm sad to admit that I never left. I've been holding my own in all kinds of weather, with my dungaree jacket and fingerless gloves, enjoying the great outdoors with my ever-trusty companion, an absolutely fucking freezing can of brew. I always tell my pals that I wish I could feel things like fear, pain, and the cold, just so I could relate to them. Nothing like the bravado of playing the tough guy to turn your life into misery. Oh, the fun, fun, fun you can have, with beer 1 and beer 2, frozen snot in your nose and a hole in your shoe. Apologies to my friend Theodor Geisel (Dr. Seuss) for that. On the other hand, being where everyone isn't is kind of nice in itself, even if you have to freeze your ass off to be there.

The thawing and the longer days certainly keep me at a further distance from my dark and gloomy side. More people to horse around with, a little more jump in my step. Hope springs eternal when spring is in the air. Warmer weather does, however, raise tensions. Cold weather is an unrivaled police force. The beat of life sometimes is one and the same as the beating of the war drums when it comes to the Bronx. Hibernation brings new life and a hardy appetite for mischief back to the streets.

We're hanging on the corner one Saturday afternoon, me and Bobby, when we hear disco music. Bobby hates a lot of things, including most types of people, but he absolutely despises disco music.

Bobby: "Where is that shit coming from?"

Me: "I'm gonna go out on a limb here and say it's coming from a radio owned by either a ginzo or a rican."

Bobby: "They need to turn that shit off right fucking now. Can you tell where it's coming from?"

Me: "I'm trying not to listen. My god, it's the fucking Bee Gees they're playing!"

Bobby: "If I spot the window it's coming from, I'm going to throw my beer bottle through it. No way I'm letting anyone play the fucking Bee Gees in my neighborhood. There has to be rules. The motherfuckers!"

Me: "If there was any doubt that the Italians would ever recover from the collapse of Rome, disco music erased it. What self-respecting man would prance around like a fruit and think it was cool? Or for that matter, think it's okay. It's not fucking okay! Save yourselves from being excommunicated from the white race, for Jesus' sake."

Bobby: "Wait. I think it's coming from around the corner."

What Bobby and I discovered when we turned the corner was three of the younger kids from our block with a boombox. By now, the Bee Gees had been replaced by Donna Summer, and the trio of little assholes were mimicking John Travolta with these hideous dance moves. Bobby was furious, no time to stop and take a breath. I started to mention how I love Donna Summer, how she does things to my groin that border on unnatural, but I caught myself.

The kids were like 13 or 14 years old and were younger brothers, or friends of the younger brothers, of some of our friends. In Bobby's mind, this made the whole situation even more intolerable. I was feeling empathetic, not for the three little brats, but for Bobby himself. His level of distress was apparent, his sense of dismay was biblical. Why hath thou forsaken me? To be turned on by your own people. Playing fucking disco music in the cradle of our existence.

Smote he must, and so Bobby doeth.

The music came to a dead halt as Bobby smashed the boombox across a brick wall. Pete Townsend's routine of smashing his guitar at the end of a concert is pure amateurism in comparison. All the king's horses and all the king's men would need a day just to find all the pieces, never mind put the fucking thing back together. The little bastards didn't dare raise a stink. Thou doth protest too much, thou get your ass kicked.

Bobby: "It had to be done."

Me: "You bet yer ass it did. You're a better man for doing it. You taught those kids a valuable lesson. They're gonna realize that you did it for their benefit. Maybe not today, but they will."

Bobby: "Yeah, I feel better now."

Me: "For what I just said?"

Bobby: "I wasn't paying attention. What did you just say?"

THE BRONX

I woke up the other night to take a leak and noticed that the kitchen light was on. Mom never forgets to turn it off, so I suspected she was still awake. Mickey was sawing logs, and I managed to step over Danny without waking him, so my mother never noticed when I approached the room. I heard ma weeping softly and figured she had the old pictures out. She liked to take them out when we were all asleep to keep us from seeing her cry. When we looked at them together, we all somehow managed to avoid the sad memories to focus on the happier times. It rips my heart to pieces to know how much she suffers, how she'll never truly be free of her grief. He was clearly the love of her life, and she was his.

The wedding pictures show an unmistakable glow, as if the altar was at the feet of heaven, and the two of them were being whisked away to their own private Eden. Then there's the photos of the family holidays and gatherings, each one holding a special memory, each one another piece of him she'll never get back. Ma loved her life then, and everything about it. Don't get me wrong, there's still a lot of things that can put a smile on her face, and the old gal is as tough as nails, but I pray mightily that she can someday wash away more of that pain. I need to do my part to help the process. So far, I fear, I'm just making it all worse.

There's a photo I've sequestered from the family collection of my father as a boy of about five, standing next to my grandfather. I keep it hidden from the others and consider it a private possession The picture was taken in Ireland and Pop, as we call him, is standing proudly in his Northern Irish police uniform, a holstered gun at his waist, as his little boy, head tilted upward, gazes at him adoringly. My grandfather is a giant of a man at six-foot four, and his bull neck, stout chin, and elegantly strong hands, make this photo that much more striking. It provides me with the assurance that I come from good stock—that I have what it takes to be a man.

Pop, as we've learned, lived a conflicted existence as a policeman in the North. Catholic by birth, he joined a predominantly Protestant force because he believed he could be a difference maker. My father told me that his father could never understand how people who were by most accounts starkly similar, could find so much room to hate each other.

Born in Tyrone to a farming family, where education and work opportunities away from the farm were far and few between, Pop seemingly scored a coup in becoming a man of the law. But therein lay the great conundrum. Assigned to a post in Belfast, he was viewed as less than by his fellow officers, and as a traitor by his fellow Catholics. Undeterred, at least in the beginning, he assured himself that a man of principles, steadfast on always staying on the side of what is fair and right, and trusting in the benevolence of his fellow man, could persevere through anything.

By my father's account, if a man was drunk and hit his wife, our Pop wouldn't hesitate to lay down a strong hand, be he a Catholic or a Protestant, Orange or Green. If a hungry kid was caught stealing food, my grandad would be lenient and empathetic, caring more about the child's current circumstances than the origin of his birth. Dad said that his old man, to the best of his recollection, never mentioned hating anyone. Only that time and time again did he come away dismayed and disappointed, both by those he worked with and those he strived to protect.

So great was the conundrum that a man who viewed neither side as the enemy could be considered the enemy by both. It was only after numerous death threats against him and his family, threats entirely perverse in their reasoning, that Pop finally decided it was time to pack up and leave. He didn't want to raise a family in a land of turmoil, where hate had the upper hand.

A friend who had left years before and was now a successful businessman in New York, offered him a job and a place to stay. So off he went, wife and two young sons in tow, saddened by his inability to influence the hearts of his fellow man, to a land where his faith in humankind would once again be confronted.

If you asked my dad or my grandfather what was the most important thing in life, they'd tell you something along the lines of it all lies in how you treat your fellow man. They'd add other stuff like being kind and generous and trusting in God. They always played it by the book and look what it got them? Okay God, explain that to me.

Chapter 14

Man or Mouse

I won't be able to provide any whys and hows to this tale, I'll just tell you I woke up on the beach in Rockaway. Earlier the previous evening, me, Bobby, Lukie, and Big John piled into Mickey's shitbox and drove out to Rockaway for my cousin Kaitlin's eighteenth birthday, which was held on the boardwalk in frigid conditions, with a keg of beer as the centerpiece. We were drinking on the ride out, enough so that we somehow convinced Mickey to blow through the toll and take the gate with him. No sirens, no cherry tops, we just kept right on moving as if we'd paid the toll. When we arrived, Kaitlin's shindig was in full bloom, and we were delighted to see that most of the assembled crowd were her female friends. The few guys that were there before us were all right types, your general run-of-the-mill shanties.

We wasted no time catching up in the consumption department, and the buzz got some sting. My cousin was delighted to see my brother, but me less so. I'd caused trouble at her sixteenth birthday, which was held in pretty much the same spot, by cutting open my foot on broken glass and bleeding out like a pig to slaughter. The long and short of it is that I had to seek medical care, and the party ended abruptly. She has yet to forgive me, and I certainly get it. I'd probably hate to see myself show up at my own party.

When you're outside freezing and you want to keep on with the keeping on, you need to create body warmth with action. The music was excellent, with a heavy emphasis on the Stones, and I was dancing like a fool. I even did my Jagger routine when "Honky Tonk Woman," maybe the finest song in history, came blaring through the speakers. I latched on to this one gal, who was on the short side, but had a pretty face. It was hard to get much more of a read on her because she was dressed as if she was going dog sledding in the Alaskan tundra. Somewhere along the line, I must have decided that I was overdressed as well and stripped naked down to my waist.

Yet again, I had fallen prey to my inability to avoid being a jackass and would pay the consequences. Numbness of the mind becomes numbness of the body and absolute numbness is a ticket to nothingness. Nothingness is nothing to be proud of but it's also nothing to be ashamed of so there's nothing to make of it. Dig me? Whatever happens from this point on has nothing to do with the conscious me. You know, that other guy, before he got drunk.

It was in this barely clad state that I awoke on the beach, with my little dancing partner cuddled at my side. She was still bundled up like the Michelin man, so it was clear that no forbidden fruit had been picked from the vines.

I fought hard to remember how we ended up here, but the few brain cells I'd retained, with 'a few' probably being an overcount, failed to assist me. I can only imagine how horrific I must have appeared, but when I prodded my new friend awake, the look of terror in her eyes told me all I needed to know. With a quick, "I have to go," she was off and away, likely counting her lucky stars for being alive. I'll admit, the sand in her hair and the stink of beer on her breath extinguished any potential pining I might have carried over from the previous evening. As I watched her scurry across the sand, I really felt like chasing after her just to find out, once and for all, if she was fat or skinny under that balloon of a coat.

Filthy and smelling like sewage, I labored towards the boardwalk hoping to find my comrades. Fortunately, for me, they were all asleep in my brother's car and had not cast me to the wolves. I roused them from their fitful slumber, four bodies in a grotesque tangle of flesh, hair, and bodily fluids. Lukie was moaning like a wounded animal, and when he managed to free himself from the car, he let out a yowl after placing weight on his right ankle. Apparently, he'd been drunk enough to sleep through the pain but now had an utter reminder that he was injured.

When I inquired as to how it happened, Big John tried to tell me but couldn't contain his laughter long enough to explain. Finally, I was told that Lukie, caught in yet another Rod Stewart inspired frenzy, had somehow whirled himself over the boardwalk rail and plunged a solid 10-12 feet into the sand. Knowing he had hurt his ankle; I presumed a logical explanation. "He landed on his feet?" I asked, puzzled as to how that was possible. What occurred, and it's a forever memory for us all, is that Lukie, perfectly unscathed from the fall, badly sprained his ankle trying to kick one of the many responders who rushed down the stairs to see if he was okay.

It was one helluva uncomfortable ride home for my boy, Luke, with the car too small and crowded for him to rest his ankle comfortably. Every time he grimaced and swallowed a howl of pain, we'd all do our best to stifle a laugh, but it was damn near impossible. By the time we hit the Van Wyck, we were all in synchronized hysterics with every moan. The more pissed off he became, the more we piled on. It's never anything personal, it's just the way things are. If you do something sensationally stupid, you should expect to get your balls broken.

Lukie knows this as well as anyone, so he won't hold any grudges. He'll be laughing along with us in a day or two. Falling over a rail, headfirst down ten feet or so into the sand, while doing a spinning dance move, is some really funny shit. Turning your ankle trying to kick a good Samaritan is beyond hilarious.

Growing boys need good basic fun. Let off some steam. Fuck 'em if they can't take a joke.

The wisdom of a lifetime a minute at a time. No harm, no foul; no foul, no fun.

THE BRONX

I finally got the balls to pack up a workout bag, hop the 4 train, and head on down to the Morrisania boxing gym. This beat cop from our neighborhood, Officer O'Toole, saw me sparring with some older kids a year or more ago, and suggested I take my skills to a real setting. He said he knew a thing or two about the sweet science, and could tell from watching me that I knew how to mix it up, but that I lacked the proper technique, and that the Morrisania gym was the place to go, if I wanted to be the real deal.

He knew, from previous strolls through our block, that I had a passion for boxing.

O'Toole told me I had fast hands and a solid chin but so do lots of guys. He also told me that the large majority of wannabe pugilists never climb the three steps up into the ring because tough guys don't want to find out that they're not as tough as they think they are. They'd rather just go on pretending. Climbing through the ropes and standing tall, when it's only you and your opponent for the whole world to see, is another matter altogether.

Like just about everything else in my life, pretty much the story of my life, I procrastinate like a motherfucker. Day in, day out, I tell myself I'm gonna do it, and day in, day out it doesn't happen. I keep telling myself that I'm too busy, that I need to work and make money, that I'm not in good enough shape at this exact moment. Then there's that same tired nonsense about there being no gyms in our neighborhood, that the darkies and chicos get handed things, and that's why I have to get my ass on a train and go into some gym where I'm probably the only one with white skin outside of the people that run the place. O'Toole told me that if I ever get up the nerve to show I should ask for his pal and ex-partner, fella name of Tommy Boyle. Said Boyle was rough around the edges but soft on the inside.

I consider myself to be in shape. On any given day, even hungover or with close to no sleep, I'll bang out 500 or more push-ups. Every chance I get, I'll hit the weights at the school gym or in the basement of one of my pal's buildings. I can still get around the reservoir twice, even with that one crazy steep hill towards the end, at a better than decent clip.

To be honest, I'm as vain as they come, and I have a penchant for constantly checking myself out in mirrors, preferably with my shirt off. The weird thing is, I'm never satisfied with what I see so I just keep rattling off the push-ups hoping the scenery improves. As much as my vanity gets the better of me, more than anything, I want to be prepared for when I need to prove my muster. But the whole time, it seems, I'm that guy that O'Toole talked about, the guy who's actually afraid to take the plunge. The chump who's too terrified to open the door to his soul and find out there's nothing inside.

The train door slides open, and I exit onto the platform on 170th Street. There's no familiar feelings for me here, no safe spots for me to duck into to buy time. The whole time I'm racking my skull for a reason to turn around and get on the northbound train. Maybe the gym isn't open, maybe Boyle's not there anymore. I'm talking to myself now, people thinking I'm nuts. Have some balls, be a fucking man, I keep repeating to myself. Don't walk away, don't be a God-damned candy ass. I feel the moisture on my hands, the incessant beating of my heart, but I will myself to keep on with the task at hand. Then I see the building, and as I move closer, I hear those magnificent sounds: the clatter of the ring bells, the slapping of the leather, the grunts of combat. And then there I am, standing at the entrance to the gym, the frightened white boy, hoping to prove to the curious inside, that I'm anything but.

The gym was as dumpy inside as it was rundown on the outside. Had I not been so uncomfortable, I'm sure I would have pictured it with a certain respectful awe, but at the moment it cast a surreal, foreboding shadow. There were two main rings, and they were both occupied with guys sparring. The walls and floor of the place were gray painted concrete. There were exposed pipes and hanging wires, and no signs of a locker room. Heavy bags and speed bags were everywhere, and they were abuzz with motion.

Kids as young as ten or eleven mixed in with adults, banging the bags or jumping rope. If you suddenly found the urge to be around a cluster of badass motherfuckers, this was the place to be. Hard, lean muscles in abundance with a confident arrogance to match.

Whether it was my ego or just paranoia, I expected to be noticed upon entrance. If I was, it was barely. Nobody seemed to give a shit, at least as far as I was concerned. There wasn't going to be anyone in this modern colosseum intimidated by me, and I needed to have that same attitude towards them. Fact of the matter is, I was shitting bricks. Still, I didn't want to be one of those chumps O'Toole talked about, the ones who were too tough, in their own minds, to really find out if they were tough at all.

I suspected the lone Caucasian I spotted, the older bald-headed one, was Tommy Boyle. He was standing at one of the rings, his elbows on the canvas, barking instructions up to a pair of pugilists who were banging away at each other. It was then I noticed the second white guy in the gym; he was one of the two swapping leather between the ropes. Turned out to be Tommy's kid, and he was damn impressive. His opponent, this tall, skinny, Black kid, was even more impressive. The bell sounded ending the round and the two fighters embraced before climbing outside of the ropes. So white kids with boxing gloves weren't as rare as I'd thought they'd be here. I was sure I'd be the only one. It didn't make me more comfortable, quite the opposite.

One more excuse I couldn't use to head for the exit. White boys were welcome here, they just needed to know how to fight.

I took the first seam that opened to approach Tommy. I introduced myself and told him O'Toole had sent me his way. Tommy beamed a wide smile at the mention of his former partner. When I told him why I was there, he welcomed me as warmly as a grizzled ex-cop, ghetto boxing gym manager was capable of. Tommy had spent a career putting kids like the ones in here in jail. Now he was doing his damndest to keep them out. He motioned to an older Black man to come over, and then introduced him as Snuff. Told me Snuff would give me the lay of the land and set me straight on the rules of the house.

Snuff had been a professional prize fighter in his day, he told me. Said he got his nickname from his tendency to snuff out his opponents like roaches under a shoe. It was easy to believe when you saw his hands, which were like sledgehammers. His clenched fist looked to be the same size as my entire head. He asked me to repeat my name, said he was hard of hearing. But when he asked my name a third time, I realized the problem wasn't his hearing. Snuff, like so many like him, was permanently punch drunk. I bet the guy's corner never 'threw in the towel' once. Fighters like him want to be the ones to make that decision. Snuff was living authentication of where the no-quit-in-me approach takes a fighter along a one-way, dead-end road to Palookaville.

When Snuff asked me if I had ever boxed before, I lied and said I did, which was somewhat true. I just never did it in a gym. He showed me around, stopping here and there to explain how things worked. Said Tommy wanted commitment. You either came when you were supposed to, or you shouldn't bother to come at all. "Boxing ain't no part-time thing, ain't no game like basketball or Parcheesi, you all in or you all out, no in between." Snuff was lucid one minute, and then he'd drift off muttering incoherently about God knows what the next.

Eventually, I found out that the monthly gym fee would be ten dollars, but that they'd take whatever I could afford. I could use their gloves and headgear, but I definitely needed my own mouthpiece and hand wraps. Then he told me some shattering news; Tommy doesn't let any newcomers spar for at least six months. "You put in the work, you show some skill, and you get to fight, real live like," is what Snuff said. I didn't know how to tell him that I didn't have six months to give so I just stared blankly ahead. When Snuff asked me for my name again, I just said *'fuck it'* to myself and walked toward the exit. I thought I'd depart as quietly as I'd entered but that wasn't to be the case. The gym was filled with street kids who can pick up the scent of a wounded animal a mile away. "Chicken-shit honkie bitch," was probably the nicest thing they said.

What I should have done was just keep right on walking the hell out of there, but my rage was like a boiling cauldron now, and any chance at reason had banished. I was probably angrier with myself than with them, but the devil had a firm grasp on my tongue, and there was no preventing what was to come from my mouth. I turned and glared back at the lot of them and belted out, "I have this thing called a job, something you motherfuckers wouldn't know about since you're all on welfare. I wish I could play around all day like you lazy bastards." Needless to say, it didn't float with this particular breed of feral beasts.

Had Tommy not been watching and moved to slam the doors of the gym behind me, keeping everyone with a mind to attack me inside, I would not have fared too well to put it mildly. So, I headed back home thinking, at least for the moment, that I had proved my iron by standing up to the taunting crowd. When reality set in, I realized that what had transpired was another feeble attempt by yours truly to accomplish something meaningful.

Maybe on Halloween, I can put on a robe with trunks and a pair of gloves and pretend to be a boxer, but you'll never be even close to the real thing until you put in the work and earn the right to climb the three or four stairs up to the ring and through the ropes. You can't be tough by talking tough or acting tough, but you can be a coward by just doing nothing. My trip to the gym was a whole lot of empty noise. Call me a pussy why don't ya, not like I have a leg to stand on.

I can live with being a lot of things but being a coward isn't one of them. Take no chances and you take no crowns. Irish Spring, manly yes, but it doesn't wash away the stench of cowardice.

Chapter 15

Greeks, Italians, Cliff Hangers and Damsels in Distress

This lady had been coming into the gas station on a regular basis and I've been helping her out with questions about her car. She told me that she and her husband were on the outs and that he had always taken care of the mechanical stuff. Giving her a hand hardly makes me the proverbial Good Samaritan, as she is quite easy on the eyes, and has a voice that's half purr and half rasp, kinda like Julie Newmar as *Catwoman*. She also doesn't seem to favor bras, nor should she; the display, from all angles, is absolutely captivating.

When she pulls in, instead of staying in the car and waiting for me to approach, she hops out and greets me with the kind of smile that evokes Novocain, because it pretty much incapacitates me. When I pop the hood and lean underneath to check the fluids, she'll sometimes lean in next to me with her hand on my back. If she asked me to lick off all the grease and grime on her engine block I'd do it without hesitation. If she asked me to do it while on a leash with a dog collar around my neck whistling "Yankee Doodle

Dandy," you bet yer ass I would be her obedient musical canine.

Each visit, which is usually once or twice a week early in the evening, concludes with a friendly goodbye and thank you, but feels to me like something a little bit more. When I return to sanity, and do some step-by-step cognitive reasoning, the idea that this enchanting beauty, for one a decade or so my elder, could have any romantic interest in me whatsoever, I'll dismiss it as pure absurdity. Yet, when I see her car pulling in, my heart will beat like that big brass drum in the song. A boy can dream, and Tinker Bell can be part of that dream.

On one visit, she asked me my name, and told me hers was Angela. We got to talking and came around to discovering that I actually went to grammar school with her baby sister, Joyce. Joyce, my classmate for eight years, was no slouch herself, but we were just little kids then. This grown-up version of Joyce was infinitely more appealing. It was kind of busy and I kept getting interrupted but then something magical happened, she pulled her car over to the side and said she'd wait for things to clear up, and then we'd talk some more. Holy shit, I thought, this can't really be happening. It's like Farrah Fawcett jumping out of the poster on your bedroom wall and snuggling under the covers with you.

The place empties out and there I am, sitting next to Angela on the hood of her car. I've already offered to change the oil in her car and rotate the tires, for free, seeing how taking care of a car is not something she's used to doing. She tells me uh-uh, no charity. She'll let me do the work only if she can reciprocate by making me a nice, Italian dinner, at her apartment, after the job is done. I told her that I can't exactly show up at her place with my grease-stained duds and how I'd have to go home and shower first, and she blows my mind into the stratosphere with an offer to take a shower in her bathroom pre-dinner.

When she says, ". . . don't worry, I won't peek." I damn near cry with jubilation, but being the suave, composed man about town that I am, I simply gulp and nod my head, as my eyes turn a dead gaze into the abyss. I'm not sure if I'm more Igor or Frankenstein but I will sure as fucking hell do as commanded. To die happy would be to die at this exact moment. What have I done, God, to deserve such a sumptuous bounty? I am wary of the old adage, if it seems too good to be true it probably is, but a fool and his fantasies are not easily dissuaded. Which swings me back over to God with an urgent plea to make it be just true enough for it to stick.

Before Angela leaves, we set a date for the following week. When the boss is long gone for the day, and I have the place to myself. I'll pull her car into one of the bays to do the work. She can go home and get things ready and then I'll drive her wheels over to her block and park it. And then . . . and then . . . and then . . .

This woman has done what no other female has even come close to. She has enabled me to stop obsessing about Mary, the lovely Irish lass of my deepest desire, who generally occupies at least 50% of my idle thoughts. Angela has even topped her, currently inhabiting at least 99% of my ruminations. I ache with anticipation by the second. The other 1% or so of my brain activity is directed towards the Almighty, begging him to close the deal.

The week goes by slowly, but the time is nigh. Twenty-four hours separate me from my personal Eden. Then I see Angela's car pulling into the station. I tell myself she is merely swinging by to remind me of tomorrow, as if I could forget. She pulls her car over to the side and gets out.

There's an odd look on her face and my heart sinks. Her husband is back in the picture, they're gonna try and work things out. He's moved back in; the car is topsy-turvy. She apologizes and leaves, taking with her the exotic ambitions of this devastated kid from the Bronx. I pray that I can find a way to resume obsessing about Mary. I also remind God that he reneged on our deal, and that he owes me. I tell him that since Angela is off the table, how about a little help with Mary? Or maybe a different hot chick ten years my senior just to tide me over for a bit?

THE BRONX

Our neighborhood contains what may be the two of the greatest acrobat/climbers known to man. PT Barnum would have signed them both on sight. Either one of them could have scaled Everest in half the time that that English fellow, Sir Edmud Stickuphisass, or whatever his goofy name is, did it. My boy, Mahoney, routinely shimmies his skinny ass up a light pole, seemingly in seconds. Then he'll make his way, arm over arm, to the middle of the arch, and then hang with one arm a good twenty feet above the street. It's many a pair of sneakers that he's rescued from this high altitude. Those things are tossed up there with the intent of permanence, never to be retrieved. Hah! Not with Mahoney about. He's half man, half ape. Or more like half Irish, half ape. Or maybe he's three quarters ape, since most Irishman are half ape to begin with. I'll leave the math to you.

As for any unclaimed sneakers, Mahoney has no need to keep them. He already has the best dressed feet in the neighborhood, courtesy of the backdoor sneaker business he runs out of Modell's Sporting Goods. Seems he took a page from my blueprint to create an export business from his place of employment. He'll even customize size and color for some customers. I am currently wearing a sweet pair of blue and white Clyde Pumas that my man gave me for my birthday. Mahoney would like to be a police officer some day. As they say, it takes a crook to catch a crook. My boy should climb the ladder fast, all pun intended.

THE BRONX

Then there's my man, Eddie Shannon, perhaps the greatest one arm cliff hanger in the Western Hemisphere. Eddie, usually after he's had a few, will find his way to the nearest rooftop, loop himself over the ledge, and dangle by one arm, feigning desperation and calling, 'Help, help' to anyone who will listen. Anyone who's seen the routine in the past will look up to the source of the bellowing, and say something to the tune of, "Oh, it's just Eddie." However, the gullible in our midst, like my dear beloved mother, will utter something to the tune of, "Oh my goodness gracious, Jack, there's some poor man about to fall off the roof, help him!" To which I'll reply, "Oh, it's just Eddie," leaving my mom, and anyone else within earshot, stunned at my nonchalance It's only after I call up to Eddie to see if he wants me to get him a drink of water, or perhaps a cigarette, and he answers from six stories above, "Sure, Jack, that would be great," do they begin to understand my lack of emotion from the spectacle we are watching unfold. Then the crowd of would-be rescuers, mostly neighborhood parents, will disperse muttering disgustedly things like "I hope the bastard falls, teach him a lesson," or "I feel like going up there myself and stomping on his goddamned fingers." This episode of Eddie's daredevil psychosis will conclude like all the others, with a nod and a wink from our man, as the police and medics escort him to the awaiting ambulance. Then he'll be off to Bellevue or some other psych facility where he'll get the type of individual attention he could never hope for at home where he's just one kid in a family of eight.

I will say this, Mahoney and Crazy Eddie have the wheels turning in my head to start jotting down a rough plot for a Hollywood production similar to *The Dirty Dozen*, where these two misfits are set loose in a war zone somewhere and basically save the day by climbing all over planes, tanks and whatever else they need to climb over to seal the deal.

I picture Eddie hanging, one-armed, from the wing of a plane 10,000 feet in the air, and then climbing atop and kicking in the window of the cockpit, killing the pilot and copilot, and then rerouting the nuclear bomb carrying aircraft to save millions of lives. Meanwhile, Mahoney will have ascended an air traffic tower jutting through the clouds to rearrange an antenna or two to divert other enemy planes and send them crashing into the mountains. Civilization, as we know it, will remain the same courtesy of my boys. I'd call it *The Heights of Heroism* or some other ingenious tagline that will pull these gullible movie types in by the droves. You have to admit, I'm onto something here.

THE BRONX

The saying goes, "In the land of the blind, the one-eyed man is king." My version of my life on Creston Avenue would be, 'in a world of mental midgets even a dumb fuck like myself can seem to have half a brain.'

Sal: "Hey, Jack, how you doin', you needle dick, faggot-ass motherfucker."

Me: "Sal, I believe that's verbatim to how I greeted you the last time I saw you. Or, for your sake, word for word. Though, admittedly, I stand amazed that you could have remembered it in its entirety, and in the exact sequence. I'm tempted to refer to you as erudite, though there's little fucking chance that word has ever threatened your vocabulary."

Sal: "That's one of them Greek gods, no? Some of those chicks are really hot. You know what they say about the Greeks, right?"

Me: "They say the same thing about the Italians."

Sal: "Up yours, Jack. Don't compare me to no fuckin' Greek."

Me: "When you stop and think about it, an exercise in futility for a man of your astounding intellect, the Greeks and Italians have a lot in common, with the backdooring just one of many shared traits. In fact, there are far fewer differences, with the only one coming to mind at the moment being bread. I'll give it to you, you got 'em on the bread. But both cultures like cheese, wine and especially all types of oil. Greek men and Italian men dress like fruits and overindulge in hair products. They're also hairier than the average sheep dog. I could go on and on. Perhaps the most apt theme tying the two societies together is that they've both been in a steady decline for the last ten centuries or so."

Sal: "You and your big words, Jack, like you're some kind of dictionary or something. Youse fucking Irish are, you know, you're . . . ah fucking forget it. You're a scumbag, Jack, that's all."

Me: "See there you go proving your mental acuity again. I love you, Sal, you fill up my life in ways only you can."

Sal: "I like you too, Jack, but not that way. I ain't no Greek."

Me: "Wanna go over to Science High School and play some hoops?"

Sal: "Yeah let's do it; show them Jew boys and spades how the game is played."

One would have to admit that I'm one funny son of a bitch. "Laugh and the world laughs with you, cry and you cry alone."

Chapters 16

The Cavalry Is in Town but that Could Be the Problem

When I'm working the stick at the Alibi on a Friday night, there's no predicting how the crowd will fill out. The first few hours are always the regulars and the occasional surprise, but pretty tame all around. After nine and until closing, it's anyone's guess. Sometimes, a group of ten or more will show up *en masse*, having left another bar together because the place wasn't showing any promise.

Lately, my hometown gin mill has a little buzz, and when word gets out that it's the place to be on a Friday night, the bar can fill up in a hurry. You'll see guys from neighborhoods around that you're sure have never set foot in the place. Then, if you're lucky, groups of girls will stream in, locking in a guaranteed crowd for hours to come. There's nothing more exciting to the average young maverick than being in the midst of fine-looking ladies, and thinking they've got a chance. I make sure the music flows as much as the drinks, so the energy never gets sapped.

Often enough, I have to pull in another bartender, preferably my brother, Mickey. It can get so busy that

157

your head spins, but the ding ding of the register and the swelling of the tip jar are natural stimulants. I try my best not to imbibe because a drunk bartender is a careless one, and carelessness can bite you like a rat trap. By one or two a.m., you'll be dealing with a lot of intoxicated people, not all of them well-intentioned.

I try to be preemptive when I see trouble brewing, maybe get lucky and prevent a brawl from happening. I have no tolerance for sleaze bags that try to take advantage of drunk females, and I'll kick them the fuck out if they keep it up. It's wishful thinking for the most part, because even the most steadfast of barkeeps can't shutter every window before the storm gets in, when that tempest is a concoction of potions blended together in human emotions, with a wick dipped in healthy parts booze and drugs. A spilled drink here, a shoulder bump there, a girlfriend disrespected, money stolen off the bar and boom!—the genie's out of the bottle and the shit has hit the fan at tornado speed.

You do what you can do to restore the peace and resume the festivities, but sometimes it takes 'the boys in blue,' New York's Finest, arriving on the scene, to beat some sense into the skulls of the knuckleheads. A few cold ones for their efforts, the law enforcement officers head out, and the party continues—if you're lucky. Irony being, without a crowd large enough for tempers to flare, the tip cup stays small. If a little turbulence is the price of a nice, fat money jar, then upheaval it will have to be. I'd rather have a fat lip and a fat wad of cash in my pocket, than a night of peace and poverty.

As I've said, some people will show up out of the blue that really astonish me. You're like 'what's he doing here?' They're the types that I wouldn't have expected to see walk in here in a thousand years. Sometimes they're those 'faces that come out in the rain' that Jim Morrison sings about. Shit can get strange; it surely can.

Such was last Friday night. The Alibi was humming, and things were merry. Then I heard some loud rumbling that grew in intensity, and then subsided to a low roar. Headlights shot through the windows of the bar partially blinding me. I hopped over the bar and went to the door to see what was up. Damn if it wasn't Marlon Brando and the rest of the cast of *The Wild One*. Well, almost.

Outside, lined up on the sidewalk, was a group of Harleys, six or seven best I could tell. Not in the street mind you, on the sidewalk. As if they were begging for someone to tell them that they can't park there. There wasn't anyone brave enough or foolhardy enough to educate them on proper manners and parking etiquette. I didn't say a word myself, just went back inside, hopped over the bar again, and waited for the fun to start.

The new guests were mostly people I knew. Kids that I went to school with and even hung out with every once in a while. But they were a different breed altogether from my usual circles.

These gents cast a shadow over whatever ground they stood on, and if you were in their vicinity, the ground you stood on as well. The easiest cut to the chase description was that they were simply tough motherfuckers, but it went beyond that.

They confidently strolled in, knowing full well that they were making an entrance that the patrons would stop to watch the parade. They gave off an ominous glow, a searing radiance that burns to the quick if you light the match, intentionally or not. I couldn't help but feel like I was being pulled into a scene in a Wild West saloon. With this posse, you play the hand you're dealt, you just hope it's not the dreaded two pairs, black aces and eights.

Returning to the Wild West theme, these cats were definitely in the renegade camp, more Black Bart and Jesse James than Wyatt Earp and Wild Bill Hickock. There was even a real live Bart among them, a muscle-bound quasi lunatic with the last name of Lyons. Like Johnny Cash's Sue, you're bound to grow up quick and mean in the Bronx with a name like Bartholomew, and my man Bart could be that and more. But in the here and now, live at the Alibi, these bad guys weren't all that bad. They were on our side, and we were on theirs. Just cut them a wide enough berth, and be generous with the buybacks, and life will be hunky dory.

The tell-tale determining factor of whether you're tight with someone, or not, is if you can freely and mercilessly break their balls. A perfect stranger would risk his life calling Bart a faggot, but a man like me would be remiss not to. You do 'it' to reopen the door to your friendship, enabling him to return the favor. He'll feel unwelcome if you just say something like, ". . . Hey Bart, it's nice to see you." He'll be thinking, *what the fuck did I ever do to this guy?* Then when you've established a jovial rapport with the new patrons, everyone else can relax, confident that these scary looking motherfuckers are here for the same reason as they are, to have a few laughs, and more than a few drinks.

There turned out to be eight of them, who arrived on six bikes, six males and two females. I knew one of the gals, Gina, from grammar school, when we were both pious young Catholics.

Besides Bart, there were three other males I knew and two I didn't. Nalon, the tattooed wonder, was one of them, and Skinny Billy was another. The ringleader, Brendan

Burns was the third. All three were roughly my age but the two guys who I'd just been introduced to, who I'd never met before, were quite a bit older, maybe in their early twenties. Everyone nodded, grunted, or shook hands to complete the introductions. The two young ladies stayed in the background at first, as if afraid to talk, but their tongues loosened up considerably after the first drink. The stuff that came out of their mouths from that point on would make even the crudest sailor turn crimson with abashment.

One of the older guys was the younger brother of a local police legend, a badass Jew undercover cop name of Freddie Feldman, also known as triple-F, as in 'Oh Fuck, Freddie Feldman is here!' Probably the baddest Jew any of us had ever heard or seen. The Jews we knew, and they were few, were on their way to becoming doctors and lawyers, not kickass cowboy policemen. Feldman was rumored to have three tears tattooed across as many knuckles, one each for the perps he reportedly gunned down. I've seen him around a few times, and he looks the part; wild long hair, bulging biceps and a menacing glare. Just a few months ago, he apparently shot a Jamaican drug dealer dead on the roof of a building on 197th Street and Decatur. He then left the guy dying while he hopped across roofs, and down fire escapes to pursue the accomplice. Real live action movie shit. The younger brother, Mark, was tall and lanky, hardly his older siblings double, but an anomaly in his own right—the rare Jew biker.

The other of the two older guys, a mysterious being named Richie, was built like a fire hydrant. He didn't talk much so it was hard to figure him out. Rumor had it that he'd just finished a 30-month bit in state prison for beating up someone with a hammer who had tried to rape a girl that lived in the same building as him. Beat the guy to a pulp and nearly to death.

When it comes to these types of stories the truth never quite gets told. You get bits and pieces, downplays and embellishments, but rarely an accurate account. Either way, I was going to dance gingerly with Richie. Everything about him felt like a reminder not to put your hand in the cage.

Nalon must have gotten his first tat when he was in the second grade, and one every month thereafter. The kid was seventeen and had no open patches below his neck. Went from pasty skin and freckles to being Ray Bradbury's *Illustrated Man* seemingly overnight. Nalon was a pretty easy-going dude though, and not the brawling type. With Bart, the aspiring Hells Angel at his side, he didn't need to be.

Skinny Billy was unique in his own way, but not in the way you want to be unique. His life was a series of tragedies that had altered him beyond repair, or so it certainly seemed. Never an outgoing personality, he had always had a laid-back way about him. Not too much this way or that way, kind of just in between. Though he was lean in build, the 'skinny' tag originated from his usual greeting which had always been, 'what's the skinny?' That phrase of address had left him like so many other aspects of his being. In the course of eighteen months, when he was fourteen and fifteen, he lost both of his parents to cancer, and his little sister to a hit-and-run driver. As awful as it was to lose both parents, it was his little sister's death that haunted him the most.

He had taken her out for ice cream to get her out of the apartment, a dwelling that was racked with despair. Billy had said how after that the world changed from light to darkness in the wink of the devil's eye. His sister had been so happy to have ice cream with her older brother and escape into a more light-hearted world, at least for a short while. Billy remembered looking at her as they approached the Grand Concourse, the glow emanating from her, the rosy cheeks with an ear-to-ear smile. She had been skipping and got a little ahead of him, barely off the sidewalk and only a couple of feet into the street when a car, moving recklessly at an accelerated speed, veered into little Susie, sending her flying in the air. Her head hit with a sickly thud and her body went limp.

The impact shattered her skull and knocked her out cold. She never regained consciousness and was pronounced dead just hours later. Billy blamed himself of course, a guilt that creeped into his bones, and rattled them incessantly. But he reserved his greatest hatred for the heartless bastard who cowardly took off, and to this day had managed not to get caught. The bystanders all recalled the harrowing pleas for help from Billy, the animal desperation in his voice as he knelt and held his sister. No one, unfortunately, got a license plate number or even a decent description of the car and driver.

They did, however, somewhat confirm what Billy thought he saw himself, that the driver had dark skin. Billy had never been a hateful person, but he was beyond that now. He hated the niggers and spics. He hated God. He hated most things, in fact. Life held little meaning for him outside of a burning need for vengeance. Now, he was a scary character, someone who you could only guess at. The empty look in his eyes. The weird hat pulled low on his brow. Every drink I handed to him went down in a gulp or two. For a small guy, the liquor did little to change his demeanor or appearance. Conversation was minimal and the angry stare immutable. I couldn't bring myself to charge him until I had to, simply because he demanded I do so. "No fucking way, Jack, I don't want your sympathy." So, I charged him that one time, then lied to him thereafter, pretending that the drinks were already paid for by his friends. I couldn't find it in me to do anything but.

THE BRONX

Brendan Burns was indisputably the leader of the pack. I'd known Brendan from the fifth grade on, when he transferred into our school, having moved into our neighborhood from the north of Manhattan. Back then, he was a small, slight kid with glasses who was fond of reading Hardy Boys books. In other words, he was ripe to be picked on, and he was. It was around that time that he became an enigma to me and remains such to this day. He proved to be one smart son of a bitch, with a master vocabulary even back then. But those who goofed on him were quick to discover another side to him altogether. Brendan was a tough motherfucker inside and out. The bookworm with the quiet demeanor would have his nose between the pages, pretending to be oblivious, while simultaneously devising a plan to take down his hecklers.

It's almost absurd to comprehend how this 'Clark Kent' of a kid could change costumes so abruptly. The mild-mannered literary bookworm one second, to the brash kid, glasses neatly folded on the desk in front of him, standing toe-to-toe with his adversary, daring him to make the first move. If you didn't respond in the affirmative, he had you from that point on. When you're challenged to a fight and don't engage, making up some limp excuse to back out, there's a certain comprehension that passes man to man. One knows that he has established superiority, and the other knows he'll be the subordinate in whatever relationship survives.

The ball busting ceased almost as quickly as it started. Everyone settled in and Brendan seized the floor. He learned to rate the upper hand early in those first couple of years at his new school, and he seemed to have kept it. The skinny unimposing frame was gone, replaced by a formidable, wide shouldered torso, to complement the swollen biceps and meaty neck. It's the rare individual who can own you physically and mentally. I'm still yet to figure him out, even a little. I just try not to be cast under his spell. When a guy has the world by the balls, you do your best to keep your own balls from his grasp.

Mysterious aura aside, Brendan is a lot of fun. A funny fucker in the mold of the urban mick. Quick-witted and merciless, fast to a phrase and adept in delivery. He was also a famously cheap bastard and was rumored to still have his communion money folded safely in his little blue suit. Loved to flash a wad of twenties, and let you know he had the ability to be a big spender if he wanted to. He'd swear up and down that he just bought a round of drinks, knowing people knew he was bullshitting, but not caring to challenge him. Somehow, he made you feel lucky that he let you buy him a drink. Even luckier that he even acknowledged.

Brendan and I have the distinction of having been thrown out of the same high school within a month or so of each other and ending up in the same center of abundant learning, St. Joe's, on the rebound. Both of us are smarter than the average bear, and that commonality earns both sides a little mutual respect. Our new school is as big a waste of his time as it is of mine. We both have big designs on life and that is not the place to nurture them. Things have to be bigger and better out there; there's no other conception of the future that'll fly. My man, Brendan Burns, knows I'm nobody's punk so he doesn't try to pull me into the fold. There's plenty of others who he'll manage to sweep in. Lord knows there are those who will drink the potion. It's an acquired taste that I don't plan to come by.

One of my favorite Brendan Burns stories is the one I share with the crowd at the bar. He laughs when I mention the game 'manners,' which was purely his invention. The way it worked was that anyone who signed onto the game had to agree to one major stipulation, that provision being that if you cursed within earshot of any of the other participants, you needed to audibly pronounce the word 'manners' as loudly and clearly as possible. If not, you'd be eligible to be punched anywhere between your waist and your neck until you did. There was no maximum on how many times you could be bludgeoned before you got the magic word out. I was pretty good at not getting caught and Burns was even better.

One early afternoon in the eighth grade, Burns and I were on the lunch line at the school cafeteria, with him several places in front of me. He's the type of guy who always, and I emphasize always, knows his surroundings. That includes geography, incidentals, and people. Who, what, where and why—examine and prepare, steady and ready. Basically, the kid doesn't trust anyone or anything and is psychotic enough to think he's being watched. In this instance, he was, by me, but I managed to coyly stay out of his line of vision. Brendan approached the lunch table, took a look at what they were serving, and clearly disgusted, murmured under his breath, ". . . how do they expect you to eat this shit," absolutely confident that there were no 'manners' players anywhere within a mile.

Though safely obscured, I was close enough to hear the word 'shit' quite clearly. Given Burn's mental acuity and absolute need to never lose at anything, I knew this was an opportunity I would likely never have again. I pounced like a leopard in the darkness—swift and unobserved. Sliding to his side, I brought my right fist on an upward arc blasting into his kidney. His body went slack on impact, and he dropped his lunch tray and fell to one knee. Everyone in the lunchroom turned towards the commotion to see the untouchable Brendan Burns bent over in pain. By now, the look of disbelief in his eyes was gone, replaced by an intensely angry stare in my direction. If I understood what was going through his mind at the moment, and I doubt I knew the half of it, he had already somehow calculated his response. He did not jump at me in retaliation. Rather, he composed himself, filled his lunch tray, and calmly told me that he hadn't cursed, and that I'd made a grave miscalculation.

For even if he had cursed, and I was well in my rights as a 'manners' gamer to have punched him, I should have more prudently considered the consequences of my actions. Brendan told me that what he had just endured at my hand was actually something that he now welcomed, because it would make his retaliation that much sweeter. He assured me that his revenge would come, and that I should consider myself as prey from this moment forward. The biggest, baddest lion doesn't need to pursue the weakest in the herd to have his dinner. Nor does he need to eat on schedule. He can lurk in the weeds and wait patiently. When the meal does come, it will be precisely what he prefers. The Brendan

Burns lion would have his cake and eat it too. Nothing could change that. His day would come, and mine with it.

After an extremely short period of elation, dread overcame me like a man on the eve of a date with the electric chair. The high fives and pats on the back for taking down the king, were of no solace. I was fucked and I knew it. I ceased cursing altogether, even at home in bed. We live on the first floor, and I would envision Burns on the street outside listening through the open window, ready to scale the short distance to the window and into my bedroom. I even called his house a couple of times to make sure he was home, but his mother, likely coached by him, would refuse to acknowledge that he was there. When I'd see him at school or on the street, he wouldn't treat me any differently and was usually downright jovial. He would wait however long it took. I thought of trying to quit the game but feared I'd be branded a coward, so I reluctantly hung in.

I successfully avoided slipping up for months. I even managed to be on the giving side with some of the other 'manners' crew. My diligence was steadfast. I remained painstakingly careful. Eventually, the game would end, and I'd retire on top. That was not how it unfolded. Unfortunately, for me, Brendan Burns would exact his revenge in such an improbable way that it could only have been him who could do it.

It's a Saturday afternoon, and we're the home team for a varsity CYO hoops game. I have arrived in style, with my droopy, purple, and gold, Pete Maravich, LSU socks, a necessary contrast to our dreary Kelly green and white school uniforms. It's an eyesore, sure, but a needed one. You want the crowd to notice you. We're playing another Catholic school from down on 165th street. One-hundred-percent ghetto kids, papists or not. They're in first place and we can tie them for the league lead if we beat them. My humanity loving teammate, Robert Salvano, refers to them as the 'jumping jungle bunnies.'

These kids can get up, there's no two ways about it. Anyone who tells you it's a fallacy that black people can run faster and jump higher than us white folks is a dumbass motherfucker. This is science man, and every game of basketball I play against the darker persuasion is just another test case in the affirmative. Our coach, Mr. Baxter, who also happens to be our gym teacher, keeps telling us over and over that we need to 'outthink' them. It's tough to outthink someone whose crotch just sailed past you at eye level, but I get his point. If we're gonna win we're going to have to avoid turnovers and stupid plays.

The visiting team is big and imposing, downright scary to some—fourteen-year-old children in men's bodies. Afros and sneers. Little kids in the audience must be thinking they're at the movies and that there will be unpleasant surprises. The only white person on their bench is a nun who's some kind of coach, but not the head coach. During pregame warmups one of them actually dunked. The last time we played these guys, at their gym, a fight broke out after the game and we needed the cops to escort us out of the building, not in handcuffs but for our safety. The locals, mostly parents and older siblings of the players, were waiting outside the postgame, with the intent to do us harm. It's the kind of experience that sticks with you. I remember feeling like the *Hunchback of Notre Dame* up in the tower looking down at a sea of torches. I also remember that nun over there blaming the whole thing on us. She did have a point.

Our guy started the whole thing by purposely taking out the legs of one of theirs.

Because of the history, and also because it's a big game, our auditorium, which seconds as our basketball court, is packed. The contest for first place has brought in all those who love to watch a competitive game of hoops. Some others are here for a different sort of sport. The fight that occurred the last time, and the potential for an encore, has attracted a fair amount of our hometown hoodlums. These are the types who only enjoy sporting events that involve some type of serious violence. They consider basketball a sissy sport and would otherwise not be here. Brendan Burns is one of them.

The game lives up to its hype. My boy, Danny Smith, our resident superstar, is on fire and is keeping us in the game. Our foes are running and flying all over the place. They are well-coached and disciplined, and better than us, but we manage to hang. Maybe it's the adrenaline from the home crowd. The ref stops the game more than once to warn Mr. Baxter that our team will get a technical foul if he can't keep the crowd from hurling nasty slurs at the visiting team. A couple of kids are escorted out.

I feel like I'm playing detached from reality. I've actually scored a few impressive hoops and I'm buckling down on defense. That's when it happens. I get called for a foul that I didn't think I committed, and I mutter 'bullshit' under my breath. I'm near the baseline where there's spectators. They can hear what I just said. Brendan Burns, alas, has heard me as well. He steps forward and in the bat of an eye punches me so hard in the abdomen that my feet feel like they've left the floor. I crumble in pain, gasping for air. A stunned audience struggles to comprehend what has just happened.

Brendan Burns calmly walks out of the gymnasium. I recall his words as he hit me, *Don't forget to say manners, motherfucker*. Manners—he wins again.

I didn't tell them the long version of the story as I was busy running back and forth filling drink orders. There are customers that don't like my two-ingredient maximum but that's too fucking bad for them as I simply cannot spare the time to be shaking and mixing fruity, bullshit cocktails. If you were looking for a nice bar with a real bartender, you should have found somewhere else to go. Like Nick the barkeep in *It's a Wonderful Life* who says something along the lines of his place having 'hard liquor for hard men.' Well, I serve cheap liquor for hard-up men—and women for that matter. Anyway, they were all laughing uproariously at the 'manners' story. Brendan Burns had a sly grin and a twinkle in his eye, always delighted to lap up the spotlight. I'm sure he also remembered how disappointed he was that the brawl he cheerfully anticipated had never happened.

So fortunately, nothing frightfully interesting transpired with this crew. Skinny Billy and Richie barely uttered a word. Burns held court with a host of party goers who migrated his way. Mark the Jew had people leaning in to hear stories he was telling about his older brother. Nalon slowly but surely got legless drunk, and Bart was Bart. The two gals stayed close to their men with the only separation coming when Bart lifted the chick who wasn't Gina over his head and bounced her in the air like a volleyball. His hands were not discreet as he did so,

The only close call was when Skinny Billy and the mysterious and eerie Richie offered to intervene and toss out Louie, the strung-out Puerto Rican who stopped in to hit up anyone he could for a little cash. I told them that it wasn't necessary as Louie was a frequent visitor and pretty harmless. They told me to let them know if I changed my mind. Thankfully, I didn't. Before they departed, Burns suggested I visit them some day or night over at the parkway where they staked their territory, maybe go riding with them. I took it as a distinct honor and told him I might very well. Any time this crew enters and exits without an incident is a home run for the establishment. I was rounding the bases when they were gone.

Instincts can neither be explained, nor can they be dismissed. It's like you don't know but you do know—when you can't kick that feeling of foreboding no matter how hard you try or how long you kneel with your head pointed up towards the sky.

Chapter 17

Black and White with a Sprinkle of Green

Me: "Hey Al, what's happenin' my man. This is my boy, Knucks, the guy I told you might be interested in purchasing some of your black-market goods. I can vouch for him, he's as dumb as a stump but as trustworthy as they come. He's like a dog with amnesia who keeps forgetting he's been kicked."

Knucks: "Fuck you, Jack. Yo, Al."

Al: "You a friend of Jack, you a friend of mine. But I gotta be keeping you white folk on a leash, never know who's the man and who ain't, who's strivin' and who's jivin'. But Jack say you cool, I give you a pass."

Knucks: "You play the game but the game don't play you."

Me: "What the fuck is that gibberish, Knucks? Excuse me, Al, my boy here is not used to conversing with black people. In fact, you may be his maiden voyage. He's trying to be way cooler than he's capable of, and he's not capable of much."

Al: "That's awright, Jack, I aint never expectin' white motherfuckers to be cool anyways. You a needle in a haystack when it comes to legit street smooth and white skin. That's why Big Al in your corner. Hey Knucks, it true how you got your nickname? Your brother punched you in the head?"

Knucks: "That's a load of bullshit. Jack's telling lies."

Me: "Fuck up, Knucks, I'm not the one who even gave you the name, though I wish I'd been clever enough to do it. Then why do you think people call you Knucks? They just pulled it out of thin air?"

Knucks: "Everybody just started calling me that for no reason."

Me: "And you just kept answering to it? You see the shit I'm burdened with, Al? It's my service to mankind. To the least of mankind. Hapless fuckin' dopes like my man right here."

Al: "The white race always gonna be a mystery to me. You peoples is all batshit crazy. But you, Jack, you can be Jamaican all day long. You no bumbaclot, Jackie. Your man, Knucks—well, we just be seeing about dat. Pleasure doin' bidness yo. Pleasure making your acquaintance.

"Jackie, you know me luv ya."

Me: "And I love your black, island ass as well, Al. God bless Jamaicans big and small. Later, bumbaclot, or bumble bee, or bubble gum, or whatever you fuckers call each other."

THE BRONX

I should have known something was up when I turned the corner on Creston Avenue headed for home and felt like I was suddenly on display. People weren't saying much, in fact, there was nary a peep, but the expressions on their faces told me there had been an odd occurrence, and that the event was taking place in my apartment at this very moment. It had a similar feel to the time a limo had pulled up at the fire hydrant and none other than Frankie Valli hopped out of it carrying a bouquet of flowers. He had come to see this woman named MaryAnn who lived on the fifth floor of our building. She was closer to a girl than a woman, probably eighteen or nineteen, but she was smoking hot, too hot for our neck of the woods, and she was about to be proposed to by a living legend.

We were so excited we never even thought about trying to steal shit out of the limousine. People stood, jaws agape, stunned into silence by what seemed to almost be a miracle. Frankie fuckin' Valli in our backyard! This had a weirdly similar feel. Maybe that *Good Housekeeping* Sweepstakes guy was in my very living room handing a nice, fat check to my mother this exact minute!

What I found when I walked through our door was something equally startling and unexpected, a Black man and woman sitting on our old, beat-up couch with glasses of Coke in their hands. The Sweepstakes has better odds I thought to myself. Upon my entrance, they both immediately stood and took a step forward to greet me. The man had a goatee, glasses, and was sharply attired in slacks and a blazer. He reached out his hand and said, "Hi Jack, I'm Duke, it's a pleasure to meet you." I shook his hand, but I can't remember if I even said anything in reply. Then the woman sprung forward, wrapped her arms around me and proclaimed, "Hey baby, I finally get to meet you. I'm Mary, Mary White."

As I recovered from the shock of what I had just experienced, I put the names together and remembered that Duke and Mary White were my mother's coworkers at the restaurant. I just never thought that Mary White was anything other than white and that Duke was more Duke Ellington than Duke Snider. This was *Guess Who's Coming to Dinner* in stereo. Now I completely understood the reaction of my neighbors as I approached the building. I could almost hear the voices saying, *'two niggers just went in the McGee house.'* Oddly, instead of being mortified, I felt a rush of pride. Eat your hearts out you goddamned ignorant bastards, the McGees are out there in the world, living and playing with all shapes and colors, a kaleidoscope of humanity. Kissinger went all the way to China to change the arc of human relations, and all Jack McGee needed to do was walk into his living room.

My mom was giddy at having her friends from work in our rundown little apartment. You can bet she knew it would cause a stir, and she absolutely did not give a shit. Not even a little.

She knew Mary and Duke for what they were, honest and decent people, and the neighbors could just go on believing whatever they needed to believe. After five minutes of sitting and talking with them your only regret would be that you didn't know them sooner.

Duke and Mary were an item but were not married. Duke's wife, his high school sweetheart, had died of cancer just a couple of years ago, and Mary was only the second woman he'd ever so much as kissed. Mary was divorced, having walked out of an abusive relationship. I remember my mother telling me about Duke's wife passing, and how everyone at the track, from the managers to the bus boys, had pulled together to help him in his time of despair. It was the same every time life took a whack at one of the workers, whether it was illness, financial, or whatever. They pooled resources and helped ease the burden. I just never pictured the Duke I had envisioned looking anything like the guy I was sitting across from. Mom would occasionally share descriptions of her coworkers but clearly didn't think characteristics like skin color were essential to properly illustrate a person or their character.

Mary's laugh is infectious and her hugs mesmerizing. Having that woman embrace me and tousle my hair was not something I could ever grow tired of. So here I was, rubbing skin with the other side, and loving every second of it. She's good chubby, Mary is, like a cherub, and she has a Tina Turner purr to her voice that can hypnotize better than a snake charmer. She wore a classy pearl bracelet and a gold cross necklace. She smelled of lavender. She's as white as any white woman I know, maybe even more so.

Duke is Sammy Davis Jr. cool. He too has the type of distinctive voice that puts you at ease. Marvin Gaye or Al Green, like that—silky smooth. He knows everything there is to know about boxing, dating back to John L Sullivan. He rooted for Frazier over Ali because he likes fighters not talkers. He asks me to show him my stance and immediately tells me my feet are too close together. He opens his palm and tells me to nail it with a right cross. "Whoa, easy tiger!" he laughs, as he shakes his hand in pain. I don't know if he's putting me on but it's enough to make me crack a smile and feel good about myself.

I remember Brother Brian telling me something along the lines of judging a person's value by how they make you feel when you're around them, and even more so after they've left. He said that if you've left someone feeling better with your presence, then you've made a positive difference in their lives. And that alone is a tremendous thing. I would say, without hesitation, that Mary White and Duke had just done that for me. They also tore apart my prototype depiction of what I've always numbly referred to as 'them people,' or simply 'those niggers.'

Duke said that he and Mary and my mom got along so well because they're just 'everyday people,' just like the ones in the Sly and The Family Stone song. As my mom is prone to say, 'you'll never learn anything if you don't take your head out of your ass.' Mine, apparently, has been jammed up there for quite a long stretch. It feels nice to pop it out if for just a short while.

THE BRONX

The adventures of my life, at least since I've been fourteen or so, often feel like they transpire while I'm in a trance. In other words, they just seem to happen without me being fully aware of what's exactly going down. Whether it's me flying into a rage at the drop of a hat or shooting off my mouth without contemplating a single premeditated thought, and then immediately wishing I hadn't said it, I often end up wondering how I could possibly have done what I just did. Going from point A to point B is more like a sleepwalk than a journey. Add alcohol to the mix and the separation of mind and body becomes total disjointment, where the guy committing the deed is not the same guy, he thought he was just a few minutes prior. Thus, was me at the Meatloaf concert.

Meatloaf, that fat bastard who can sing like a mother-fucker, was hot on the scene but not sizzling enough to be selling out big arenas like Madison Square Garden. Amazingly he was scheduled to play at Pace University, which is located in some town up north where rich people live in unlocked homes with cute wives and bratty kids. And, lo and behold, we had a real, live, bonafide in. The guy we had the in with wasn't necessarily okay with being the 'in' in the equation, but that wasn't of any real concern to us. What mattered was that we were going to get our hands on some tickets.

This kid was a student at Pace, and he was the first cousin of our friend, Kenny. This guy, whose name was something really fucked up like Brad or Scott or something equally nauseating, had let his cuz know that he was on the student recreation committee and could get his mitts on some tickets. When Kenny told us this we were like, '. . . well, what the fuck are you waiting for?' and soon enough we were in. Kenny was reluctant as hell to be part and parcel to the release of wild animals on a pastoral college campus, but it's not like he had much of a choice. Once the cat was out of the bag, he needed to decide between hitting up his cousin for the tickets or catching a severe ass whipping.

So, the day came and there we were like the Clampetts, loading up the wagon for a trip to civilized society. Oh, and by the way, Meatloaf, like a bat out of hell, we'll be gone before the morning comes. Yeah, when the night is over, we'll be 'gone, gone, gone.' But more often than not, we'll leave an impression, and will be remembered long after we're 'gone, gone, gone.'

Word had it that this being a college venue and all, alcohol would be strictly prohibited. What wasn't prohibited was the alcohol consumed beforehand, and any booze that passed in unnoticed. So, the party planners, of which I was one, had a twofold strategy. On the way up, a trip that they said would take 45 minutes or so, we'd drink beer with the occasional slug of Jack Daniels, with the intent to get lubricated jiminy quick and dirty like. Someone, I'm not sure who, had the brainstorm that liqueur in a wine sack was the way to go. I thought shoving a pint of Smirnoff down the front of my pants was the way to go but eventually was convinced otherwise. Not only is straight vodka like drinking battery acid but the potential clinking of the bottle would make concealment a challenge. When a bunch of idiots are swapping ideas, it's a sure bet that the eventual conclusion will be idiocy extrapolated.

So, we loaded up a couple of cars and headed due north to a place that definitely did not bear any semblance to our beloved Bronx. We were in my brother's car with Bobby upfront and me, Lukie, and Mahoney in the rear. Meatloaf blared loudly from the cassette player, a *hors d'oeuvre* for the main course awaiting us at Pace. We drank heavily, all the while fretfully attempting to pour blackberry brandy into the minute holes in our wine sacks with Mickey seeming to go out of his way to drive through every fucking pothole in the road. Why blackberry brandy, the curious might ask? Because it was a better choice than creme de menthe or peppermint schnapps. Or, that's what we believed anyway. And we wouldn't end up smelling like we'd doused ourselves in cheap after shave lotion.

The way the tickets worked was that we had sets of two that weren't necessarily together. Pace had been forced to transform a 2,000-capacity performance theater into a rock arena, and they'd let the various student committees organize everything, including security which would be a gaping hole of inept strategizing. Basically, the whole thing was handled haphazardly, creating a level of systematic chaos. We were far from the only rowdy drunks making their way indoors.

The wine sacks turned out to be an exercise in over precaution. I think I probably could have rolled in a keg of beer while yodeling like a lumberjack. But we had what we had, and it was my intention to make good use of it. So, Lukie and I found our way to our seats and got ready for an evening of entertainment. None of our friends were seated anywhere near us as best we could tell but it didn't matter. I felt like Jimmy Cagney on top of the tower in *White Heat* yelling down at the coppers, '. . . look at me, Ma, I'm on top of the world.' If the world was gonna go up in flames tonight, I was gonna be in the middle of that fire.

It was during "Paradise" by The Dashboard Lights that I elbowed Lukie and told him I was going to jump onstage. By now, both of us had sucked our wineskins dry. Like any sound minded friend, he grabbed me by the shoulders, stared straight into my eyes and said, ". . . do it, motherfucker, do it." What choice did I have?

Meatloaf's sidekick was now front and center—black leather pants painted onto her tight body, her voice majestic, feeling like her vocals were meant specifically for me, only for me.

But it wasn't the whole Jack McGee, it was him of body but not of mind. The lyrics 'Do you love me, will you love me forever' were like a direct question that I was compelled to answer. My heart thumping to every word she sang; my desire escalating fiercely. The world now reduced to just the two of us, me and her. The distance between us no longer insurmountable. I heard, 'I gotta know right now,' and shortly after that the . . . 'feeling came upon me like a tidal wave' and I dashed forward and leapt onstage.

The college recreation committee had done a lousy job providing security around the stage and a person of my adept mobility, even in a compromised state, could not be contained. The adrenaline surge was as if I was shot out of a cannon. Meatloaf, stunned by the approach of a deranged lunatic, stepped back from my path allowing me undisturbed access to the object of my yearning. The striking woman with the angelic voice and snugly fitting leather pants did not appear to be happy to see me.

In fact, she was terrified, as was her corpulent companion. The music ceased as hands and arms embraced me. I managed to wriggle free long enough to raise my hands to the crowd, which had erupted into a mixture of cheers and boos. Security scurried to reclaim me but before they could toss me into the waiting arms of my captors, I managed to flip roles and toss one of them instead. More cheers erupted, or at least that's how I recall it. Meatloaf, I found out after, had threatened to walk off stage. My girl, his girl, had needed to be calmed sufficiently to continue.

I tried spotting my friends as I was aggressively herded to the exit, but to no avail. A man not in the midst of his friends, is at the center of his enemies. Anyone who did or could have approved of my antics was nowhere to be found. I was surrounded by haters, but I was oddly loving every minute of it. Sometimes a man just needs to do what he has to do, regardless of which area of his brain is supplying the instructions.

Based on the circumstances I've presented, as I remember them, I was really left with no choice. The spell had been cast upon me and I was at its mercy. I'm pretty sure that's the same argument David Berkowitz (Son of Sam) presented in regard to his neighbor's dog compelling him to go out and shoot all those people. Sound reasoning, it seems, is an elusive aspiration for those who search for reason through the murky lens of booze and insanity. Blackberry brandy, despite having similar qualities, is not Windex, it will not clear the view. Fate is a time in one's existence, thrust upon those who may or not be ready for it. My fate this fine evening, it would seem, was to be the chuck chop in a mound of Meatloaf. If this was indeed a moment dictated by fate, then yours truly was up Fate's Creek without a paddle, as the punster might say.

If God was watching over me at that point, it was like he was mostly watching a football game and sipping from a beer can and remembering every once in a while, to look back over his shoulder to see what the kid playing with matches was up to. He helps me get out of one jam and then a big play in the game grabs his attention, and while he's screaming at the television, he once again drops me from mind and sight just long enough to let me slide into another dilemma of my own making, or not, depending on your concept of God.

Unceremoniously tossed from the concert, drunker than a brewery rat, and with no concept of where I was geographically, I was not exactly in a position of advantage. My boys couldn't find me, and neither could I find them. My ride home had vanished, I was a man adrift. A stray cat off the beaten path, a rolling stone with no direction home. I was the guy with the shovel, the one digging his own grave. Tired and bedraggled, I figured my options would be clearer in the morning after I caught a few winks. As the man himself would say, the man I had just recently danced alongside on a concert stage, I was all revved up with no place to go.

My best recollection is that I stumbled upon a smaller sized building and probably thought I could find a place under a stairwell, or in a janitor's closet to sleep. I've certainly managed to obtain my beauty rest in stranger, less desirable places. There's a faint memory of me fiddling with a locked door and then deciding to kick it in to gain access. It seems I entered the establishment on a higher floor with no apparent cubby holes to slide into. What there was instead was a series of doors rather close to each other. It turned out that one of those doors was ajar, and further perusal proved it to be unoccupied. God had not forsaken me, or so I thought. Goldilocks had a choice of three beds, but mine was limited to two. I chose the one with the bigger pillows.

The rest of the night, what remained of it, unfurled like a Gene Hackman movie. I was startled from my drunken stupor by a woman's screams. Apparently, the sight of a complete stranger, slumped unconscious in her bed was not appealing to her. Neither I'm sure, were the blood stains on her pillow that I'd left from an open head wound I'd incurred in my earlier adventures that evening, or the puddle of urine I'd somehow deposited at the foot of the bed. The lass's frantic screams brought bodies rushing to her aid, bodies that now blocked my exit.

Whatever shut eye I had managed was insufficient to allow me to regain my composure. I was still solidly in the abyss. There was no time to stop and explain. There was no reasonable explanation to be had even if I tried. I jumped into a standing position, let out my best werewolf howl and slammed through bodies until I was out of the room and into the hallway. I was of course unaware at the time that I had 'committed an assault.' I just knew I needed to get as far away from that place as fast as my dumb ass was capable of.

I ran for the nearest exit in a state of panic. My head beating like a tom-tom at war time, complementing the war paint dripping down my face from my open wound. My throat was parched, my legs wobbly, but I gamely trudged on. The few in pursuit stayed just close enough behind to know my whereabouts. No one seemed inclined to engage me physically. In the background, I could hear sirens, and the sky blinked cherry tops. The manhunt was underway.

By now, I realized I had been in a college dorm, so the police would be looking for someone who didn't look like he was college material, i.e. the plastic spoon alien from the lower ghettos. As I ran outside, I fortuitously happened upon a bike rack and, with God now back in the picture, the bicycle I grasped was unlocked. So off I went, pedaling like a motherfucker down a road to somewhere. As I steamed along, I was temporarily blinded by the lights of a cop car that, amazingly, drove right past me. Maybe at first glance, I appeared to them to be no less than a studious young man out for a late evening/early morning session of vigorous exercise. It must have been the second glance that altered the narrative because now I heard screeching tires and the flickering lights that seemed to dim into the background were glowing brighter again.

They were in full pursuit, and I was the naked prey. Or nearly naked anyway, having had the good sense to have gone to bed fully clothed. In yet another stroke of brilliance, I realized I was not going to out pedal a cop car. So, off the bike I came, and into a patch of woods I went.

Again, car tires screeched, but this time they were joined in concert with slamming doors and loud voices spewing expletives of an assorted verbiage. I remember one dutiful policeman yelling, 'stop running you little prick because if I have to shoot your ass I will.' I figured he was bluffing so further into the woods I galloped, only to find out that the woods weren't exactly a dense forest but merely a temporary haven from the visions of my pursuers.

I came out over a highway overpass which left me with few viable escape paths.

Desperate times call for desperate measures, so Robert Redford and Paul Newman be damned, over the rail I hopped, with a mighty 'ohhhh shit!' for emphasis. It was a solid fifteen-foot jump, and it landed me plum in the middle of a two-lane highway. God once again took his eyes off the football game to check in with his charge and made sure that no cars were speeding along when I landed. Good man, that God fella. The cops, probably of the Barney Fife caliber, were not about to follow me down onto the road so their hunt was stalled. I ran further up the road and frantically started waving cars down. It didn't take long for a Good Samaritan to pull over to the shoulder, roll down the passenger window, and invite me into the passenger seat.

My on again, off again, Creator above must have become distracted again because the man who picked me up was an off-duty policeman from the very same local force that was chasing me down. He had been home, probably watching porn, or something of equal intellectual stimulation, when he received a call from one of his coworkers filling him in on the massive manhunt happening in his very own backyard. For the perpetually bored fuzz in a sleepy, one-horse town, I was a happening event and an unfurling drama that absolutely could not be missed. I probably had just added three stripes to this fellow's uniform. He'd probably have his own float in the next town parade. He managed to fool me until we were right upside a police car and there was no way I could break for freedom.

Now in custody, I was put in a cell out front of the police station where I could be viewed like a wild animal in the zoo. There was a feeling of tremendous excitement in the air, a sense of jubilation that I did not share. I could almost conjure an image of the local populace outside calling for my execution as a few of them tossed a rope with a noose over a tree branch in the public square, ala Quasimodo in the castle spire. I desperately jogged my memory to recall the worst thing I'd done that evening. People do commit horrendous acts in a blackout, that much I knew. I just didn't know what hideous crime I had committed, only that it must have been bad. I asked the men outside my cell for two things, aspirin, and a cup of coffee. I wasn't quite ready to call mom.

The menu offered in this penal establishment was quite a few grades up from the Riker's new inmate special, which is one slice each of baloney and American cheese on stale white bread, with the bread being one of the few white things in Rikers.

I was shocked when they asked me if I wanted anything on my burger, and if I wanted fries or onion rings. It was like they were paying you to be locked up. Who said crime doesn't pay? I opted for the bacon cheeseburger deluxe with fries. They also offered me more coffee and as much cold water as I could drink, none of it tasting like it came from a bathroom faucet. My head was still pounding but I was definitely feeling better, well enough to participate in the little fireside chat that was about to begin.

They asked me if I needed a lawyer, and I told them that would depend on what I was being charged with. "Trespassing for one, disorderly conduct for two, and assault for three," is what the cop told me. I told them I got the trespassing and disorderly conduct bits but that I was clueless as to who I could have assaulted. I told them everything I remembered and held nothing back. I figured what I was telling them sounded a lot less bad than what they were going to tell me. I also asked them where the hell I was, starting with the state. Eventually, they let me call my mother who, upon hearing of my circumstances, actually didn't seem terribly surprised. She was, however, exceedingly pissed off. Skipping work to come and bail me out was not a decision she arrived at easily.

I was released to my mother's care and supervision, and the original charges against me were reduced to misdemeanors with the assault charge completely thrown out. The chick who claimed she had broken her wrist when she was knocked to the ground during my dash from the dorm room, had actually broken it by punching me in the back of the head as I thrust myself through the crowd of people blocking the door. My brother, Mickey, told me she ended up being some bull dyke with spiky hair. Sexual preferences aside, I'd have advised her that to truly harm an Irishman you don't want to aim at his head. So, God was back in the game and off I went with my freedom in hand. My criminal escapades wouldn't land me on any most wanted lists or get me any votes for the bad guy all-star team. Maybe, an honorable mention for the most misdemeanors in one fluid stream.

I found out a few days later that I had made the local paper, *The Pleasantville Times*, on page two no less. I was like, '. . . holy shit, don't they have anything newsworthy to write about?' I also figured that if the *Daily News* covered every story like this one in the Bronx, you'd have to read through the equivalent of *War and Peace* before you got to Dagwood, Blondie, and the weather. Needless to say, I wanted every possible copy of that newspaper I could lay my hands on. As they say in Hollywood, there's no such thing as bad press. I'd exerted a lot of time and energy to earn my spot in that rag, and I wanted written proof to support my celebrity status.

Another thing they say in Hollywood, or somewhere anyways, is don't let the facts get in the way of a great story.

Well, I had plenty of facts to lean on, but the newspaper left out a lot of really pertinent stuff. So, I might be inclined to embellish the facts a tad going forward—come out sounding like Steve McQueen in the *Great Escape*. Obviously, I have the looks to match. And God, speaking of the devil, actually did end up hanging with me until the bitter end, landing me safe at home in my spacious abode in the Bronx, NY. I'll be sharing this claim to fame with everyone who cares to listen for quite some time going forward. Gonna' ride this baby as far as I can take it. Or at least until I find a way to top it.

THE BRONX

They say that everyone in life gets visited just once by the White Horse and when they do, they need to jump on it and ride, but you're supposed to avoid the dark ones like the plague. That's seeming less clear to me these days because sometimes the dark ones are whiter than the white ones. It's kind of a moot point because whatever the color, I only seem to come in contact with donkeys and circus ponies.

CHAPTER 18

Loose Screws and Lug Nuts

When I'm bartending, I'm forced to listen to a lot of really stupid people say a lot of really stupid shit. And a really stupid guy, who is really drunk, will take that dumb wittedness to levels once thought unachievable. Then, he'll share the inane nonsense over and over again with the utmost confidence, as if his pearls of wisdom are so profound that they have the capability to forever alter your life for the better. He'll pepper in a continuous stream of phrases like, 'you see where I'm coming from?' or 'that's the god's honest truth,' and I have to bite my lip before I scream out something like 'I have no fucking idea where you're coming from' or 'do you really think God is that stupid?' but I don't.

Such was the case the other night with this clown, Bruce, who works for Ma Bell. The guy is a blowhard on his best day, and an outright torture in general. I cringe when I see him walk in the bar. Things are just starting to pick up and Bruce, who was already intoxicated when I started my shift, is blabbering some nonsense about the art of barroom brawling. That's the other thing about drunks and conversations, they transpire at extremely high decibels. Like a blowhard with a blow horn.

Now Bruce doesn't know the tiniest thing about barroom brawling. He's fat and out of shape and has a yellow streak to boot. If he's ever been in a real fight, it's either been with a female, or he's surely gotten his ass beat. That's a fucking ironclad guarantee. I'd even take the average female over him, particularly if it was one of the local mothers like my very own dear mom or Mrs. Mahoney. I witnessed Mrs. Mahoney beat this local hoodlum, Ralphie, to near death with a high heel shoe. No messin' with that whirlwind of femininity when she's protecting her brood.

So, here's our man, Bruce, he of fat mouth and body, telling these other idiots how you have to always throw the first punch. Approach it like a Western, stare the guy down and then draw before he realizes what's going down, and take him out in a whisk of manhood. Then before he gets up, assuming you've managed to drop him, which apparently Bruce has done numerous times with ease, you put your foot on his prone carcass and advise him to avoid further pain and embarrassment, by staying down and conceding to the better man. Just like that, bang and it's over. You get the girl and the beer, and drink of the golden, fucking, Viking chalice. Couldn't be easier.

What Bruce is failing to remember is that not too long ago, he meekly reached across the bar and took a poke at me in a fit of anger motivated by some contrived slight. His sissy slap of a punch had zero impact, and I immediately hopped over to his side of the bar, got him in a choke hold and dragged him across the floor to the door and threw him to the concrete outside, real Western like. I could have reminded him of this, but I didn't. One thing was for sure, ol' Bruce is no Jesse James. Damn, he's not even half the man Annie Oakley was.

The actual key to a successful barroom brawl is frankly not that complicated and involves one simple strategy, i.e., don't be drunk when fighting. The booze will melt away your inhibitions, prompting the drunken fool, who would never in a sober state have the balls to engage, throw a punch, or brazenly challenge a would-be nemesis to a battle.

Conversely, the grog, depending on the consumption amount, will render you physically compromised, leaving you with the dexterity of a wet noodle. Hence the wobbly gait, slurred speech, etc. Most people are stupid enough to think they drive better and fight better when they've had a few to loosen them up. Meanwhile, they're being untethered from reality and any hint of their minimal capability. I've been shocked at how easy it's been to break up brawls between the ossified by getting in between the paper tigers and pushing each away in different directions, using just one arm per idiot.

Now that's not always the case with a man of monster dimensions, with physics being the culprit there, but as a general rule it's gospel. A really inebriated individual will drop like a domino with very little force applied. Try hitting a baseball or shooting a basketball when drunk. Or even better, try lighting a cigarette on a stovetop. I've done that one and I can assure you it's a difficult task in a sotten condition. It took a good long while, too long if I remember correctly, for my eyelashes to be restored to their natural fullness.

I unfortunately do not always take my own advice and have partaken in fisticuffs while being nearly legless drunk. Fortune has held me in safe stead though, as I've had the providence to go up against equally hapless fools. A sober brawl involves tactics and guile for the sake of survival. You need to size up your opponent and maximize your skills. You can come off looking like Jack Dempsey if you're straight and use a similar mindset versus a drunk. I walked into a situation where some ape, who probably outweighed me by 50 pounds, was about to annihilate my brother, Mickey.

They were already outside the bar when I arrived on the scene and the local prizefight promoters were arranging for a 'fair' fight. I had no doubts that my beloved sibling was in for a colossal ass beating if events proceeded, so I stepped in to take his place. The goofball, who was not from our neighborhood, politely agreed to fight me instead but vowed to get my brother as well immediately upon my destruction. I agreed to his terms and the movers and shakers allowed me to step into the circle and pinch hit for Mickey.

I found myself surprisingly calm given the circumstances. My mind went into combat mode and my strategy became crystal clear to me. I would let the drunk lunge at me with the first punch, and then slide to his side, the same one from where the punch came from, get into a crouch with my fists poised for action, and then unleash a straight right to the side of his noggin. It worked like a charm. One punch knockouts are the stuff of legends. The fact that I had an almost insurmountable advantage by being sober, and that he was stupidly drunk, would not be in the morning sports pages. The entire story would be that one punch, and the man that threw it.

My recent exploits up north resulted in the various people of authority mandating that I spend more time with a doctor of the mind. I think they considered me a younger version of Randall McMurphy from *One Flew Over the Cuckoo's Nest.* Like Randall, I would admit to being enamored with 'fucking and fighting,' but never viewed either as a mental disorder. I do believe I would have gotten along a little better with Nurse Ratched than he did, however, as I find her rather cute, and the uniform was an added touch.

So, back on the couch I go, spilling my guts to yet another bearded, sweater vest wearing weirdo who, to make sure he has all the boxes checked, is also smoking a pipe. He introduces himself as Dr. Fried, 'not Freud, ha ha,' and my first thought is, *do you have to be a Jew or a German or perhaps a German Jew to be in this field of medicine?* Dr. not-Freud makes sure I know he's Ivy school educated, with the implication being that a lowly gutter rat like me should be fall-down grateful to be in such fine company. He also reminds me that I'm here before him at the request of the State of New York disciplinary system, and my second thought is, . . . *if you're such a whoopie doo fucking genius why are you taking cases from the state?* I always figured these Hah-vid types only had offices on Park Avenue where rich ladies with nervous conditions paid big money to talk their way into getting sent away to one of those country club nuthouses where they can get permanently stoned on sedatives and play croquet, and maybe sneak into the bushes with one of the youthful help.

This freak has me really uncomfortable because he was stroking his beard with his thumb and forefinger while staring blankly ahead in total silence. After what seems like an hour he opens my file on his lap, and mumbles 'hmmm' over and over as he leaves through the pages. He closes the folder, finally looks in my direction, and says, "okay, let's get started." He runs down the usual questions about family life and school, and then acknowledges my father's murder as if it was just another variable in this strange mosaic of life. If he's feeling sorry for me, he's doing a nasty fine job of concealing it. Then out of left field he tosses out, "have you ever had sexual contact with another male?" I reply, rather angrily, "no fucking way," and add a look of dismay to emphasize the absurdity of the question.

Now, I'm thinking that if this faggot head shrink makes one move in my direction, he'll be lisping all further questions due to a lack of teeth, which will be swirling around his mouth like Chicklets. He kind of apologizes as he explains that he knew the question would upset me but that he needed to ask it. I was waiting for the usual explanations as to why I did the things I did and acted the way I did but Doc took a less conventional approach. He said that my 'child within' wanted to come out but that I wouldn't let him because I was too hung up on my desperate cling to masculinity. He told me it's okay to get in touch with my feminine side even if I wasn't gay. What I wanted to tell him is that there was no 'even if' and that if I did, in fact, get in touch with my feminine side, she'd be a lesbian who likes girls as much as I do.

Mercifully, the egotistical prick wasn't going to give me a second past the forty-five minutes he was paid for. I could have mentioned that we started fifteen minutes late but that would be like asking a bank robber to come back and shoot me after he'd already gotten away. Out the door I went before he could schedule another appointment.

If the State of New York thinks these sessions will keep me on the straight and narrow to a reformed life, they have underestimated my ability to spot a fraud when I see one. Another session or two with this nut job and I'll be serial murderer material. Practically the whole time I was sitting there, I'm thinking to myself, *hey, I could do this shit for a living.* Give me a couple of classes up at the big H with the geniuses and I'll flip the switch and swap roles with my man Zigmund here. I'd shrink his head down to the size of a penny, and since he already has the beard, he'd just need a little bronzing at the local beach, and he'd be a dead ringer for Honest Abe on the one cent piece.

If you told me I was great, I might believe you for a minute or two but if you told me I was fucked up in some way, shape, or manner, I'll obsess on it for an eternity.

Chapter 19

Brother Brian Gets Smarter Still, Jack Not so Much

My final days at my institute of higher learning are approaching and I cannot fucking wait to leave that dump in my rearview mirror. Brother Brian has been on me to make a decision on my future, one that he insists should include college. He dropped a bombshell on me by telling me that he would also be parting ways with St. Joe's and would, in fact, be trading in his Irish Christian Brothers collar for a wedding ring.

"So here we are, Jack, the two of us misfits departing from this place at exactly the same time. And while we're at it, please refrain from putting Brother in front of my name. From now on it's just Brian, and no mister nonsense either. I'm still too young for that."

"Okay, Pops."

"Ya bastard ya."

"Are you really getting hitched Mister Brother Brian? Sorry, it's kind of weird for me to just call you Brian but I'll try my damndest. It's just that you're more like an uncle than a cousin, a role model and all that. I feel like I owe you that type of respect. You've helped me quite a bit and that's not something I take lightly. If I can ever pay you . . ."

"Oh, stop with that gobshite, you owe me not a thing. You may not realize it, but you've probably helped me more than I ever helped you. You see, Jack, as I've told you often enough, I see myself in you. You're that kid keeping it all inside and not allowing yourself to breathe, and that was me as well. I don't want to stay that way one more damn day. I was you, Jack, I am you for Christ's sake. Let's get out of this strait jacket together. I have a plan, but you need one as well. I'm getting married to a wonderful woman, assuming she shows up at the altar. It'll be a new start for me, a new life.

Now hear me out, this is what I need from you. I've talked to a good friend who's in the administration department at Fordham College. They've got a scholarship program that's sponsored by some rich guy who lost his father at a young age, just like the two of us did. They can't come out and say it but the gentleman is partial to the Irish. Long story short, you're in if you choose to be. I told them all about you and they're excited to meet you. Told them you're smart in ways they'd understand, and even smarter in ways that they wouldn't. Won't cost you a plug nickel. Whadda ya say, lad, will you do this one thing for me? I can talk to your ma and give her the details if you want me to. I know for sure what she'll say. C'mon kid, tell me we have a deal."

"Sheez, Brother Brian, I mean . . . man, that's pretty incredible that you did all that, and for me no less. I don't know what to say. Can we change the topic for a second? Who's this fine lass who'll be taking your hand in marriage? You never . . ."

"Jack, do you think by now I can't figure out when you're dodging me. She's a great gal, and I'm a lucky man. Now stop your *feckin* sidetracking and get back to what I just asked you about. Will you do this one little favor for me, man? Can we come loose of the vice together?

"You're such an intelligent lad, Jack, use what God has given you, for Christ's sake!"

"Yes, sir, I understand. By the way, I think you said 'Christ's sake' twice and completely neglected the Jesus, Mary and Saint Joseph's."

"You're such a wiseass, you little bastard. One other thing before we wrap this up, just so I can have my facts straight, or at least some approximation of what's true and what isn't. These people have already taken you as you are, nothing in your past can change that. They may ask, they may not, so now it's more for personal curiosity. There's always been some nonsense buzzing about concerning yourself, and a man can't take anything at face value these days. I heard the reason you were tossed out of your previous school. There won't be any judging done here."

"You mean for when I shot the fire extinguisher into Mr. Water's math class? He was a hard man to like."

"Jaysus Christ, that's not what the little bird told me. Did ya really? You're a piece of work."

"Maybe for the time I turned out the assembly hall lights when the Cardinal came to visit?

"I did everyone a favor, that guy couldn't have been more boring, and he simply would not shut-up. I bet most people didn't even notice because they were already fast asleep in their chairs.

"And, by the way, they could never actually prove it was me that did it. That definitely had to factor in though. I don't mind coming clean now because they've already done with me what they would. Water under the bridge, as they say."

"Jaysus Christ, again! I shouldn't be laughing, it will only encourage you going forward, but you've given me a mighty kick to my funny bone. I've heard that man speak, for hours it seemed, and getting him off the pulpit is certainly a gift to your fellow man. No, not that either. What I heard was that you had a relationship with your French teacher."

"Well, I am not ashamed to say there's some truth to that, but it's not the reason they gave me the boot. I was already gone before they found that out. Besides, it's a romance language and I took the definition to heart. Do you know any French, Brother? The way it rolls off a woman's tongue? Like how she would say *bonjour*. A soft, easy little bon, followed up with a kind of whistling, as she drags out the *joooooooour*. And in order to get the Frenchie sound perfect she has to pucker up her lips like she's blowing in your ear. I don't know how that flies in Ireland but to a kid from the Bronx it's a friggin' aphrodisiac more potent than anything that the little Chinese street merchant has in his cart. You can buy all the rhino horn dust you want but I'll take the French girl with the short blond hair and nice legs any day when it comes to inciting the ol' pecker."

"You've a magic wit there, Jack, there's no denying that. Are you aware that you could have likely filed charges against her? It works both ways with adults having sex with the underaged, it doesn't matter if the offender is male or female."

"Press charges? You nuts? There was no crime committed here. Doesn't a crime require a victim? I never fought her off for a second. It was like a dream, I thought I hit the lottery, died, and went straight to heaven. I have two regrets about the whole thing: one, that it didn't happen sooner and, two, that it had to end."

"Please tell me you've moved on from this, c'mon lad?"

"I had no choice. She disappeared into space. Probably on Gilligan's Island or something. If there's anyone still nosing around looking for her, tell them there's a tenner hanging out there for her phone number. Hey, I'm just joshing. Yeah, it's over and done with from my angle.

"Besides, I've promised myself to this gal, Mary, even if she doesn't know it."

THE BRONX

I, of course, asked for some time to chew things over. Here's this man sticking his neck out for my benefit and not getting the result he probably expected. What kid in his right mind would turn down a free ride to a college that would ordinarily cost you an arm and a leg? Well, that's not to say my mind's made up but something about the whole thing just feels too weird to me. These college kids aren't my kind of people, though I'll cop to having a thing or two for those preppy girls in their plaid skirts and gleaming white teeth. I've been squirming behind desks for 12 years now and I think that's the limit to what I can stand. I'm just not the academic type. Sure, I love books, I read everything that's worth reading, but the only use I have for a textbook is to maybe use it to substitute for a leg on the couch.

I didn't find out until after he was dead and gone, but my father apparently wanted to name me Dylan, after Dylan Thomas, but my mom thankfully talked him out of it before the birth certificate was stamped and final. Besides if you know me even a little, there's no name that would have ever fit me other than Jack. I'm a Jack through and through.

The old man was quite the literary demon, I remember, always falling asleep with a book on his chest. His father, my Pops, was the same way. The two of them wrote letters that would have put Shakespeare to shame. Always quoting some mick or another, Behan, Beckett, or Yeats or even that nut job, Jimmy Joyce. Beautiful stuff, sure, but nothing to help you with the bills.

Besides, what am I gonna do with the piece of paper they give you at graduation other than wipe my ass with it? I just can't picture myself in some stuffy office doing accounting or, worse still, some lying son of a bitch lawyer trying to screw you out of your last dollar. Though given my penchant for stringing along a horseshit story, something I'd likely be damn good at. "Ladies and gentlemen of the jury, please listen eagerly as I captivate you with a patch of deceit wide enough to cover the infield at Yankee Stadium when the skies open up . . ."

Fuck all that. The craziest thing about it all is that it's got me thinking about the exquisite, dare I say, enchanting, Mary. How college would improve my chances of stealing her heart. She'll wind up with one of these studious types who can communicate with her on her level. Get rich, live in some castle with her goofball of a husband, and forget she ever spent a day in the Bronx. And definitely fail to recall even a trace of my sorry ass. Or maybe not. Maybe the Bronx stays in the girl as much as it stays in the guy. Maybe is a very big maybe though, and a betting man would need some very wide odds to make that wager.

I promised Brother Brian, soon to be plain old Brian, an answer within a couple of days. I need to mull it through and there's no better place to do it than on the corner of Creston Avenue with a bottle of the devil's brew in my fist. It's the one place that never gets weird to me.

You don't stand a chance if you don't take a chance they say.

Chapter 20

Requiem for a Rogue

Word came down, and it came down hard: the passing of the legendary Bill Kennedy aka Willie the Rogue. Sam the deli man had phoned the police because he hadn't seen or heard from Bill in a few days, an absence two days longer than any he could remember over the twenty plus years he'd known him.

The last disappearance he could recall was the time, quite a few years back, that became the oft repeated, and now legendary, 'apron story,' named for the line the Rogue delivered upon resurfacing. A younger, dapper version of the man had done Sam a favor by delivering a box of groceries to the apartment of a local lush by the name of Connie.

So, off he went, nattily attired with a clean, white apron draped across his front torso. The groceries had included a couple of six packs of the Rogue's favorite beverage, Premium Rheingold Beer. Connie was a frequent call-in customer of Sam's deli who rarely left the house and was known to drink at all hours of the day. Sam also knew she didn't eat properly and was concerned enough to implore Bill to convince her to eat something, though not perturbed enough to exclude the beer from the order.

Connie, despite being a hopeless sot, was still young enough to have retained some of the attractiveness she had possessed not all that long ago. Which was more than ample enough for a man of the Rogue's taste. What transpired in the apartment that day remains a mystery, one that will pass to the grave with Willie the Rogue. The little that was known was that Bill went off the radar until the following morning when he popped into Sam's deli with an ear-to-ear, shit-eating grin. Sam immediately tore into him, asking where the hell he'd been, and included quite a number of expletives in his criticism. The Rogue, a little hot under the collar (and a little not) from the onslaught, shot right back at the deli man with, "what are you so goddamned mad about, I brought back your apron!" This instantly erased Sam's wrath and brought him to tears with laughter. There and then the 'apron story' became neighborhood folklore.

When the police arrived at Bill Kennedy's third floor apartment there was no noise from within, and their bell ringing, and heavy knocking drew no response. The building super, who had accompanied the men in blue upstairs, suddenly remembered he had an extra key and ran quickly to retrieve it. One of the cops later told Sam that the Rogue was found lying peacefully in his unkempt bed with his hands folded across his stomach, and what appeared to be a grin on his face. "Sheepish in life, sheepish in death" is how Sam put it. His overall appearance could be described as tidy, with his boxers and standard white T-shirt no worse for wear, and black socks pulled up to his calf. He looked as if he was expecting to be found this way, dead as a doorknob but still, in his own way, a man about town.

The rest of the apartment was certainly not tidy. It was the disheveled ruin of a man who, disguised from his true self, did all his living outside the confines of his abode. Out there he was the charming, beloved Willie the Rogue. Inside he was a poor, broken down man of no accomplishment who never had a wife or a family or a career. The debris strewn about told the story of a man who subsisted on beer, filterless cigarettes, and cheap, ready-to-eat food. It was a place to lay his head at night where no one asked to come in, and no one was invited.

Sam had a number for Bill's only known living relative, his sister, Martha. Upon hearing the news of her brother's passing, Martha was initially somber, thanking Sam for passing on the news, and thanking him for being such a kind friend to her brother, who was her only sibling.

Soon after that, Martha began to quietly sob, telling Sam things like, 'he wasn't always like this,' or 'I tried to get him to come live with me and my family,' 'he was never the same after his older brother had passed when he was a teenager,' 'he was such a great guy to grow up with.' Sam agreed to meet her when she came from Ohio to deal with her brother's affairs, which meant signing his death certificate and getting a box, and maybe a cheap headstone, for this final leg of his trip.

Sam also shared that she came across to him as a lady with class, educated and such. The low sobbing on the other end of the line had nearly broken Sam's heart.

A legend to all of us who knew him. Willie the Rogue would nonetheless be denied a hero's farewell. No twenty-one gun salute, no doves released from a cage. He did receive, however, thousands of toasts as we celebrated his life on the corner of Creston Avenue, his corner, our corner. We also pledged, as we forced down the cans of piss with Rheingold labeled on them, that we would never forget the man. Not forgetting Willie the Rogue would be easy, getting used to not having him around was a matter altogether different. Sam gave Martha an apron to bury our friend in. He swore it was the same apron from Bill's story. I could picture Bill standing behind Sam as he was telling us this, winking his eyes and smiling proudly.

God is still sandbagging me, but I do believe he does, on rare occasions, send me hints that there really is a heaven, and that even roguish 'bums' might get the red carpet when their final day comes.

Chapter 21

Bronx Potpouri

I am thinking of writing an Irish cookbook. Maybe add in a chapter crisscrossing the Irish love of fine cuisine with their amorous nature in general; how food clashes with romance, how a certain dish consumed by a certain Irishman might compare to his passion for a certain type of woman. The book will hardly be a tome. It will be concise in its expression, perhaps matching the length of an exposé on Irish porn stars or, for that matter, an illustrated edition of classic Irish erotic art.

It's what can be referred to as a 'leaf through' book, something you can peruse over and over. At the moment, it's just a kernel of an idea but certain individual perceptions I have are bringing it to life. For instance, take the Irish predilection for ketchup. To the uninformed, it's a simple condiment but to the clever Irish chef it's a sauce, a glaze, or even an ingredient. Let's not even get started on the artistic dimensions enveloping the core food of the Irish diet, the common brown potato. The uses for the multi-faceted spud, that oblong bearer of nutritious and enlightening starch, are almost too many to mention.

Irish cuisine, to date, has not made it to the forefront of fine dining, In many ways, it's a babe in the woods on unsure legs. Its story has never really been told. My objective in this would-be-publication is to set a base, a solid foundation, for the great Irish chefs of the future to expand on. It will need to not only grab the reader on a subject they would normally have very little interest in, but to implore and motivate them to create, and to then forge forward into a realm the Irish have never breached. It will, of course, also have a few 15-minute easy-to-make dishes for the less sophisticated cook. Included will be anecdotes of various forms that meld the food to the greater world at large.

Let me return to the clash of food and women from the Irish perspective. I have a mother, sisters, aunts, and beloved females of all stripes in my life, all who I admire and respect greatly. So, it is with hesitance that I would even use the word ugly in reference to a woman. But let's compare an unattractive woman to a bland piece of meat. This is not to say that the average Irishman is a sight to behold so the comparison can be easily switched to a woman's perspective.

One of my fellow barkeeps, Robinson, has a theory on women that goes along the lines of every woman 'having a time.' Some women's time comes immediately. They walk into the bar at eight p.m. and they're already the equivalent of a veal parm dinner at a premium guinea restaurant. For now, it's a better comparison than an Irish dish, but that's what the book will try to change. Other women, Robinson explains, fall into other-hourly frames of attractiveness. The late, late bloomers could run to 4 a.m. and beyond before attaining a level of desirability.

Conversely, again, in defense of the female race, some men never reach a time at all; they are eternally in purgatory.

All their romantic conquests will involve an exchange of funds.

The object of the cookbook would be to bring all Irish dishes to 'a time' when they're acceptable for consumption via the addition of ingredients, or some new, ingenious method of preparation. If successful, I will have expanded the horizon of the potato, beer, and boiled meats of all varieties. Adorn the woman in jewels and her magnificence increases. Add ketchup, Guinness and maybe some A1 and there's a chance that the warty frog of a piece of meat transforms into the handsome prince with a peck from the delectable mistress. A little kiss and ba-boom! The formerly uneatable now caresses the palate, and the digestive system lives happily ever after.

Now, this is all a silly pipe dream as I've never cooked a real meal in my fucking life. My basic premise is that the Irish can do anything better than anyone else if they choose to, so why not cuisine? Though maybe not the 100-yard dash—those motherfuckers can move! The other point, maybe, is that the Irish have been blessed with taste buds so neutral that pretty much everything tastes the same anyway. A good meal for a mick is just stomach coating for the preferred refreshments anyhow. Instead of a cookbook, it might be better served as a contribution to a medical journal. After all, could anyone other than a stout Irishman survive sufficiently on a diet such as his?

THE BRONX

I drove my Triumph down to the playground on Bainbridge Avenue where Brendan Burns and his devoted acolytes hang out most days and nights. If any of these guys are gainfully employed, they're doing a more than credible job of hiding it. The motorcycles are always parked on the sidewalk and the local cops could give a shit less. They view these characters as allies against the creeping encroachment of the less desirable from points southern. The devil you know, etc.

Most of these loveable individuals are still in their teens but that doesn't make them any less formidable. They are, make no mistake, not a crowd to be fucked with. The playground is theirs, as are the streets around it. You don't stay without an invite. The boomboxes play Zeppelin and the Stones, and the songs are not meant to dance to. When you hang here you do it with the usual dose of ball busting but maybe with a more cautious edge. Not all of these guys are of a high intellectual capacity and a skewed interpretation of a barb could easily lead to violence. Confucius says to spare the mother jokes if you don't know the mothers.

On a typical night, you'll find Brendan Burns playing demagogue with the usual assortment of henchmen— Bart, Skinny Billy, and Nallon, and a small army of motley, wannabe, bad boys. The girls, many of them Irish Catholic, are not the storied chaste ones; they are not starting anything too late. In the warm weather, halter tops are all the rage and any growing boy who doesn't admit to being stimulated is either a liar or a fag. When I'm in the midst of these people, I feel like I've upped the ante on my social disease. If you want to be known to be of a certain element of cool and ghoul, there's no better place. 'McGee is hangin' down at *the schoolyard*' is what I hope people will say. He must be as bad a motherfucker as the rest of them.

Quart bottles are all the rage, Budweiser, and Colt 45. Athletics is not. Unless you include wrestling, slap fights and arm wrestling. On certain days, weights appear, and you'll see shirtless, tattooed torsos hoisting metal plates in the great outdoors. Just because you didn't play football in high school doesn't mean you can't hit with animal ferocity. Burns has said that all sports are just lesser versions of the ultimate sport, hand-to-hand combat. In his mind, if you take down an individual, *mano a mano*, you are the better athlete. If he's wrong, it doesn't feel that way when you're mingling here. I can take all these cats in a game of hoops, but they'd rather bounce heads than balls any old day.

It's a certain type of element inside these chain-linked fences, and the local periodic table includes many elements that are useful, and many that are not. And even more that are outright dangerous. This element makes up for in hazard what it lacks in usefulness. Lie with dogs and you'll catch fleas. Dance with the devil enough times and you're bound to two-step to hell, the old soft shoe on a bed of nails, as Mick Jagger croons, '. . . don't play with me, cause you play with fire.' At the root of every inferno is the cinder that started the burn, but at the peak of that inferno is the smoke that blinds you.

With my usual crew, like my brother, Luke, Bobby, Mahoney, and such, even guys like Sal, we get into a lot of mischief, but the majority of the harm is done to ourselves. In the playground, the lineup has little issue with extending the harm outside their circle. These boys don't mince words or try not to offend. The niggers and spics are the enemy, plain and simple, and need to be dealt with. Faggots are abnormal and nauseating. That mythical being, 'the man,' is working around the clock to fuck you over. Liberal Jew judges and politicians try to integrate schools and neighborhoods while hiding comfortably in their nice houses in safe neighborhoods.

The consensus these boys share and abide by is that you need to take matters into your own hands. If you do nothing, you lose. Next thing you know, they're living in your building, robbing your shit, preying on your sister. The motherfuckers aren't even human. Let one in and the floodgates open. Pretty soon they're everywhere, destroying your block just like they did the one they came from. Only a coward would allow that to happen; only a coward would stand around and watch it go down. Inaction is for the gutless and the timid. If you ask any one of them what they're afraid of they'll look you right in the eyes and tell you they ain't afraid of a fucking thing. Hang around here long enough though and you get the sense that there's quite a bit that scares the shit out of them, they're just too fucking thick-headed to see it.

In a sense, I'm no different. I find myself here in this place, at this time, because I'm really no more distinct than most of them. I'm testing my manhood, proving it in fact. If I can hang with the baddest of the bad, doesn't that make me a bad motherfucker by osmosis?

I make my way through the chain link fence and into the den of the beast. The ones who know me nod or say hey. The ones that don't look me over with a mixture of curiosity and disdain.

Burns, as usual, is at the center of this society. There's a lot of new faces, many of them wearing the colors of a gang named the Henchmen, their jackets festooned with images of darkness, most prominently the grim reaper and his bloody sickle. I think to myself, these guys are losers and misfits, many of them will be dead before they're twenty-five, but here I am somehow wishing I could be one of them, at least for the night.

Nallon pulls me aside and asks me if I heard what happened to this goofy kid from grammar school named Pratt. I tell him, "No, what happened?" He's like, "Oh fuck, this will blow your mind." Tells me Pratt was drunk and got into it with Joey Burke the other night right here. I didn't know Burke well but what I did know was that he was from a fucked-up family and that he and his brothers were bad fucking news. Pratt, I knew, would have been a fish out of water in this crowd, pretty much a jester to be toyed with.

Nallon told me Pratt had kiddingly asked Joey, who was less than a week removed from a bit upstate, if he took pole from his fellow jailbirds. As dumb and reckless a query as only the dumbest of the dumbest fucks could ever utter. Burke immediately pounced on him, flailing away at Pratt's skull with punches but was subdued quickly. The ass backwards thinkers among them are trying to prevent Joey from a parole violation, not really caring one way or the other about poor, helpless Pratt. Pratt's well-being was of small consequence. Joey Burke stormed away stewing with unsatisfied vengeance. No one really saw where he went.

Nallon then continued with the final part of the story—Pratt was found beaten to a pulp on the sidewalk outside his apartment building. Joey Burke had apparently followed him home. The kicker, Nallon said, was that Pratt was discovered not just bleeding from his head, but also from his anus, his pants pulled down to his ankles. Jailhouse justice, inside or outside the walls. My immediate thought was that, *Hell yeah, Joey boy took pipe upstate*, but I kept that to myself.

The answer to Pratt's question to Burke the previous night now struck me as pretty damn obvious. The type of rage displayed by Joey Burke could only have been sparked by an affirmative rejoinder to that query. It was a safe bet that Joey had indeed taken pipe while behind bars. You don't lose your shit like that unless the needle points towards home. It was an equally safe bet that Pratt would never ask that question, to anyone, for the remainder of his being. "And Pratt's parents never called the cops?" I asked Nallon. "Not if they know better." is what the man came back with.

It doesn't take me long to figure out that I'm unlikely to hear anything this day in this playground that will stimulate my intellect. Common consent that I'm not a pussy is accomplishment enough. The mood, let's call it convivial darkness, is not alluring. I'm not sure exactly why I stick around. I really don't like these people. The more I hang the creepier they all seem, even the girls. My interpretation of cool needs recalibration. Still, I stay. I beat a bigger guy in an arm wrestle. I win at cards. I make some muscle-head look inept in a slap fight. I am nobody's bitch and people take notice. Maybe the allure is greater than I gave it credit for. Yeah, I'm getting pulled in. Yeah, it feels pretty good. Also feels pretty darn weird.

THE BRONX

Ma took the bunch of us over to Throggs Neck for a barbecue at Duke and Mary's house. We all squeezed into Mickey's car and off we went to the other side of the Bronx. Barbecues are not something that happens often in our lives, but it seems like lately 'the times they are a changin'. White folks heading over to the black folks' house, the ones who moved on up before they did. Like George Jefferson welcoming his new neighbors, not the other way around.

Call it what you will but Duke and Mary served up some bonafide stereotypical delectables. If Black people eat southern fried chicken and barbecued ribs it probably has very little to do with the color of their skin, and a whole lot more to do with the fact that the stuff is goddamned, fucking delicious. My brother, Mickey, who told our mom he wasn't going to eat anything that 'they' touched, and threatened to bring his own lunch, is eating like he's going to the chair and not expecting a call from the governor. The dumb fuck is even expounding on the use of horseradish on certain foods even though, prior to today, he likely never even tasted it.

If you were to judge happiness by the amount of barbecue sauce a person has all over him or her, we were a blissful bunch. Ma seems to be the only one in the family capable of getting the digestables in her mouth on the first try. My little brother and sisters have forsaken the fine manners they've been taught by our mother and are conducting themselves like hyenas at the carcass of a wildebeest. Mary and Duke just keep shoveling food our way with gargantuan smiles on their faces. I'm tempted to ask and see their fingers to see if any of us McGees have managed to bite off one or two of them in the process. I'll tell you this, I wouldn't be risking my digits with this crowd.

Duke apparently has owned this home for over twenty years. Like my aunt and uncle out in Rockaway, he saved his nickels one at a time. Always worked two jobs, including twenty-five years with the MTA as a motorman. The job at the track has been his 'side hustle' for another couple of decades. Raised two kids here, both with families of their own now. Mary moved in only after Duke had consulted his son and daughter, and after what she refers to as an acceptable period of time. She knows she can never replace Duke's, Bunny, and she has no intention of trying.

Mary said the neighbors on either side are like night and day. The family to one side is German and were orphaned in the war, came here separately, and found true love in the good ol' US of A. The man, Herr Richie as Duke calls him, owns a local deli, and is, according to Duke, the most generous man he's ever known, handing out food to anyone who might need it. Richie, or Mister Lange as our beloved ma has insisted we address him, is sitting with us as we eat. He brought along what is undoubtedly the best potato salad and pickles known to humankind. Mr. Lange calls Duke his baby brother and kids around that they look so alike you can barely tell them apart.

The neighbors on the other side are a different story. He's Italian and she's Irish, and they have never taken to having colored people, more likely expressed as niggers, in the yard next door. Duke said he pays them no mind. And it works both ways he went on. "If you shut out the bad, it can't use you up and chew you up. But if you keep your eye on the prize, that being the good, it just keeps on multiplying. Like Herr Richie right here—he's the gift that keeps on giving, one set of neighbors like the Langes makes me a lucky man. Don't matter what's on the other side. Those people have wasted a lot of their lives stewing over nonsense that never came to roost. I spend a whole lot less time thinking about them than they do thinking about us," is how Duke concluded.

Mary adds that Duke and his missus got more than even without even trying by having kids who were better students and athletes than their non-friends across the fence. "Bet that burns their ass and then some," is how she finishes. Duke reminds her that it was never a competition for him, and he wishes them the best. Us McGees are all giggling at this, and it occurs to me that we've taken the side of the bad guys in this movie of real life. Throw in the Nazi deli owners and we may have just swapped allegiances to our sworn enemies without even realizing who are sworn enemies were in the first place.

If Ghandi showed up this very minute in a white robe and sandals, I wouldn't be the least bit fucking surprised. We would have to apologize for consuming cow meat I imagine, unless those spareribs are pork. Yet another idea for a sitcom! I need to get this down on paper before I lose any more of my ingenious concepts to that old, ordinary way of thinking.

THE BRONX

Me: "So Sal, tell me again how your mother caught you jerking off?"

Sal: "Oh man, it was not good. I thought I was the only one home and I was standing completely naked by the window of the bedroom, you know, for an extra thrill, almost wishing some chick was watching."

Me: "Like some old wash woman thinking it's her lucky day to chance upon the Italian Stallion beatin' his meat? And you actually admit to this? You are one fucked-up individual. What did your mother say?"

Sal: "Nothing at first. She kind of made this noise like she seen a ghost and then pulled the door behind her."

Me: "Then what transpired?"

Sal: Nothing. I acted like nothing happened. I got dressed and went in the living room to watch TV."

Me: "Did you deposit anything on the window ledge of the bedroom or the vicinity?"

Sal: "Nah. She caught me before I shot a load. Besides, I was in my parents' bedroom. Their windows face the street, mine don't. And I got enough class to spit it out into a container and then wash it."

Me: "Like the family pasta bowl or something like that?"

Sal: "Nah, just a coffee mug."

Me: "Jesus fucking Christ! You said your mother didn't say anything 'at first'—did she say something later on?"

Sal: "Yeah, she reminded me that it's a mortal sin to use your seed outside of marriage and having babies. Then she muttered something about now knowing why the Vaseline jar was nearly empty."

Me: "I thought your culture encouraged the males to prove their virility, in whatever form available. Need it be a hole in a wall or a goat. I heard a story about some Italian mother jerking her son off in a hospital bed to convince herself her baby boy was still alive and kickin' after a car accident."

Sal: "That must have been Puerto Ricans."

Me: "My apologies. I tend to loop the ginzos in with the ricans and greeks. When it comes to carnal pleasures the whole lot of you are pretty darn creative."

Sal: "Whatever you just said is bullshit."

Me: "Your mom gonna make you pay for the Vaseline you've been using?"

Sal: "She better not. Besides, my little brother probably uses more than me."

Me: "Good thing you didn't use her olive oil, that shit's expensive. I need to split. A little parting advice—next time you choke your snake yell 'Ma, you home?' and then do it every two minutes until you've completed your task. Shouldn't need to do it more than a couple of times."

Chapter 22

Money Isn't the Most Important Thing in Life but It's Right Up There with Oxygen

The money keeps rolling in. I'm working my usual jobs at the bar and gas station, and with summer upon us I'm set up to work construction by the day. I'll be working some crazy hours with the three different stints, but I'll be taking in more dough than the average high-class pimp—maybe get myself an outfit to match. They're gonna have to start calling me King Cake because I'll be rolling in it.

My Uncle Pat did me a solid and called in a favor to a guy he used to lay cement with. Local twenty-six of the Cement and Concrete Laborers Union. 'The Irish local' as it has been explained to me. I was given the number of some mick by the name of Hennessy, a full breed, with a brogue and all to prove it. It tickles me how these green horns who have barely been in the country more than a couple of years can land these high paying gigs. My uncle Pat informed me that I was to hand Mr. Hennessy a hundred bucks in cold cash and to do it as nonchalantly as possible. The c-note would find its way back to me in the form of overtime pay in my first check, without me actually working those extra hours. Robbing Seamus to pay Eamon, or something like that. Seemed fair to me so who was I to question it?

When I called Hennessy, he told me to meet him at a diner on 86th street in Manhattan. He bought me a cup of coffee but never asked me if I was hungry, and it was apparent that he didn't give a flying fuck if I was, or if I'd arrived from Biafra that very same day. I slid him the hundred and he deposited it in his pocket without a word or a gesture. Deal's a deal and, as I said, the math worked fine for me. Hennessy told me I'd be working at the southern tip of the city at a new place that was getting built, called Battery Park City. He also mentioned that I should dial back my date of birth a year to support my claim that I was eighteen, the minimum age to be a union member.

But today and tomorrow there was to be a wee twist to the work schedule—I'd be working in the northern section of the borough clearing debris out of a burned-out three-story building on 88th street off of York Avenue. Turned out ol' Hennessy had himself a side hustle with his own little unregistered construction company. We'd be toiling all day for Hennessy Enterprises, but getting paid as if we were down at Battery Park pushing wheelbarrows full of cement, courtesy of whatever bank Mr. Bigshit developer was transacting with. I stuck to my approach of refraining from curiosity, unconcerned how the money came my way, only that it eventually did. Economy of scale that added up in the end, whether that scale belonged to an armadillo or a snake.

I spent the first two days of my apprenticeship working alongside four off-the-boat micks and the token Black dude. Despite being the only non-Irishman in the lot, the darker cat seemed to be the one in charge when Hennessy took his leave, which was pretty much most of the time As fate would have it, he and I shared the same name, so to avoid any confusion in identifying the correct Jack, as if the stark contrast of our skin color wasn't quite sufficient, the four donkeys took to referring to us as Black Jack and Baby Jack.

I told them that for the sake of simplicity, since I could barely understand any of their Gaelic gibberish, that I would call them Fuckhead one, two, three and four, with the assigned numbers being totally arbitrary, and that each could be whichever Fuckhead they chose. They took this in stride, actually finding it beyond hilarious, and spent the entire day alluding to each other with the byname I had suggested, i.e. 'give me a hand here, Fuckhead,' or 'pass me the sledgehammer number one Fuckhead,' or 'for fuck's sake, ya feckin fuckhead, do your share of the work.' Black Jack, meanwhile, chose to leave us all nameless outside of 'boys' as he did Hennessy's bidding, repeating over and over, 'come on boys, hustle up, time is money.'

Within two full workdays, the six of us had gutted the place down to the charred floorboards and beams. It got to be a contest between us to see who could toss shit with the most accuracy from the second and third floor windows into the dumpsters below. The fire hadn't left anything inside worth a shit, so outside of the occasional appliance and copper piping, and other assorted metals, stuff Hennessy planned to sell for scrap, everything got tossed. We worked like animals and it was a miracle none of us fell through a floor or out a window. Hennessy's wisdom of allowing only one beer per man per day, and that being at lunch, proved to be a fortuitous strategy. The cheap son of a bitch even managed to cough up an extra twenty bucks per man to help pay to replace the clothes that had been ruined by working knee-deep in soot.

My best guess is that Hennessy pocketed himself a couple of grand without breaking a sweat. Taking the train home looking like a chimney sweep didn't bother me a bit, but my mother was none too happy with the trail I left from the front door of our apartment to the bathroom, and made sure the next morning, before I left the house again, that I was on my hands and knees with rags and soap cleaning up after myself.

The following Monday, I was at a real live construction site. I was in awe of my surroundings, more the men than the machines. Little old me amidst the great alpha males of society. Muscles and tattoos in abundance, the air reeking of machismo. Every hardhat featured an American flag decal, many matching the images of the ink on their biceps and forearms.

Proud union men they are, and united in their hatred for all those things that threatened their flag, be it commies and pinkos, or freeloaders and get-overs.

White and Christian, as if they'd walked off the Mayflower. No beating around the bush with this crew— they made it clear where they stood and you either aligned or you kept your mouth shut. The greenhorn Irish knew enough to play along, as did the non-English speaking Italians who came across the sea for six months of pay that matched five years' worth on their home side. Then back to their little towns and villages and the simple life, only with a little extra dough in the oven.

Basically, the pay was too nice to fuck with, so you wanted to stay on the good side of things, keep your opinions to yourself, nod your head, and laugh along with everything that was said, no matter how distasteful you found it. I learned the language quickly and avoided using offensive terms around them like negro, latino and gay. Why confuse the meaning by saying something like 'Spanish homosexual' when 'fag spic motherfucker,' was so much better understood? And if it rolled off your tongue just right it could even sound like a single word. So, unlike the micks and guineas newly arrived from points distant, I was speaking the same language as my countrymen on day one. Jack McGee was certainly born, just not yesterday.

On any construction site, the laborers are the lowest of the low—bottom of the pecking order, the least among us. Mutually despised and scorned, unless you actually wanted to get some real work done. Then we'd be the beloved peons doing the shit you'd never want to have to do yourself. Heavy and dirty, that was the job for us. Carrying steel, pouring concrete or banging away at a rock face with your jack hammer. No sitting around and reading blueprints or fucking with a measuring tape. Basically, you got paid the least but did the most work. That's why I was bunched in with the foreigners and the distinct minority of the darker skinned. If your old man, a long-standing card carrier himself, had gotten you the job, it wouldn't have been as a laborer. You'd go through an apprentice program on your way to becoming a full-blown carpenter or electrician. That's the American way, isn't it?

No great history scholars in the bunch. Most, selectively ignorant to the concept that someone not that far up in their family tree had been a lowly immigrant themselves not all that fucking long ago. Besides, who were the true bad guys, they'd ask? How about those pencil pushing, sissy cocksuckers over on Wall Street getting rich off the backs of the working man? Or the niggers and spics on the welfare rolls living the high life on your tax dollars? If you had to take sides these were compelling arguments for convenience's sake.

The site was ripe with hustles, everyone with their little scams. It seemed like they all carried their union manuals in their back pockets. The lathers on our project refused to work because we'd be laying concrete within two hundred feet of a crane. Measured it out by foot and showed our foreman the bylaws to prove it. Each trade had their own set of rules, except ours it seemed, but being a grunt isn't exactly a trade to begin with.

I learned right off the bat that there was an art to doing as little work as possible. The older tradesmen did their jobs to the fullest and went home. The younger guys, cats not much older than me, took pleasure in beating the system. Hypocrites, it seemed to me, with the balls to call other people, different people, lazy and shiftless. The idea that you got paid as much as the next guy but did a fraction of the work pissed me off royally. In the long run, I was no union boy. I'd out hustle the hustlers, but in the right way, with smarts and sweat. But at this point, all I had was a somehow—somehow, I'd figure out a way. My old man used to tell me that if I worked hard and kept my nose clean the rest would take care of itself. I wish to hell 'itself' had taken care of my pops.

The logic in these circles is that when you're busting your ass in the sweltering heat the only effective way to truly quench your thirst is by drinking beer. The coffee breaks were Bud Tall boy breaks for most. I researched it when I got home and found out it was total horseshit. Water was the way to go even if it came out of a garden hose. Get on a scaffold with a couple of pints in your gullet and you might end up like my friend, Cliff. But my man, Cliff, did it from forty stories up and nothing here was even beyond four or five. No matter the height it wouldn't be a barrel of laughs. Confucious says that a tightrope walking drunk and his life will soon part. I'm no Chinaman but that's a fortune cookie I'm taking to heart.

THE BRONX

They're digging up the street outside our apartment building and it's opened a Pandora's box of nasty living creatures that have made life indoors a living hell. My little sisters wake up at night screaming because they see what they think are rats crawling around near their beds but my stupendous vermin stomping skills have proven them to merely be oversized mice. The things that creep me out though are the freaking water bugs that are almost the same size as the mice. More than once, I've slid on my sneakers and found the dirty bastards squirming around my toes. Our old neighbors who had the means to leave have left and have been replaced by welfare moms who all seem to have at least five kids each.

The building was recently sold to Albanians, the only people brazen enough to deal with the lunacy, and the miserable sons of bitches are trying to force out anyone with lower rent.

Apparently, the city will pony up more cash for the welfare cases than what we're paying now. The garbage never seems to get put out and some of the new tenants conveniently, for them, toss it right from their windows to the alleyway down below. I have told my mother that I'm saving up every penny I make to help us get the fuck out.

Mickey and my little brother and the girls are all in, and together we'll find an exit.

In the meantime, I'm coming home late at night from work and having to walk past groups of Puerto Ricans smoking pot and gulping down *cerveza* while blasting their *samba* music. I've tried to be polite and ask them to turn down the music and maybe get the fuck out of my way when I attempt to go through the front door of the building. They nod their heads, and their presumed leader, an hombre by the name of Paco, lowers the volume to appease me, but once I'm inside the shit goes right back up.

I'm way out of patience and running the war plan through my head where, once we're gone, I come back one night unexpectedly and light every last one of their spic asses on fire. I'm coming for you *cholos*, bet on it. Before that day comes, however, I'm taking a baseball bat to that boombox and shattering it into pieces all the way to San Juan. These motherfuckers picked the wrong man to harass. But the writings on the wall, we need to get our asses out of Dodge.

Not all the buildings around here have the same dilemma and most of my friends and their families are still around but the ratios are changing between them and us. It feels like the tempest is swirling and the eye of a malicious storm is nigh. Jack McGee needs to make things happen and he needs to do it *tout* fucking *suite*. If my old man was still alive, we'd have been gone by now. I'm praying to my pops and telling him I got things under control, and I will die, if need be, defending our family. People that work hard day in and day out, pay their bills, and keep their noses clean shouldn't have to put up with this shit. I'm trying my damndest to keep a cool head and give them the benefit of the doubt but I'm no Jesus Christ—there will be no turning of the cheek.

I ran into Mary on the street and man, I tell you, she looked even more spectacular than the last time I saw her, and she looked downright goddamned gorgeous then. I had just got off the train after a day of toil at the concrete and cement camp, and there she was walking right towards me. I was scared shit that she'd walk right past me as if I didn't exist but instead, she hollered a sweet, "Hey, Jack!" and actually came over and gave me a light hug.

Normally, I wouldn't have been taken aback by a female's affection, given my manly appearance accentuated by my shirtless, and magnificently contoured, upper torso, but this was MARY for Christ's sake! Before I could stop myself, I blurted out, "Wow, Mary, you look fantastic" which was the absolute truth, but not something I wanted her to hear from me right then in that particular manner. No Cool Hand Luke was I. Like sitting on a royal straight flush and yelling, "I RAISE YOU!" before anyone has even placed a bet. Who was I kidding though, she could see right through me. I was smitten with this kitten, and it was impossible for me to hide it.

You know when you're talking to someone you really like, and time just disappears? All the grains of sand in the hourglass goes from top to bottom in the bat of an eye. I was in a groove and I could have spent the rest of my life in the here and now in a state of unmitigated bliss. The kicker was that she seemed to genuinely like being around me. I wanted to desperately reach out and just touch her bare arm or stroke her hair, anything to be closer to her. She had to run, and so did I, so we started our goodbyes. I summoned up the courage to ask her if she'd ever be up to grab some ice cream, or even go to a movie with me, I simply couldn't just let her walk away.

"Sure Jack, that would be nice," is what she answered. Again, it was not what I expected—I thought she'd have an excuse lined up to let me down lightly. Then off she'd go on the trajectory of her life, the one with the college and the wealthy boyfriend and the house in the suburbs, not too far off in the future. I skipped away in a state of euphoria, with the phone number from the object of my deepest desire clenched in my sweaty mitt. I made sure to memorize that precious telephone number before the ink ran and the number became indecipherable, a sequence of digits that would become etched in my brain, locked in like a steel trap. Jack McGee was in like Flynn! Jack McGee had arrived! I found myself singing lyrics from a *Mary Poppins* tune as I weightlessly glided away, "it's a jolly holiday with Mary . . ."

"Somewhere a queen is weeping; somewhere a king has no wife. And the wind cries, Mary"—boy does it ever. Here's your chance boy, don't fuck it up.

THE BRONX

My boy, Bobby, pulled me aside to ask me what the hell I thought I was doing with myself. He wasn't beating around the bush; true friends don't do that. When you know someone from the age of five and pretty much see them every single day for the next twelve years or so, they become more like siblings than friends. He's the guy I want in my foxhole, and I hope and expect he views me the same way. Bobby is one tough motherfucker and doesn't take shit from anyone, but he also has a heart of gold and a profound sense of loyalty when it comes to his pals.

Bobby: "Jack, what are you doing hanging around down in the schoolyard with those creepy fucks? They're into some bad shit down there. They are not nice people, maybe there's a few that are okay, but most of them are a bunch of fucking degenerates. Bad people make bad people out of nice people if you're around them enough. C'mon man, your the smartest fucking guy I know, big words and books and all that other shit, so why are you too fucking stupid to see what you're getting your dumb fucking ass into? Look, I'm sorry to lay into you like this but it's been bothering the shit out of me. I hate to admit it, but I worry about you."

If you knew Bobby like I know Bobby, you'd know that for him showing emotion comes in fits and starts, if it comes at all. He had to work himself up to approach me with this. As for telling me he is genuinely worried about me? Colossal achievement on his part. This man wears nothing on his sleeve, nothing. Normally he'd just slap me in the back of the head and tell me to 'wise up.'

Now, looking him in his eyes as he spoke, I knew that he meant what he said. Not about me being smart and that crap, but that he genuinely cared about me.

We could have gone on for another twelve years never openly expressing any emotions to each other and it would have felt perfectly normal. There are things you sense that will never require words. He has my back and I have his, no matter the situation. If you fuck with him you have invited me into the fray by default. But telling someone, with words, how you feel about them? Nah, that's far from normal. It's not how things work around here.

Me: "Thanks, Bobby, I appreciate you asking, seriously I do. I'm just fucking around a bit, changing the scenery up. Those guys ain't my real friends, far from it. I wouldn't trust them as far as I can spit. When push comes to shove, they couldn't give a flying fuck about me. And I'm not putting my head on any chopping blocks for any of them. I know this sounds ridiculous but it's like this fascination I have with serial killers like Chuckie Manson and the other lunatics roaming around out there; I like to know what makes them tick. Call it a hobby. I think I'm shrewd enough to know when to pull my hand away from the fire. If these guys do anything that I think is too nutty, I'm out. I'm not inclined to get my ass locked up just to prove I belong.

Really though, brother, thanks for putting this out there. I know you want to keep me from doing something stupendously stupid, maybe even something I'm gonna regret for the rest of my life. I promise you; I'll watch my ass. You kinda got me choked up, pal. It's nice knowing I have friends like you. You're the best."

Bobby: "Alright, Jack, I believe you. Just keep your eyes open and don't let down your guard. Think like you're in the ring, stay on your toes, don't drop your hands. These clowns aren't worth your company. Figure out whatever it is you need to figure out but do it fast and move on. The sooner the better with those fuckheads."

Me: "I hear you loud and clear, my man. It'll be a short-lived experiment, God's honest truth. I'm touched, brother, you got me kind of emotional, grateful and stuff if I can be truthful. I don't know if I should kiss you or hug you?"

Bobby: "How about neither you fucking fag."

Me: "A little peck on the cheek?"

Bobby: "How about a little kick in your balls, or should I say your pussy?"

That's another thing about my bud, Bobby. Whenever I'm around him, my use of a four letter word beginning with the letter 'f,' or derivatives of such a word, ratchets up exponentially. There's no real explanation as to why that is. Maybe I'm overplaying my cool card. Convenience perhaps, laziness more like it. I shouldn't make excuses.

My dad used to say cursing was the language of the weak-minded, but even he slipped from time to time. I know it ate at him when his kids heard him curse. He would say that if you think cursing makes you sound tough, you're sadly mistaken. Makes you sound ignorant is more like it, he'd say. The words of Brother Brian ring in my ears, ". . . be the man your father would want you to be." I'm gonna try and reign it in, add a little class to my approach. Honor my dad's wisdom, keep it from drifting out of my life. Take it to heart and keep it there next to my Pop's memory.

THE BRONX

The money keeps pouring in (I know I keep dwelling on this topic, but I can't help myself) as I hop from one gig to the next, often leaving one job to go to another. I'm cutting down on the gas station hours, mostly because it's the lowest paying of the three, but more because there's only so many hours in a day. Half the time, I'm so tired I couldn't tell you what day it is. I read something about sleep deprivation and how it can really fuck with your decision-making process. I'm hoping that explains away most of the idiotic stuff I seem to be doing of late.

The story I read said something along the lines about how your ability to reason, and your correlating actions thereof, are seriously impacted by your lack of sleep. Said something about a person being 1,000 times more likely to commit a murder if he hasn't slept in a couple of days. Now I don't think I'm about to ice anyone, but I have to admit people seem to be getting on my nerves a whole lot lately. Even my dear old mom. I opened a bank account, and I really dig watching the numbers tick up like a taxi meter but, man, it's becoming a slog. I feel like I'm getting older by the day. No time for just laying around and doing nothing, like reading a book or watching TV. No stickball, no hoops. Forget boxing. I am sticking with the daily push-up routine though and, yes, I am still a badass motherfucker, I just can't see this being the rest of my life. There's gotta be an easier way to skin the cat.

Wisdom is supposed to dictate that if you persevere along the bumpy road, it will eventually become smooth and lead you to a better place. I talk a big game but a little house with a good woman, some kids, green trees, and a few birds would do me just fine.

STEPHEN WALSH

Chapter 23

A Casual Bike Ride Through the Bronx

My mom surprised me with a letter she had kept from my dad's things—a letter to him from my grandfather, Pop. She must have figured there was some fatherly advice here that could help out her wayward child who's severely lacking the indoors presence of a healthy male role model. It was written to my dad upon his graduation from the now defunct St. Jerome's grammar school, located at the southernmost end of our beloved borough.

In Catholic tradition, you get these blue autograph books as mementos for the grand times spent getting tortured by the nuns. Seems like the custom has survived for generations because, I, too, have my own little blue book filled with obscenities and insults from my dear classmates, few who were accurate spellers. What Pops wrote, at least from my perspective, is right up there with the Gettysburg Address. Maybe even better, because the Illinois Rail-Splitter failed to put a lump in my throat, even with all those poor suckers dying for a divine cause. Well, here it is without further ado:

234

My dearest son, may your sweet life
be one of supreme happiness. Always
remember that you get exactly out of life
what you put into it, so always be honest,
sincere, and above all kind and charitable.
Pop

No long soliloquy, no powdery verse, just a straight
plunge right into the heart of human decency. Man, if I could
only end up half as good as either of these two wonderful
men who preceded me in the gene pool. Unfortunately, I'm
a long way from paying the debt I owe to each. So far, not
fucking good. If you're up there listening fellas, throw me a
lifeline, or at least a few suggestions as to how to get myself
on the path you began for me.

My dad used to kid me with what I realize now were little
pearls of wisdom that he hid within the joking. When I used
to complain about how unfair my perceived circumstances
were he'd hit me with lines like, 'a hard man doesn't need
a soft mattress,' or 'fine materials are only required for the
man who can't cut his way through the coarser fabric,' or,
'every adversity has a hidden lesson,' and all kinds of crazy
shit like that. One after the other he'd magically come up
with these phrases. He'd wink at me and laugh then leave
me to ponder the puzzle of his words. When I talked about
becoming rich, he'd always ask me what I needed that I
didn't have, then remind me to be grateful for what I did
have.

He loved telling this story about a poor man and a rich
man sitting under a tree conversing. It was mostly a one-
sided affair with the rich man going on and on about all that
he possessed with the implication that the poor man should

be envious. Yet, the poor man never expresses jealousy and keeps a warm smile on his face the whole time the rich man is flapping about how wonderful it is to have this and that array of possessions that other men can only dream about.

The poor man eventually gets in a few words edgewise, causing the rich man to get up and storm off disgusted.

Then, my dad would quiz me with, 'what do you think the poor man said to the rich man to make him upset?' He didn't expect an answer, and I never presented one other than some wiseass crack. But each and every time he'd ask me, it made me think what the poor man could have possibly said. I'd start with the cliches like 'the best things in life are free' but I knew my dad's version wouldn't be that simplistic. Another thing he'd often say, often enough that it became ingrained in my thick skull, is that you can't be smart if you can't be kind, and something to the effect that the smartest people are the kindest people. That always threw me for a loop but I imagine that the poor man in his story spoke words so laced with kindness that it irritated the rich man to no end.

That could become the end of the story but not likely from my father's perspective. Every story and incidental always came layered with another lesson that connected to the first one.

Eventually, the rich man would realize that the poor man's words, though few in number and lacking in apparent sophistication, were quite profound. Maybe they'd stick or maybe not, but from that point on he'd be a little wiser, and perhaps a tad kinder as well. What goes around comes around, be it bad or good.

So, mom has made her point through these two men of epic proportion that I was blessed to have known. No, life is not fair, but what would be truly unfair is the dishonor of living my life in contrast to theirs. I miss my pop every minute of every day, He was the smartest man I ever knew. My ma has a way of reminding me that she's no slouch herself.

THE BRONX

A couple of plain clothes cops came into the Alibi early in my shift the other night. Either one could have passed for a low-life hoodlum, so that's what I took them for at first blush. One of them, the bigger and gruffer of the two, looked at me with a big smile on his face. Right away I'm thinking this madman is stoned on fuckin' angel dust and is about to go weird on me. Then he says, "you don't remember me, do you?"

"Can't say I do at that," says I.

"I arrested you a couple of years ago," says he.

The cop, whose name I learned was Desmond Crotty, proceeded to tell his partner about the night he encountered me on my first motorcycle, a goofily chopped Honda 360 that should have come with training wheels. To a fifteen-year-old punk barely through puberty though, it was my monster, the pride and joy of an aspiring Hells Angel. Crotty, who was a biker himself, could barely keep a grin off his face as he described the events that led to my unceremonious arrest.

But first, my recollection of how the fireworks began. I had been at Orchard Beach for most of the day leading up to that evening. When me and my band of inebriated chums arrived back at our beloved corner, the first thing I wanted to do, needed to do, was fire up my badass Honda

360, the one with the extended fork as previously described, and do a little stunt driving for the assembled crowd.

It was one of those glorious summer evenings when the beer tastes like Coca-Cola, and the girls in their halter tops glisten the horizon with their impeccable beauty. Miraculously, the stubborn Jap bike started on the first plunge of the kick starter. Down Creston Avenue I flew, standing straight up like Charlton Heston riding his chariot in *Ben Hur*. After parting the crowd twice, once south bound, and then on the northern ricochet, I slid nearly sideways into my crowd of drunken friends and hopped off the bike as if I was Steve McQueen in the flesh.

My boys were hooting and hollering and taking playful swings at my head and torso, when I thought I heard my prized cycle driving off behind me. Sure enough, Johnny Downs, local junkhead, had procured my machine and was off before I could say a word. My boy, Knucks, heard him say, '. . . tell McGee I'll be back in a little while.' A barbiturate freak with one good eye, and a wallet full of atrocious photos from Vietnam, was navigating my motorcycle through the streets of the Bronx to God-knows-where. I was extremely pissed off. 'A little while' turned out to be more like an hour and a half, and I was 90 minutes angrier and several feet deeper into my hole of drunkenness, when the Nam junkie returned with my property.

I did what any sensible drunk would have done in my circumstance, namely get on that son of a bitch and take off in a gust of fury. That's where the cops come into the story.

I headed up 198th street towards Jerome Avenue, like a bat out of hell one might say. It was at this intersection where my encounter with the men in blue would commence. At the red light, I was cognizant enough to obey my instincts and slow down a bit, but still too far out of my mind to halt completely, so the stop-and-go was about 90 percent go and 10 percent stop. That's when I heard the sirens. I would later find out that the two cops, who were parked under the el train facing North on Jerome Avenue, were contemplating what they were gonna order for dinner, and, if I know my cops, where they were gonna get it on the arm.

Here I was, faced with the decision to either succumb to my punishment and admit defeat, or take off like a lunatic in hope of escape. I took a quick appraisal of my circumstances which went something like this: no license, no registration, no insurance, stolen plates, severely impaired operator, running a red light—not an ideal time for a conversation. Okay, maybe I didn't take all of that into account, but I should have. In any event, let the chase begin, me on my 360cc Honda, them in their Plymouth.

Thus, I hurled uncontrollably along Jerome Avenue, weaving between el pillars until I hit the open expanse of the two-laned road, the shrill of sirens following me like a heated laser.

Despite my skill as a motorcyclist, I didn't make it too far. Just south of Bedford Park Boulevard, I made the ingenious on-the-spot decision to veer sharply left through the gas station, ironically the one that employed you-know-who, on my way to Harris Field where, at least in my mind, I could take the bike to a place where cars couldn't follow.

As fate would dictate, I arrived at that point in time exactly in concert with a disembarking Number 4 train from the neighboring station. So once again, decisions, decisions for the impaired mind. In the spate of what couldn't have been more than a couple of minutes, I needed to make another fly off the cuff, live as you breath, momentous selection. The stakes were a bit higher this round as I had to opt for either smashing into a parked car or continuing through the crowd and maybe killing someone. Where this wisdom came from, I'm not sure, maybe it was from that inner goodness that lives inside each and every one of us, but I chose to take my just medicine as I careened into a stationary mound of steel.

So now, back in the realm of the Alibi Bar, it was Officer Desmond Crotty's turn to complete this tale of rebellious youth. Crotty turns towards his partner and fills in the punchline. He does, while he conveys the tale, have a wide smile across his face, which holds its form despite some belly laughing.

"So here we are chasing this little prick on his little Jap piece of shit, waiting for the little fucker to crash any second, but somehow he manages to stay upright for way longer than youda expected. To be honest, I'm almost ready to call off the chase because it's time for our dinner break and I'm as hungry as a fucking bear. Whether this kid gets arrested and locked-up, or dies in a fiery crash, is almost irrelevant to me at this point. Cheeseburger and fries are all I can fucking think about.

"So, I take my foot off the gas a little thinking I'll catch up with Evel fucking Knievel some other time and place. Still, I'm watching the kid as he pulls a wild turn into the gas station.

"We're close enough to witness and hear the thud when our bartender friend here bends his motorcycle into an accordion on the side of some oil tanker of a car. Meanwhile, our boy here is airborne, kind of like the Flying fucking Nun, over his handlebars. I turn to Stewart, who I was riding with that day, and I say to him, 'I bet you dinner the little bastard is dead,' and you, like the ghost of Houdini, got up and ran. So, give me a beer on the house and I'll call it square for the dinner you cost me."

I was glad to give him his beer and call it even though I actually owed him way more.

Also, I didn't exactly get up and run. I limped awkwardly a few feet before my mangled body collapsed under my concussed head. It was what Officers Crotty and Stewart did next that created my debt. They skipped their dinner to drive me to the hospital. If I remember correctly, my mom and her friend, Fran, ended up springing for their cheeseburgers and fries at the hospital as they waited to process my arrest. But even more important than the ride to the hospital was that they ended up charging me with crimes on the right side of me being Irish and, even more instrumentally, white. Misdemeanors across the board, they also chose to skip my court date which left the judge, some bald-headed Jew hard-on, with no choice but to slap me with a few fines and send me on my way. The luck of the Irish is getting lucky enough to get arrested by a fellow Irishman. Like the leprechaun says about that fruity, marshmallow cereal, it's 'magically delicious.'

THE BRONX

I'm hoping to run into Mary again so I can get her to commit to that meek promise of a movie and some ice cream. She seems to have disappeared into the Witness Protection Plan because I haven't seen hide nor hair of her in a dog's age. I can assure you that she's never too far from my thoughts, which are mostly daydreams of our shared bliss. I remain intimidated by her smarts and feel a need to exhibit some level of intellect on my part.

My Uncle Joe has referred to me once or twice as a 'clever son of a bitch' when I've made some wisecrack or another. So, my strategy is to regale the object of my desires with some first-rate poetry written solely for her benefit. If the communique falls into the wrong hands, I will steadfastly deny any involvement in its creation. The fruity end of the poet's pen must stay within the fruits of an artsy society. A fellow of my manliness could not possibly have authored such gibberish! To be on the safe side, I'll add in some bits of humor to keep my pride intact.

After quite a few fits and starts, and anguished editing, the following is what I plan to present to my beloved, upon the next fortuitous occasion of our crossing paths:

Oh, lonesome heart on asphalt street
Doth pray again his love to meet
So deep in bliss he does not seek
To kick the pigeons at his feet

This boy, this man, can only hope
She sees him not an interlope
She'll see him in a different scope
Not merely as some jackass dope

The skies will open, come apart
The arrow searching for the heart
When chance meeting gives him start
This sweet vision of timeless art

Oh, fine maiden of this dirty city
View me not with scorn nor pity
Rather sing to me an Irish diddy

Transform my heart from sad to giddy

Please think of me as one with you
To cite the lines as if on cue, I love you Jack, I really do
But even more than a million times two
If you'd clean the dog shit from your shoe

That may not be the final version, but it'll be close to the finished product. I need to get up the nerve to give her a call, she did give me her number after all. I just can't help thinking that she's out of my league and just being nice to me because she feels sorry for me or something. Using the word love, if only in jest, could send her running for the hills.

THE BRONX

Brother Brian called me to invite me to his wedding. The man works fast, he barely just got engaged. Bagels to donuts he was seeing this chick well before he turned in his collar.

Maybe even engaging in fornication prior to marriage, God forbid. Also told me he took a job as a social worker with the city of New York and will be working out of an office on Bedford Park Boulevard. Basically, on the home turf. I may never get rid of this guy. Be damned lucky if I didn't.

He did, of course, shoot me some more advice and badger me a bit about college. 'Use what you have,' 'take what you're given,' 'never take your good fortune for granted,' and on and on, and, of course, at least a few mentions of doing my father's memory justice, and taking some of the pressure off my mother by getting an education and keeping my dumb ass out of trouble.

I think my life would be progressing much faster if this concrete desert I live in didn't have so many oases in the form of the local bars and Sam's Deli. I can't recall the last weekend when I was sober from Friday through Sunday. With the crazy hours I put in busting my ass, I feel like I'm entitled to a little fun with the fellas. My boys are my life, and my life is my boys. I go where they go though, they never seem to go very far. It seems like an eternity since I was outside the borderlines of New York state. Sometimes, I'm not even sure I have been.

I had a female teacher in my first high school who asked me if my motto in life was 'if it feels good, do it,' and I think she was onto something. My aspirations never seem to get past the immediate stage despite me talking a big game. I go from flash point to flash point, no long-term plan to speak of. Next dollar, next drink, next fight, next fornication. A blueprint of mediocrity and despair if you think about it. Probably the reason why Sunday nights always come with thoughts of doom and gloom. Monday morning, real life starts anew. Real as in too real. Like the saying goes, 'procrastinators are the leaders of tomorrow.' That's me in a nutshell—I'm always a day away from doing something special. From here to eternity, one miserable day at a time.

I'm not digging this college thing. I hated every day of school I ever attended; made me feel like a pigeon in a coop. No way I'm spending my life in some office pushing pencils. I'd go out of my fucking bird.

My blueprint of life pretty much dictates that there is no future when the past just repeats itself day after day. Still there are glimpses of hope and moments when I feel with absolute certainty that all will work out just fine and even a little better than fine. Is it possible to be an egomaniac and not like yourself at the same time?

CHAPTER 24

Crossing the Border Just a
Few Blocks Up the Way

They're coming, man, they're coming. Every day they get closer; every day there's more and more of them. Putting the roaching in encroaching, the motherfuckers are eating up our space one concrete foot at a time. There's no more wait and see, the inevitable has arrived. The spics are coming, the spics are coming, and there's no flag waving revelry to greet their arrival.

It's time to move on, leave the blistering summers and frigid winters and piles of backyard garbage of the Albanian ruled edifice in our rearview mirror. Goodbye to all the *papis* and *mamis* and their bastard *hijos* and *hijas*. Goodbye to the Black Hand of the double-headed eagle. No longer shall we abide. I'll be back with a parting gift though, something nice and special. Something that leaves a lasting impression, something to be remembered by. Count on it motherfuckers, set your clocks.

Me, Mickey, and Mom are pooling our resources and getting the six of us the hell out of the netherworld. We can't be humans here; we can't close our eyes and hope it goes away. We're moving five blocks north to another country. In a couple of weeks, on the first of next month, we're going to the promised land—hallelujah Jesus, bless God in heaven. I can stay and fight, but I can't expect my mom and little siblings to do the same. Resettlement in a little Italian enclave with its own nighttime volunteer security force. Sure, I break balls on the paesani, but those people know how to keep a neighborhood safe, clean and segregated. Amen.

THE BRONX

Moving day. Pack up all our expensive furniture and family heirlooms, the three-legged couch, and the foldable TV trays. The one delicate thing that I will treat like a newborn baby in a cradle is our RCA console colored television. Yes folks, the McGees watch their favorite programs on a designer TV from the originators of the rainbow hued broadcasting phenomenon.

No second best for us when Sunday nights bring along *Ben Hur* or *The Sound of Music*. Julie Andrews and Charlton Heston just like they were in your living room. Tony, Maria, and Officer Krupke putting their hands in our Cheez Doodles bowl.

Mickey pulls up in the rented U-Haul that we immediately nickname the Paddy Wagon in honor of those shanty Irish hoodlums of lore. It's the crack of dawn as we reverse the Bronx tradition of moving out in the middle of the night. The moving crew is our motley assortment of friends.

Moving out of this shithole is a celebration and we will treat it as such, though the beer and sandwiches will be under lock and key until the job is done. Let these clowns front load the drinking and it will be a very ugly process.

The whole thing shouldn't take all that long—for a family of six we really don't have all that much to haul. As good as it feels, it's still bittersweet. Melancholy seems to be getting the best of me. This place was my life. This place was my very existence. Any iron existing in my body, mind, or soul, was forged here.

Good ol' ma is on pins and needles watching us load the truck. Can't say I blame the gal, witnessing the proceedings up close and personal. There's clearly a lack of a keen engineering mind to take charge of the organizing and proper placement of the individual items of furniture. Most of these *jamokes*, if they worked in a supermarket, would be tossing tin cans on top of the bread and tomatoes at the bottom of the bag. They are more concerned with expediting the assignment to get at the beer and sandwiches, than protecting the McGee family fortune.

Somehow, my boy, Luke, has anointed himself as the go-to guy on the inside of the van. I say 'somehow' because had he been interviewed for the job, he would have been shown the door abruptly. If I'm looking for someone to entertain me, Luke's my first call. If I'm trying to figure out how to maximize the space inside a rig, I'm not so sure his name pops up. Besides, despite it being barely beyond the cock's crow, I believe young Luke has the smell of alcohol on his breath.

Pulling Mickey aside I explain the circumstances and query him as to suggestions. We both decide that we should flatter Luke into being in charge of something he excels at, namely disc jockeying the boombox. No task has ever been made more difficult by motivational music—loud, pulsating, our-kind-of motivational music. Give the locals, the newer ones anyway, a little taste of their own medicine. Alas, I don't believe an earthquake or the second coming of Jesus (pronounced Hay-zooz by some) could wake these fuckers at 8 a.m. on a Saturday morn in the bucolic Bronx, NY.

Mahoney, he of mountaineering fame, has supplanted Luke as foreman, and by all appearances is doing a splendid job, When the lad puts his mind to things he can be quite capable. His stewardship has put mom at ease. When Mahoney becomes the answer to your prayers, you're not rolling the dice for big stakes.

The U-Haul is packed to the brim and we're gonna pull this thing off with one move. The really delicate stuff, like our RCA console and some lamps and the ilk, will be transported separately in a couple of cars, wrapped up all safe and sound like. Another Bronx tradition is to leave the vacated apartment in a sorry state as a parting gesture to the scumbag landlords, but ma will have none of that. We take every last piece of garbage with us and then sweep, and even mop the place tidy. Not the way I would have voted but my mom has a wisdom about her that I never question, or will ever question.

Stage front once again finds Mickey back at the wheel commandeering the rig as the *Beverly Hillbillies* theme song resonates in the background. Off we go to the Land of Milk and Honey, where nighttime noises are limited to the sweet sighs of restful sleep, and no one steals your car or your sister or the umbrella you left out to dry.

I've been involved in these neighborhood moving parties many times in my day, and it never ceases to amaze me how many of these nutjobs (beloved nutjobs) insist on escorting the cargo while hanging onto the outside of the truck. Five or six in the back and another few hanging on perilously along the sides. Bobby, the master of cool, even manages to drink a Bud and smoke a cigarette while hanging onto the mirror on the driver's side. No biggie for big brother, Mickey, as he has no intention of using that mirror anyhow. I think to myself, . . . *do none of these guys think of John the Bat and his permanently scrambled brains as they ride along? No fear of the same fate?* It's at that exact moment of cogitating that I realize that one of the strap hangers flapping in the wind is none other than the man himself, double-triple batshit crazy Johnnie boy in the flesh.

In truth, we're barely moving a half of a mile away. In the Bronx, one block can be a great distance. Five blocks is like the distance between San Francisco and Dallas. Night and day are like night and day—sleep when it's dark and be awake when it's light out, not vice versa, though I'll likely not be following those rules on the weekends. What's most important to me is that Mom gets some peace of mind, and my baby sibs are safe.

I promised myself I'd return to my childhood home and make a parting statement. The family might have moved but me and the boys still have a stranglehold on our corner down the street from the old address. The vacant store that had been Shabutsky's candy store on the opposite corner from our little fiefdom is now a fucking *bodega*—Lord have mercy. Hard to believe it but there it is staring right at us every single second, almost mocking us, always daring us. A small matter in the scheme of things. It's not like we're going to turn over the deed to the property and walk away. It's ours until we say it isn't and I don't see us making that assertion any time in the near future.

So, to the corner I shall return, each and every chance I get, until there's no more corner to return to. Feels weird to look out the windows of our new apartment and see a different landscape. Basically, for the large majority of my life I've rolled out of bed right into my circle of friends and acquaintances. Now there's a bit of a walk, or a fast scoot on my bike, but it's the only true direction I know. The corner, Creston Avenue, oh yeah, the corner. The sacred corner. Our corner. My corner.

I picked a Sunday night for my final *adieu* to my lifelong abode. Why Sunday? Most people are home getting ready for the work week. Things are generally quiet in the asphalt jungle, or maybe just quieter. No sense of urgency or excitement that a Friday or Saturday brings. Things are still tense on the corner with the latest influx of the darker strands of stormy weather, and the crowd is thin as you'd expect. Just a few of us sipping beers, ruing the end of the weekend, keeping a lazy but keen eye on the bad guys. Every party comes to an end as does this one. I say howdy to the boys and head up the street. Not a word have I spoken as to my plans. My revenge is my secret. This Buds for me. I've been biding my time and now the final clicks of the clock are playing in my head.

Around the back alley I creep. It's dark now, on this late summer eve; darker still in the moonless backstreet. I tiptoe through the maze of garbage, alley cats and rats; rats that never used to be here but are here now. I do my best Marty Muller and hoist up a full garbage can, after kicking it a few times to scare away any rats that may be congregating within. The fuller the better; despite the added effort it needed to lug it along.

True to form, Paco's apartment is alive in rhythm and dancing, the music is ear-splitting. *The Endless Summer* meets the 'Endless Party.' Catching waves any way you can.

Some parties die harder than others. Some die at the drop of a dime, or a cascading trash bin.

The majority of my work is done. The garbage can rests beneath Paco's windows, windows that faced our own in this urban dead-end. I am sweating like a pig at the slaughter but quiet as a church mouse, no squeaks or squeals shall I emit. I've thought about a guttural accompaniment to my tossing but have decided the can will do plenty of talking on its own.

Points made loud and clear. The message will leave doubts only as to the assailant.

The side-by-side windows of the living room are wide open. Flimsy curtains shield part of the view, theirs, and mine. They're the type of curtains that you haphazardly pull shut to affect some modesty when you're doing your girl on the family couch. They won't be much of an impediment for my plan.

Ducking beneath the window, I listen for an opening. When the music gets loudest and the drumbeats spark an exaltation of spasmic dancing, I'll know with confidence that the opportunity has presented itself. I stand, grip the top and bottom of the can with one hand each, and fling it with all my Irish might. The one thing I overlooked is that the window I chose is actually closed. No bother as it just makes the explosion that much more comforting to my ears.

Ka-fucking-boom! An orgasmic thrill envelopes my body. The music stops immediately and the shouts and screaming fill the air. Quite a surprise for my old apartment building cohabitors.

Many a night I have wanted to do this. Just make the music stop, just get a decent night's sleep. Delayed gratification is the best kind they say.

There's chaos inside but outside I remain calm in accordance with my plan. I will not panic but neither will I linger, I hop a fence into the alley of the building next door. My escape will be in the opposite direction from whence I came. I know these back alleys better than the cats. When I was a wet behind the ears little brat kid an alley was just another name for a playground. Me and my boy, Mahoney, owned this place. *Sayonara*, Paco, you sorry-assed son of a bitch! Enjoy the cleanup and be sure to get a fine evening's rest. I know I will.

THE BRONX

Mom told me upon arriving home to the palace (any place is a palace in comparison to what we just left) that Brother Brian called the house again. Unfortunately, Ma Bell was able to transfer our old number to the new location so people I was hoping to avoid can still track me down. Modern technology has its downsides. Do I like and appreciate the guy? Oh yeah. Am I ducking the guy? Oh yeah. I just don't know what to tell him.

I know what he's calling for as does the woman with the keen maternal instinct that I share a home with. She wants an answer as well. For the life of her, she tells me, she can't comprehend for a second why I'd pass on a full ride to an accredited institution of higher learning. Me and my thick Irish skull, she says. She's got my Uncle Joe involved and even Duke from the racetrack. Wise men, strong men, she says. Men who know better, men who want the best for me and who have been in my shoes at one point in their lives. Forget Brother Brian! She's got that guy on a pedestal so high you'd need a pair of binoculars just to catch a glimpse of him. The patience is running thin across the panel but the level of incredulousness is plenty thick. Then, of course, there's my dad, she reminds me, and how he wanted all his kids to be well-educated.

The old gal is trying to finesse the situation, tiptoe through the minefield that exists in my head.

I don't think I want to go to college. I've hated pretty much every day of school I've ever been part of. I'm not one of them, meaning I don't see myself as some pansy-assed pencil pusher. Besides, I'm more than gainfully employed and raking in the dough. Maybe I, can get full-time construction work and keep tending bar at night, reel in lawyer type money. Save every last dollar and buy some real estate, save some more and buy some more. Keep going and going until I'm my own conglomerate, Then there's the cop or fireman route. Or, of course, I could go the USMC trajectory and travel the world, or leave it, to be honest.

THE BRONX

Well, I finally screwed up the courage to call Mary. Up to the last second, I expected her to come up with some excuse. Miracle of miracles she said sure. Maybe the kid's still got it. I suggested a movie in the middle of the week when I would have some rare free time, and the date was set. I asked her if there was anything she was interested in seeing and she told me *Rosemary's Baby* which got me even more excited. I was immediately thinking that I hoped the movie would scare the living shit out of her and that she'd be squeezing my hand and my arm and begging me to wrap my arms around her.

When Wednesday came, there I was in front of her apartment building anxiously waiting for Mary to descend to her building's lobby and then spring through the front doors right into my heart. I was as dolled up as is possible for the likes of me, i.e., a clean shirt and stain-free dungarees. My hair was combed, kinda, and a dab of Mickey's Aqua Velva had me smelling like a French whore. I was praying that Mary would view me as I presently viewed myself, a handsome son of a bitch, if there ever was one.

And then . . . she came in colors in the air, oh everywhere; she came in colors, like a rainbow. She had achieved the impossible; she was even more beautiful than the previous image of her that lived in my noggin. Lord have mercy, was it just an apparition? The long golden tresses, the piercing eyes as blue as the most pristine ocean, the smile that launched 10,000 ships, the glow of a brilliant full moon.

I was stupefied by her presence. There were a thousand things I wanted to say to her, yell to the heavens at the top of my lungs, but I merely managed, "you look terrific, thanks for coming out with me." Trying at once to be both James Dean and Cary Grant, to captivate her with an array of cool and charm.

Girls from the Bronx are my favorite kind of girl, and Mary was that prototype and so much more. Down to earth, but still regal and majestic. The girl next door on her way to wearing the tiara as Miss America. When God created the perfect woman, he must have used Mary as his model. And here she was, on a date with that part-time gutter rat, Jack McGee.

I know this sounds moronic, but I scarcely remember what she wore that night. I was in a trance the whole time I was with her. All of life's problems and complications disappeared. I was living a dream wilder than my wildest dreams. Mary, it turned out, was more like me than she wasn't. She has her own set of complications, and comes from a large family always looking to stretch a buck. A bloodline that lacks in pedigree what it has in grit, beauty with a hint of the beast. Life wasn't going to get the best of this girl; she'd be the one turning the tables, not vice versa.

Doom and gloom would be suckers to challenge her.

Rosemary's baby was every bit the scary little bastard he was portrayed as being, and I couldn't have loved the nasty little prick more for it. Mary was petrified and used my bare arm for the comfort of digging in her nails to stifle her screams. Never has a man been so enamored with a bloody forearm. If pain means love, bring on the thumbscrews.

I, of course, was not scared one bit. At least as exhibited to my companion. Ye of strength and courage protect thy fair maiden even if your life you must cede. Fear not, my dear, for I will go to the gates of hell and back, to protect thy countenance. I am thy knight in shining armor.

The night went too quick as life's most precious moments always do. I learned so much about Mary and I think she got to know me a bit. I held back quite a bit, but she seemed to genuinely like what I allowed her to see. She'd be off to college in a few weeks, headed to Upstate NY to an all girls (thank you, God) Catholic college, where that pretty little head would be taking in knowledge of various enterprises, with a focus on medicine. The whole time my mind was vacillating between two conflicting opinions: 1. *Was she too good for me?* or 2. *Was I just barely good enough for her?*

As we parted, she handed me a small strip of paper with her college address where I could write to her. I showed her my scratched-up forearm, and she profusely started to apologize, but then couldn't contain a hardy laugh. Then it gets blurry again. She raised my arm higher and then gently 'kissed it to make it feel better.' I'm not sure why that made me feel like crying, but it did. An awkward pause ensued before I grabbed her in my arms and poured every ounce of my existence into a long, lasting kiss. If I had never known true love, I knew it now.

THE BRONX

You can drift out to the fanciful sea at times, but the tide always manages to pull you back into shore where a group of numbskulls you call friends awaits you.

Me: "Oh great fortune to stumble upon this most holy of concrete paradises where I should encounter my cherished allies, Lord Sal and Master Knucks."

Sal: "You're talking like one of those English fags again. Our man, Knucks, here has taken to your Jamaican pal, Al, like you read about. Probably, his best customer. I don't know where he comes up with the money, but I bet he sells his ass. He's been walking kind of bow-legged lately."

Knucks: "Hey Jack. Fuck you, Sal. I've been pimpin' out your old lady, she didn't tell you?"

Me: "Whoa, easy with the mother jokes, Knucks, I thought we had an understanding about this? Even a classless prick like yourself should know better."

Knucks: "Yeah, you're right, McGee; sorry Sal."

Sal: "It's okay, man; I know you weren't serious."

Seismic shifts like the one just displayed to you here should bring hope to all mankind. Even the smallest of hearts and minds hold wisdom and kindness. Are you fine, young Jack McGee, a steward of decent human kindness? Wouldn't that be something? Me, the esteemed difference maker, an example of what's good in us all.

THE BRONX

Ask not whom the college bell tolls for, it tolls for thee. Brother Brian (what did he want me to call him again?) has logged in yet another call to the premises, and once again spoke with my beloved mother about the dwindling timeline pertaining to my opting into college, or not.

Ma told me he is no longer taking the tact of the kindly ex-man of cloth and is threatening to wring out my neck and put his foot a mile up my dumb Irish ass upon sight. My old lady told him, and repeated it to me, she'd pay to watch that and would have seconds with whatever was left of me. No shrinking violet she.

Then he went on to tell her that he could probably get the scholarship delayed for a semester, but he'd have to come up with some kind of excuse, like a medical situation or such. You have to admire a man of God who will lie his ass for you. I want to just tell him and my mother to allocate their time and efforts on someone who's worth it, just forget about me for now. So, my life in higher education purgatory remains in limbo.

My mother, for one, always tells me to 'get it through your thick Irish skull,' Well, ma, get yourself a jackhammer and we'll see what we can do.

Chapter 25

A Knight in Dented Armor

Today was one of the most jarring days of my life. I'm lying in my bed feeling so angry, frustrated, and confused that I doubt I'll get a wink of sleep. I'll probably spend the night strolling the streets fighting for some clarity in my head on old age philosophical questions concerning the nature of man. Or more precisely, the beast that lays inside a man.

Sunday morning coming down on my gas station shift, and all those Johnny Cash lyrics are playing out in real life: "No way to hold my head that didn't hurt, I'd smoked my mind the night before, On a Sunday morning sidewalk, Lord, I'm wishin' I was stoned." And the cleanest dirty shirt and how a Sunday morning can be downright fucking miserable depending on your state of mind, etc., etc. And my mind was in some state.

Fortunately, at least, it was one of those late summer days that started to bring in fall air. Seventy-five degrees with low humidity, a cleansing tonic for a man on a ten-hour shift, nursing a quasi-severe hangover. Wounded body or not, I still took care of business and rattled off a couple of

259

hundred push-ups. I kept my calm and was even damn right polite to the motley array of customers. The day inched along and my outcome on life improved with the waning *katzenjammer.* Then when it seemed like things were looking up, they took a highly disagreeable turn lower. As low as it can go, you'll see. Lower than I ever thought possible. And it had nothing to do with me, outside of dragging me in its wake to witness the lowest depths of indecency.

Around 2 p.m., my boy, TC, dropped by. Seven hours done and three to go but why count the minutes of Eden? TC is as good of an egg as they come. Always bringing me a cup of coffee, or a sandwich, or a freezing cold Canada Dry ginger ale. Never asking for a penny. Today, he arrived empty-handed, and I immediately realized something was up.

TC was out of breath and clearly in a huff about something. He seemed incredulous that I did not see a bunch of younger neighborhood punks pass by the gas station about ten minutes previous. He was talking excitedly about following them down Jerome Avenue, and how they were now behind that beaten-up lot that ran between the back of the gas station and the platform for the 4 train. It was the path we'd used our entire lives to hop the trains, and it was also used by junkies and lowlifes of various ilk as a sanctuary from the public eye. According to TC, this crew of dirtbags was up there now, and they had a girl with them. I didn't like the sound of that at all.

"What the hell are you saying, TC? What girl and why is she with them? Who is they? Kids I know?" I needed him to spit out what in the fuck was going on.

"Yeah, Butchie and Swee-Pee and Sal's little brother, Anthony, and one of the Flynn kids, I forget his name. And now, there's like five or six kids from Villa Avenue with them," TC blurted out. "Apparently, this girl was kind of wandering through the neighborhood and Swee-Pee started rapping with her and convinced her to hang with them. The thing is, Jack, I think she's like retarded or something, like fucked up in the head. Those little pricks are gonna do something with her. I didn't know what to do so I ran in here to tell you."

"Stay here and watch the pumps, TC. You can do that right? Okay, I gotta get back there."

I hauled ass like a man running for his life and I was at the back of the station and on that broken path in a matter of seconds. There was so much adrenaline shooting through my system that it felt like my heart was going to explode. I was operating on pure instincts with no plan. All I knew was that there was something really wrong about to happen and I had to stop it.

The lot runs a couple of hundred feet up to the train platform but is only six or so feet wide, and it's overridden with garbage and the type of shrubbery you'd expect to see after a nuclear holocaust. As I scurried up the trail like a madman, I tripped and fell into a pile of hard items, like old bricks or something, and cut up my elbow pretty nastily. It only slowed me down for a couple of seconds. I was crazed, on a mission, and a fucking tank couldn't stop me.

About 50 feet up the trail I could see the pack of hyenas, and I could hear them laughing. It made my blood curl but only motivated me that much more. What I saw when I got there was a girl who looked no older than 14 or 15 without a top, and with her shorts opened at the snap and slightly pulled down. Swee-Pee was the closest to her and appeared ready to pull down his jeans. Now Swee-Pee is about 15 or 16 himself, not much younger than me, but he's part of the younger neighborhood crew that I don't hold in much esteem. To put it more succinctly, I don't like the little prick.

Swee-Pee had a big smile on his face with his boys egging him on. I was hyperventilating and drenched in sweat but seemed to have made it in time. The bastard seemed to think my presence had another purpose and as I got closer, he scowled, "Yo, Jack, get in line bitch!" I knocked him the fuck out on the spot. He lay unconscious and sprawled on the littered floor in front of me and I can't quite explain why I didn't take my foot and stomp on his head. I know I wanted to. Must have been the grace of God because it sure as fuck wasn't something inside me. I found the girl's shirt, handed it to her and told her to put it on and button her pants. Then I grabbed her by the arm and led her back down to the street.

As we walked away, I could hear some of the halfwit mongrels muttering in the background how they were gonna get even with me for raiding their party. Sal's little brother and the Flynn kid I could give the benefit of the doubt. Too young, stupid, and curious to have the sense to not go along, the others, the ones I knew and didn't know, would hold my wrath for a long time to come. I can state quite confidently that if I had left this young lady where she was, and walked back to that wolf pack, I would have no problem swinging my way through all of their heads. Maybe I was delirious, but I sure felt like I could do it. Like I've said before, neither anger nor me are on speaking terms—anger never asks to be invited and I can't seem to throw him out once he's in the door.

Now the dilemma was what to do with the young lady in distress. I had no idea who she was or where she came from or how she ended up where she did, right here, right now. I wanted to be gentle but firm, to keep her from running off back into the grips of the animals. I brought her around to the gas station office and asked her to sit down in a chair. TC told me all was cool business wise and that he'd handled the customers that came in, no problem. But he was way more interested in what had occurred on my end. I told him I'd fill him in later but that, for now, we needed to figure out what to do with the girl, a girl whose name I didn't even know. Start with the name, figure out where she lives, and get her home safe and sound. Just like I'd want someone to do if it was my own sister, God forbid.

The girl told us her name was Jane. You could tell right off that she wasn't all there. She said she was hungry and thirsty, so TC ran across the street to get her a soda and a bag of chips. I made Jane promise me that when I was at the pumps handling customers that she'd stay put. She certainly seemed eager to please, as if she was starved for attention and we were just her newest friends. Nice kid, I'm thinking. Thank God for TC, I'm thinking even more. What if he hadn't come along when he did? One miserable event that could have changed the path of her life forever. I feel like my Pops is right there on my shoulder.

TC was on the lookout for the cops and after a bit managed to flag down a patrol car. Two guys from the 52nd that I'd never seen before, so I imagined they were kinda new. I didn't get into details about what had transpired with Jane, only that she was a wayward kid who'd wandered into a lion's den and needed some help getting home.

The men in blue, one older cop and a younger guy that looked and felt like a rookie, seemed suspicious as to my story. I insisted that the girl, Jane, needed some help, but the more seasoned of the two officers seemed to think I was bothering them needlessly. The younger one nodded along with everything his partner said, which ran the gamut from them not being babysitters, to them having more important things to do, to me overreacting to play hero.

Now I have always had the utmost respect for the NYPD, and all cops in general, but after what I had just witnessed, I was losing my cool. Correct that, I was seething. Meanwhile, Jane was just sitting there eating her chips and drinking her Coke like nothing had even happened, which didn't help with my convincing the cops as to the severity of the situation.

TC was still helping me with the incoming customers, many who were becoming way too fucking nosy, squinting through the office window as if they were at a Times Square peep show. I had just gone through a convulsion of emotions that may or may not have included intent to commit homicide. The lackadaisical approach of the law wasn't just causing me frustration, it was cutting right through my nerves. I tried to calm myself down, I really did, but it didn't work. It doesn't work when things aren't nearly this bad and it sure wasn't going to work when every rational thought in my head was like a live dangling wire in a thunderstorm.

It took just a snicker at that point from the rookie cop to ignite my explosion. There he was nodding and giggling at comments from his older partner alluding to my being a pain in the ass, when I just couldn't stand it anymore. And thus, I screamed out, "Okay officers, sorry to bother you on your day off but that young lady over there was just nearly gang-raped, yes, gang-raped! I don't know where that rates on your list of crimes but feel free to get on with your lives and go arrest a jaywalker or two. I'll get her home myself.

"How stupid of me to make this into such a big deal. Just a little old gang rape in progress and me making mountains out of mole hills! My apologies to the men in blue for asking them to do their fucking job!"

Well, saying I got their attention would be like saying the '27 Yankees were a good baseball team. The older cop, whose name turned out to be Mulvey, had not taken kindly to my eruption. He took a step in my direction as if to put me in a chokehold and cuff me, but then must have done his own bit of on-the-spot soul searching. He refrained from putting his hands on me but the fury in his eyes was unmistakable when he responded, "Gang rape? Where the fuck did that come from? You never said anything about a gang rape! Okay? Now the game playing is over and I'm the one doing the talking, and you're the one keeping his smartass fucking mouth shut unless I tell you that you can open it! You understand that?"

I had tried to be coy for Jane's sake but now she was as rattled as the rest of us. The commotion was too much for her. She was sobbing uncontrollably and repeating over and over again, that she wanted to go home. TC, a man on his way to sainthood, was doing everything he could to keep her calm, mindful not to put his hands on her given her recent trauma. He'd already gone and got her another Coke and some bubblegum and was trying to distract her into mimicking his bubble blowing.

Officer Mulvey, who thankfully was a tad more tranquil now, asked me to repeat to him everything I had witnessed starting from the beginning. I apologized for being so evasive, and he apologized for assuming I was wasting his time. We both had our reasons. My intention all along was to keep names and faces out of it. I'm no rat and never will be. Mulvey wanted names but wasn't desperate to push it. It was, after all, in his words, not an actual crime that had occurred. Nobody got hurt and there's nothing that can't be fixed.

I told Officer Mulvey, and his partner D'Amato, that all I wanted from them was to get Jane back home and to have a chat with her parents about their little girl and the perils of being on her own on the mean streets of the borough that Ruth built. I thanked them for their service to the citizens of my beloved Bronx. What they would say and do was clearly out of my hands. So off they drove with Jane in the backseat. Jane, a girl I barely knew, if at all, whose impact on me seemed inexplicable, yet profoundly saddening. I put my arm over TC's shoulder and reminded him of what a great friend he was.

So, here I lay, head on a rumpled pillow, staring wide-eyed into the nothingness of Mickey's upper bunk mattress, trying to comprehend a world where a little kid, not unlike my own sister, could be savagely preyed upon. Does it even make a difference that it didn't occur to the extent that it could have? I'm reliving the spectrum of emotions that God visited upon me today and rage may be the most consistent, but sadness and despair seem to be the most powerful. What kind of world do I live in where people can do such awful things to each other? This world, this God, allowed my father to be murdered in cold blood, leaving my mother to raise five kids on her own. Not to mention all the wars, sicknesses, and heartbreaks and on and on. Kids from my own neighborhood, from families not much different from mine, are going to do that to a defenseless kid who barely knows what day it is?

But, yeah, the rage is there. I'm nowhere over wanting to pummel these little savage pricks into oblivion. Sweet-Pee and the creeps from Villa Avenue. Yeah, come and get me boys, get your revenge. And Jane, what will happen to Jane? Is she from a screwed-up family that doesn't even give a shit? Does she have people who can protect her? Can I be her protector?

There's that sadness again, seizing me like the straps of an electric chair choking the life from me.

It's hard for me to picture a God when I pray. For me, it's not the white guy with the blond hair and blue eyes from the Middle East, miracle of miracles, that they throw at us in Catholic school. For me, mostly, it's my dad. I feel like he can hear me, that he's up there, somewhere. It's because of him that I don't worry so much about myself, but I can sure use his help with a whole slew of things. Life is just so God-damned complicated. So, we have these conversations, and he listens. How do I know he listens? Because he responds in his ways. Keeps me from doing stupid stuff and makes sure that I know right from wrong. That's not to say that I don't confuse the two on a regular basis, just that it could be way worse without my old man involved.

Counting sheep and counting problems. Multiplying numbers, too many numbers, run amok in my head. Jack McGee, battered soul, solitary in the sleepless shadows. Crying in his dark cave like a little pussy. Feeling sorry for himself, he is. He laments about black clouds and makes other sorry ass excuses. No hero, he, though he certainly longs to be.

Life goes on and I go on with it. Maybe that crazy shrink, or was it Brother Brian, who told me that unless I dealt with the demons bouncing around in my skull, that not only would they not go away, but they'd also multiply. Well, howdy-do and let's put them on the shelf for another day. The Bronx is burning and the whole world seems to be feeding on itself. A guy can cave, or he can just keep on keepin' on and do the best he can. I'm too fucking young to let this shit pull me any lower than it already has. A boy needs to live, A boy needs to have some fun. Pull up those bootstraps, boy-o. Grit and determination. Spit and elbow grease. Climb your ass out of the rabbit hole.

Chapter 26

Let Me Count the Ways

Mary is leaving in a couple of days and is busy getting ready, but she gave me a buzz and invited me to swing by to bid my adieus, temporary ones I pray. As usual, she appeared to me as beautiful beyond words, as magnificent as the most spectacular sunset. Yet, even a sunset can bring a touch of despair. "Oh, teach me how I could forget thee . . . parting is such sweet sorrow . . . thus with a kiss I die." Kiss we did, and dare I say passionately? Man, what a feeling! Yeah, Romeo, I too would consume the poison if it meant we'd be together forever, whichever side of the turf. The usual promises lovers make but don't always keep. The intention to write, an opportunity to visit, chastity and faithfulness, Yeah, but who was I kidding? She was leaving for a world I couldn't touch.

Truth be told, my chaste intentions may not survive a Friday or Saturday night when I'm drunk and on the carnal prowl. Just calling a spade a spade, a dog a dog. I'm not the type of guy who seems capable of commitment, and I wonder if I'm any better than the creeps I toss stones at. Still, when push comes to shove, I think I do respect the opposite sex more than the average jackass. That poor girl behind the train station is still stinging me like rubbing alcohol in an open wound.

THE BRONX

They say you can't hit a moving target, but it seems you can certainly ferret out a hopeless lush sleeping off a frightful hangover on his one day off, even with a pillow grasped tightly over his head and pretending to be dead. It doesn't help that said casualty has a mother who blatantly invites her house guest into his bedroom. What you might call sneaky bastards. There it was that ex-Brother Brian finally pinned down the lost boy.

A smiling no-longer-a-brother Brian took a seat on the edge of the mattress where hence I lay. Instinctively, I hastened to cover my nuts, not because I feared a predatory action from my friend, but because an image of Alex in *Clockwork Orange* and the headmaster with the iron claw popped into my head. I am often amazed at how my mind conjures up these depictions out of thin air. The instincts of a pigeon in traffic, I guess. Just five minutes earlier, I was near catatonic and now here I am identifying with the flash card of one of filmdom's greatest sociopaths. You needn't take it any further, sir. You've proved to me that all this ultraviolence and killing are wrong, wrong, wrong . . .

Mr. Brian had an earful for you know who. He wasted no time digging in deep with the self-pity scalpel, then segued into selfishness and immaturity, making sure to scrape some nerve endings on the descent. I could sense mom in the other room pumping her fist in the air while suppressing screams of glee. It would be nice if someone reminded her that the apple doesn't fall far from the tree. Am I my mother's son or a waif mistakenly switched at birth? C'mon ma, root as you may for an ass-kicking for your second son, you'll take all the credit for the genealogical piss and vinegar in my constitution.

Fortunately, the visit didn't take long. Mr. Brother Brian, the genuinely decent man that he is, managed to convey all his remonstrations in a ten-minute span. He left only after securing a promise from me to seriously revisit a college commitment for the spring semester. He also saved me a stamp RSVP-ing to his wedding, which was already at least two weeks late. My mom hugged him tightly before he left, once again thanking him profusely for his guidance.

What the guy sees in me remains a mystery. For my part, I can't imagine having a better guy in my corner, despite our philosophical differences.

It would seem that I can't go five minutes of the day without thinking of either Mary or that poor girl, Jane. Obsessive Compulsive Disorder is the medical term, but my brand has all that mixed with some of Edgar Alan Poe's *Tell Tale Heart*. Namely, I feel tortured. Why, might one ask? I'm not entirely sure but I think it 's because of regrets that I missed doing something I should have—in both cases. Or, conversely, did I do something I shouldn't have?

Invariably, these thoughts will drift over to include my mother and little sisters. Again, that sadness at what I'm not really sure. Man, life is hard. Man, life is confusing. Man, I'm one fucked up guy. I'm no women's libber but it occurs to me quite often that females get the short end of the stick.

CHAPTER 27

The Oscars—Live from the Alibi

I agreed to fill in for Hassett on a Monday night shift at the Alibi. He reminded me I owed him one for his doing me a solid in a similar situation a few months back. Complete pain in the ass for me because then I needed to get someone to take my five to ten shift at the gas station which is no small feat. Plus, Monday nights are usually disasters. You don't make much money and the customer base (think people whose lives have led them to be in a dingy bar on a weeknight, Monday night no less) is *Twilight Zone* level. To make matters worse, this Monday was Oscars night and the owner, Terry, liked to watch them from his own establishment, with his cheat sheet of predictions and an insistence on starting pools for Best Picture, Best Actor, and Best Actress.

Now all of this is disturbing on so many levels. Firstly, what grown man watches the Oscars in the first place? Then there's all those asinine categories like Best Score and Best Foreign Film that nobody gives a shit about, but always result in long-winded speeches that drag the fruitcake show on for hours and holds up the main awards, the ones we

ing, stop by some night and try some for yourself. The
ruse is quite simple. When Terry's not watching his glass, a
given when his annual broadcasted delight is in progress, I
slyly add a shot or so of straight vodka.

Saying vodka has no taste is like saying piss has no taste,
There's taste all right, it's just god-awful. Vodka also has a
turpentine quality that blends effortlessly into Alibi's rotgut
tap beer. So Terry is none the wiser and the trick generally
works like a charm, with the eventual aim at getting him
hopelessly drunk so that he's oblivious to his surroundings
and he that doth protest too little, if at all, will sheepishly
be shown the exit. He'll be so fucked up in fact that if I yell
up to the television and scream 'touchdown!' and tell him
it's the Super Bowl, he'll ask me who's winning.

Before he gets to this point, however, I'll still have to
deal with his pestering about my bartender skills (of which I
have none), and his painful analysis of the Oscars. I will piss
him off royally with my own analysis which is somewhat to
the effect of giving the Best Actress award to the hottest
chick, the Best Actor award to the guy who kills the most
people on screen, and the Best Picture award to a box office
disaster on the basis that it was likely too sophisticated
for the average dumbass American theatergoer. I will also
have to endure the other cheap-tipping, pathetic sots who
will actually engage Terry in high-spirited dialogue about
the bevy of Hollywood freaks and their chance at a prize,

273

STEPHEN WALSH

despite the majority of them having not been in a cinema since Charlie Chaplin retired.

Mission accomplished. Terry was pie-eyed by ten p.m., and I shuttered the place by midnight not giving a flying fuck as to the remaining stragglers and their textbook knowledge of New York State law that allows bars to stay open until four o'clock in the morning. If my life were to become a sequence of uninterrupted Alibi Monday nights, the movie that would best sum up the story would be either *Psycho* or *The Texas Chainsaw Massacre*.

As for Hollywood, maybe I'll have a different take once I'm discovered. Tell me you can find a better James Bond, outside of Sean Connery maybe, and I'll tell you your opinion on good looks and being a badass isn't worth a two-week old copy of the Sunday comics. Get a few gigantic movie deals under my belt and I'll be packing up the family *Beverly Hillbillies* style and heading toward the Pacific. Mom may not like it, but she gets to be Granny, based on temperament alone. Mickey's history of falling in love and wanting to get married qualifies him as dumb enough to be Jethro. Ellie Mae will be designated as a second cousin which will make her eligible to be my main squeeze. The Irish, unlike their Italian brethren or those from the more southern districts of these here United States of America, are disinclined to go the first cousin route. Truth be told, there's not a whole lotta difference between a mountain hayseed and a Bronx gutter rat. Yee-fucking-hah and off we go!

THE BRONX

I do try to stay out of trouble, honest I do, but unfortunately, I have chosen places of employment where unrest comes with the surroundings. Now, it would be expected that a rundown (being kind here) gin mill like the Alibi would serve up at least a tad of mayhem on a regular basis. Drunks will be drunks, boys will be boys, etc. However, one would also expect a gas station to be a relatively calm place with a small design for commotion. Read the fine print though and you'll understand that even a gas station, if it be located in the Bronx, can provide enough material for a crime show aired weekly on network television. My experiences, as previously related here, certainly give credence to that thesis.

Firstly, like any business in the general area, there's no shortage of people trying to rip you off one way or the other. Then there's the lack of an available restroom that seemingly gives people the right to think they can piss on the side of the building or even, in one instance, between the pumps. Ray Bradbury did the *Martian Chronicles*, and if I were to do the Gas Station Chronicles it would have a similar otherworldly quality to it. Shit happens here that might surprise you, but barely fazes me. It can be Sunnyside Gardens one night and Bellevue Hospital the next.

Which brings us to this past Sunday morning. Sporting less of a hangover than usual, the lyrics in my head were more to the tune of Arlo Guthrie and "Good morning, America, how are you? Don't ya know me I'm your native son?" than the Johnny Cash blues. Life wasn't loving me, but it had less disdain than usual.

The daily Sunday shift will never bring good luck but just avoiding any bad luck can provide sufficient inner peace. Well, so much for that because barely an hour into my shift, Bob, the owner, decided to stop by. Not only did he stop by, but the son of a bitch decided to linger. I guess the old lady kicked him out of the house and he needed a place to go, her gain being a major loss to me. With Bob there, I had to feign being busy and likewise having a general appreciation of the customers. Customers getting a measly two dollar's worth of gas and paying in an assortment of small denomination coins are pretty fucking hard to appreciate.

So, there was smiley me, the gas station attendant, sharing my love of mankind, when this interesting fellow crossed into the station grounds rolling a tire. I sort of recognized the guy from being from Villa Avenue, that bastion of Italian culture where the annual Grease Pole event brings extreme pride to its inhabitants. This guy though had blondish hair and a sallow complexion. It was unlikely that he traced his roots to the Mediterranean. He had a wiry build and comported himself as the type of fellow who could hold his own if need be.

The tire was as bald as Mr. Clean after a haircut, and clearly had problems. My man was desperate to find a way to repair it and get it back on his car. He was anxious and impatient, and also way too optimistic as to my magician capabilities. There was no way this tire was going back on the road—ever. I decided to go through the motions anyway and filled it with air and plunged it into the tire tub to check for a leak. As soon as it was submerged, it started to fizz like a shaken soda can. The thing was shot, and I relayed as much to the poor fellow. As disappointed as he was, he was still cordial and thanked me for trying. In a no bad luck world, that would have ended it.

Bob, the nosy prick, was watching from inside the office. As the Villa Avenue resident was about to leave, Bob pulled me aside and informed me that I had just provided a service and needed to be compensated. Well, he needed to be compensated, because I didn't see the point.

I was incredulous as to his demand and asked him for his suggestion as to how much I should try and paw off this poor ass fucker. One American dollar was his quoted price.

Before the guy with the flat tire was too far away, I yelled across to get his attention. He turned to look at me. It was clear in his mind that we were fine and dandy, and it would just be more small talk from me. Now a dollar doesn't seem like a lot of money unless that dollar is half of what you're carrying in your pocket and a minute before seemed like a safe bet that it would stay there. He didn't take kindly to my request. Nope, not at all.

I tried to tell him that it wasn't me asking per se and that I was being forced to do it. His mind wasn't able to process that as it had already shifted to an unstable state. He asked me if I was kidding, and I assured him I was indeed not. I then decided to confiscate his tire as collateral and grabbed it by the rim and began carrying it back to the bay area. The quick thinker in me seized on the idea that rim had some value as scrap metal. Quite frankly, I was at least as perplexed as he was. Why in god's name was I doing this? For a lousy fucking dollar from a man way down on his luck?

I didn't want to bring the tire inside, so I laid it alongside one of the bay windows that was shut. It was then that I felt a fist graze the left side of my head. Sunnyside Gardens, yessiree, we're back for the main event . . . The guy had looked reasonably capable when I first laid eyes on him, fighting wise that is, but I had given him the benefit of the doubt. Though I hadn't seen the punch from the onset, it was the curled nature of the fist that semi-landed on my noggin that erased the benefit from the doubt. I hadn't had anything against this clown a few moments ago but it only takes a heartbeat to change your world.

He had just fed a fat, juicy slab of meat to my animal instincts. Those instincts can sometimes immediately signal that your prey, when it becomes such, is ripe for the taking. That sloppy one punch gave me more than a hunch that I'd have the upper hand, or upper fist more aptly, in the ensuing contest. He also managed to trigger that deep rage that eternally plagues me. I was rendered powerless as to what would come from my innards now.

With his right arm extended over my shoulder I was able to quickly use his leverage against him by swinging him around, so his back was to me and grabbing him in a chokehold. I then proceeded to lift him up and then fling him to the ground in a twisting motion so that I landed on top of him. I heard a little thunk of his head hitting the pavement and I knew it wouldn't be a pretty thing for him. I then sat on his upper back with my knees on his arms and told him I'd let him up if he cut the shit. Quite frankly, I was surprised at how easy ol' Jack McGee took this chucklehead down. An added bonus for him that I didn't have to unleash the steel pistons. Those monsters can open up holes in people. Cat-like reflexes and superhuman strength, and God still made me good-looking.

Frankly, I felt pretty awful about the whole damn scuffle—Bob and his fucking dollar. It had all happened really fast, and I don't recall having even a semblance of a clue as to how and why I reacted. There was no strategy or forethought. Just more of that bottle of rage with the cap off.

I started yelling at the kid something to the effect of why the hell had he made me do what I did—why had he been such a friggin' numbskull? But just like he'd struck a nerve with me, I'd done the same to him with that stupid demand for a dollar and then made it worse by grabbing the tire away from him. I should have just given Bob the buck out of my own pocket. So, I was willing to climb the platform and accept the medal for being the bigger idiot of the two of us. That would be the silver medal slot, as Bob, the miserly prick, was the clear gold medal recipient.

My feeble attempt at an apology fell on deaf ears. The lad, as he wheeled away his barren tire, promised to come back and kill me and burn down the gas station, familiar themes I'd heard before in my employment at this gas emporium. Recall will tell us that my life, and the incineration of the premises, had been threatened on quite a few occasions before. I wondered if I could be held in consideration by the Guinness World Record people for most death threats against a gas attendant in history, I'll be in that book yet. Wouldn't be my first stab at the GBWR and you can bet your smelly ass it won't be my last.

Somehow, in the midst of the scuffle, and oblivious to me until now, one of the bay window panes had been shattered, a matter that now brought the wrath of Bob down on me. No mention of his missing dollar of revenue, just a rant informing me that the cost of the window repair would come out of my pay. Prince of a fucking guy. If I can get my construction job back, it'll be *sayonara* Bob, and fuck you and the horse you rode in on.

THE BRONX

It is with a healthy dose of trepidation that I'll engage in conversation with my boy, Sal, though I always feel better after having done so. Sal is not as dumb as I make him out

279

to be and has even thunder-bolted me with the occasional pearl. He tries his best not to be Italian, eschewing gold chains, hair gel, spray-on tans etc., and he even bragged to me one time about being 10% Irish, a dubious claim that I did not want substantiated. I didn't want to tell the knucklehead that it would take a helluva jamboree to arrive at the 10% figure with percentages more likely to be in increments like 12.5%, 25%, 37.5%, 50% and 75%. Well, I'm neither dumb enough nor patient enough to take on that tutorial. I do love the guy and he's as loyal as they come, and I trust the guy 100%—that's math I can square with him.

Sal's exposure to the Irish, basically guys like myself, seems to have, via osmosis, not only contributed to his mental development but has provided grudging acknowledgement (subconsciously at least) from him that we are the superior species. Yes, the Irish are their own species, and even if they aren't, they're certainly of a whole different classification than the Italians. Sal will rightly brag about having reached puberty in third grade, and he has, at the age of seventeen, a full pair of legitimate sideburns, and enough chest hair to proudly leave collared shirts open three buttons down. This is an obvious area of ethnic pride for the ginzos and as a Celt who prayed to Jesus for pubes before the first day of high school, it is a topic left best alone.

On the rare occasion, while having a little *tête-á-tête* (I may never get my French teacher out of my head), we can avoid mention of each other's ethnicity and focus on topics where we have a meeting of the minds. With both of us staunchly American, white American at that, topics concerning hippies, queers, and those other races will bring mutual enthusiasm.

Unfortunately, Sal will eventually, barely eventually, say or do something that will not allow me to overlook his Neapolitan gene pool. Such was our latest thick head to thick head volley.

Before I share that, however, I'd like to reiterate that Sal is an individual who I'd trust with my life. Knowing someone's got your back counts a helluva lot more than if they're Irish or Italian, or if they think Shakespeare is a chewing gum.

Sal: "C'mon Jack, you can't tell me that you don't like some disco songs. I mean I still like Zeppelin and shit better, but some of these songs are kinda catchy."

Now it would be hard to describe the expression on my face after he said this to me, but it was a mixture of angst and bewilderment. Like eating a lemon while watching someone jump off of a roof.

Me: "What the fuck are you talking about? Me? Disco? You're kidding me, right? You can't actually believe that I'd listen to a single note of that crap, never mind actually enjoying it. Get the fuck outta her with that shit. Jesus fucking Christ, Sal!"

Now I'm ashamed at how many curse words I used but in this case it was absolutely necessary to convey how empathically I denounced his suggestion.

Sal: "You're so full of shit, Jack. Uh uh uh uh stayin' alive, stayin' alive. You honestly don't like that song? What about that Frankie Valli song, whatchamacallit, oh yeah, 'Oh What a Night.' And, please, don't tell me you don't dig Donna Summers?"

Now this goes back to my point that Sal, despite all of his deficiencies, can still mentally box me into a corner on the rare occasion. Do I like the Bee Gees? I'd go to my grave not admitting that, but I kind of do find that tune catchy, and have even whistled it out of earshot of the human race a time or two. As for Donna Summers, saying I'd give my right arm for a night with that woman would leave me bluffing one arm shy. Add in the cooing and the raspiness and that chick can sing to me all day and well into the night, And, no, I won't grab the radio station dial if she comes on, assuming I'm alone.

Me: "Sal, please don't make me lecture you again on our cultural differences stemming from the innate qualities attached to our origins."

Sal: "What the fuck did you just say?"

Me: "In layman's terms, or simpleton language for the current audience, what I began to say was that, for inexplicable reasons, you can't help liking disco because you were born Italian. Now, I can't prove that scientifically, but I know it just the same. It's no different than wanting to own a Cadillac or needing to replace your front lawn with concrete. It's simply the nature of the Italian beast. Just as me, being Irish, have been genetically shaped to abhor music that makes men dance like fags.

"As I discussed to you on countless occasions, the Irish male has been bred through the generations to abhor all behaviors that make him look like a pussy. It's really quite simple. Look at it like this, disco is spaghetti and rock n' roll is potato. It starts from the ground up and then follows a predestined path. Nature abhors a vacuum and the *paesani*, which includes you, got sucked into the one created when doo-wop fell by the wayside. Shitty music that was preferred by Italians was left with a gaping hole. Along comes disco and vawoosh! the hole sucks it right in. So, instead of the wops going sha na na they switch to uh uh uh uh. Again, really quite simple."

Sal: "Why can't you just admit you like it you fucking liar? It might even help you meet some cute girls. Me and you should go to one of those discos just for a hoot. We don't have to dress up like them or dance, just stand around and laugh and shit. My cousin, Nico, goes to one up in Yonkers. He said you wouldn't believe the way these chicks dress— tits hanging out everywhere. What's so bad about that, huh, tough guy?"

Me: "Interesting thought, my man. Yeah, just for a hoot, why not? Have a few drinks, take in some pleasurable dance music, and rub elbows with enough ginzos to fully staff a hastily retreating Italian regiment during World War II. I think not, my pal, Sal. I think not. The stigma would be too much."

Sal: "I wish I knew what the hell you said half the time. So, you'd consider it?"

Chapter 28

Jesus on a Motorcycle

Evidently, if you read the *Daily News*, the world keeps spinning. My world, in contrast, seems to be stuck in neutral. Like bald tires swiveling in the mud. My choice to bag college, at least for now, has left me in a kind of purgatory. The back of my mind has this repeating notion that I need to go visit the Marine recruiting booth on Fordham Road but, like my boxing career, takes way more mental effort than I'm willing to give. So, every day is a new day that's as old as the last one. Yeah, as if the military and all that orderly routine fits someone with the temperament of a mouse in a box. Well, even if I toss that notion, I'll keep dreaming about being the world middleweight champ, as my ass-backwards illusions have me defending the belt before I even win it. Pretty sure every champ in history spends a couple of hours in the gym before wearing the crown.

I called Hennessy, my construction foreman, and asked if he could take me back on. I need something to do in the daytime with all my work being done at night. The mick prick informed me that they were laying people off, not hiring. Apparently, he has no open schemes to extort money. Oh well, again.

My nocturnal lifestyle has my mom in a tizzy. The sight of me sleeping in my bed at ten a.m. drives her beyond nuts. It also gives her plenty of ammunition to remind me what a fucking dope I am for passing on a full ride to a decent college. She also told me that since I'm a permanent member of the workforce, and a self-declared adult, that I need to start paying rent or sleep on my motorcycle, or ride the rails like a hobo, or anything that gets me out of her sight. Not like I blame her, as I'd be saying the exact same thing if I was in her shoes.

Anyone that works nights permanently will tell you it changes a person, and rarely for the better. It's dark at night, outside and inside; more crazy things happen at night, and more crazy people walk the streets. I figure that's what they mean when they talk about the dark side. Sleep with dogs and you catch fleas. The craziness eventually gets you and you become one of the psychos inhabiting the shadows waiting for your ghosts to join the party. Man, I feel like I'm starting to get there.

Since all the normal people are generally engaged in being occupied nine to five, Monday to Friday, chasing "The American Dream," you get left with the dregs of society to spend time with—the unemployed, the underemployed, the unemployable, in addition to the thieves, the con artists, the perpetual parolees. The type of people that can only make you feel more dumb and twice as useless. So, every morning of every new day I tell myself that things need to change. At the end of the day, I realize that the hamster wheel may have been spinning but it left me exactly where I started off, one day closer to ruin. Brother Brian, if he can find me, would tell me for the thousandth time that God helps those who help themselves. I still plan on being Daddy Warbucks, just give me one more day, maybe two at the most.

Whenever I have the dual occurrence of being off from work and simultaneously sober, the rare phenomenon indeed, I like to hop on my trusty Triumph Trident and ride it wherever it takes me. I say trusty despite the damn thing takes me forever to kickstart it. I think the mechanism was designed for a ballerina built like Deacon Jones. I kind of have to float into the air above it before bringing my right leg down like a hammer. Then, I need to endure at least a handful of sputtering attempts before the bike finally kicks over. Once it starts, I immediately need to get on the throttle and rev it like a bastard to keep it from stalling out.

A+ to the goddamn Brits for design, the machine is beautiful on the outside, and D- for the engineering, something the Limeys don't seem too great at. If it wasn't for the Yanks and our tanks and battleships and planes and bombs, the stiff-assed wankers would all be goose-stepping to the German national anthem while raising their right arm towards a picture of a guy who looks like Moe of the Three Stooges with a ridiculous mustache.

There's not a whole lot of what you'd refer to as scenic routes in the Bronx. Up and down the Grand Concourse isn't so bad but the further south you go the further south go your odds of not having shit thrown at you by the natives. Something about a white guy on a motorcycle acting cool that doesn't sit quietly with the jigaboos and the coochie fritos. Pelham Parkway has a lot of green but it's busy as shit and doesn't lend itself to a cruising, blissful state of mind. No big worries there because I ride more for the thrill than any peace of mind, though the latter somehow comes with the thrill. No zen for me but let me provide some background on where that concept was introduced to me.

We had this wacko brother at St. Joe's who came up with the brilliant idea to initiate a Philosophy class with a Catholic theology twist. The guy was a fruitcake in every sense and didn't last long before they shipped him off to the nuthouse. He used to tell us that he could pick all the winners at Yonkers Raceway if he wanted to but didn't want to use his God given gifts for evil purposes like gambling. We begged him to take us to the ponies and make us rich, but he chose to stay pure. Brother Brian was his name, which drove the real Brother Brian fucking bonkers. If you weren't a lunatic walking in on your first day, good old St. Joseph's Prep would do its best to change that classification. No one walks out of that place with all their marbles.

So, Brother Batshit informs us that the class would be centered around a book by the title of *Zen and the Art of Motorcycle Maintenance*. The idea, in his mind at least, was to combine it with the Bible and provide our class of dumbassed mongrels with the secret of life so we could get out there in the world and do less harm than good. That, I wanted to inform him, was a pipedream and a half.

He did have us though with the word Motorcycle in the title. Think chicks, tattoos, the Hell's Angels and such, and you can at least get our attention span extended from twenty seconds to a minute or so. I wanted to tell clown boy that the first rule of any presentation is 'know your audience.' Also, that this was, in all likelihood, the dumbest collection of fucking idiots to ever be in a philosophy class. These are guys whose life philosophies came to them from car bumper stickers like, 'Life sucks and then you die,' or 'Ass, grass, or gas, nobody rides for free,' To say our band of morons was in way over our heads was no different than saying that Saturday comes before Sunday which comes before Monday. Standard down and dirty deduction. Oh well, there were no surprises as to the success of the loony brother's attempt to mold the brains of the unmoldable.

The premise of the book is this weirdo freak driving around the country on his Jap bike with his kid on the back and learning life lessons so powerful that he gets stoned on Zen. What happens Zen? Funny guy me. Well, he gets Zen repeatedly every time he fixes his motorcycle or runs over a bug or some other crazy shit. The biggest problem is that I can never figure out what exactly Zen is, and if I can't decipher it, and I'm smarter than the average bear, as well as multitudes smarter than the average St. Joe's knucklehead then my classmates, it's a very safe bet that they are sure as shit not connecting the dots.

After the first week of blind stares, yawns and drooling mouths, Brother Brian II, aka the Flying Nut, gave us a test. Get this, and I kid you not, the entire exam was one question, "Was Jesus Christ the motorcycle or the driver?" My classmates love multiple choice tests and especially ones with only two options. Most immediately figured that they had a 50/50 chance at a 100.

You could see their tongues out and curled to the side, a surefire sign of confidence, as they jotted down their replies. And since they could copy the spelling of either choice from the question, they were now licking their lips with that curled tongue. It was only after our teacher informed us that our answers needed to be at least 100 words did the glows leave their faces.

I scribbled down some utter bullshit about Jesus being both the motorcycle and the driver, and how Zen was achieved when the two melded into a complete being, damn creative if you ask me. Well, I did not fare well, nor did any of my classmates. We all got zeroes. No explanations from the screwball and no answer key to compare to our stabs in the dark. This story did, however, have a happy ending when our philosophy master was removed as a teacher and sent to whatever mental hospital they send priests and the like. It dawned on me after the fact that that's Zen right there. That nutjob's departure sure provided me with some inner peace.

To tell the truth, I do get some kind of ease and contentment from riding my cycle. Takes me out of my head which is usually filled with a lethal mixture of anxiety and rage. It always seems that there's someone or some institution that I need to get even with by either bashing in their skull or burning some place to the ground. Out of nowhere, I'll feel like I need to chase someone down and set the record straight on some matter that would be a non-issue to someone without a tortured brain.

That fucked up nut of mine will be whispering to me that I'm a coward if I don't act. I could be standing right in front of someone who's talking to me and neither hear a word they say, nor care to hear it. In given situations, I lack basic human emotions like empathy, and that bothers the shit out of me. I know I'm not a bad guy yet certain people, like aunts, uncles and teachers, will tell me I'm a selfish little prick who only cares about himself. When they do, I don't get mad at them, just angry with myself. How can a guy who reads about a kid getting murdered in the *Daily News* and cries like it's my own sibling be that uncaring? But if people I respect are telling me this stuff, then it's likely true and I need to do something about it. Easier said than done because I can't stop the endless, rampant lunacy that comes with a brain at hyperspeed, and the more the demons in my head race ahead, the more I fall behind in this quest of becoming a decent human being.

That's usually the case but not when I'm on my bike and manage to catch a patch of release where I feel like I'm gliding above it all and then say these little prayers that simply ask God to assure me everything's gonna be alright. Oddly, it usually works. Man, when the relief comes, I just want to trap it and wrap it around me. That peace of mind, however fleeting, is better than never having a break from this constant state of anguish. Just a little knot at the end of my rope that I hope I can hang onto.

Yeah, maybe that Zen motorcycle author was onto something; keep things in order and strive to keep them that way and your machine takes you to the places you want to go to. Neglect the machine and you veer off course and end up in a ditch. The choice is mine. Therein lies the problem.

One of the places my motorcycle often takes me when I'm riding is down to the playground where Brendan Burns, Skinny Billy and the cast of bad boys can be found most days. Here they are, hanging around and counting time until the apocalypse. Motorcycles, it seems, have way less to do with transportation in these parts, and everything to do with image. Shallow thinking that pulls me in nonetheless. That pull that I can't escape; that need to be a tough guy. Those smarter than me say that ego and pride are lousy guides.

These fellas are an interesting lot, which I've alluded to in the past. Fierce loyalty to each other but a general disdain for most everyone else. The type of guys whose love for their mothers somehow manages to eclipse their collective hate for their enemies, known and unknown. The niggers, spics, Jews, and fags are lurking out there trying to bring down their world. For the most part, I completely disagree with them. In fact, I don't even like most of them. My true friends, like Bobby, are mystified that I let myself get sucked in. You're too smart for them, they'll say. Well, apparently not smart enough.

Personally, I like my outlaws dirty and mean, the same way I prefer my boxing gyms. Pugilism suffers from clean gyms with showers and tidy locker rooms. Pretty boys need not apply. Gyms are better when they have the stench of a garbage dump baking in ninety-degree heat.

Cleanliness makes you weak. Survival favors the filthy. Climb into a ring with rancid armpits and you climb in stronger, almost as if the putrid liquid is getting pumped into your biceps and shoulders, then leaking down to your heart. Take a few heavy shots, feel the warmth of blood flowing down your face, and you're stronger still. Suffering is an asset in the ring, just a feeding for the animal instinct in all of us. Boxing is a poor man's game, they say. You can't be hungry when you've had plenty to eat. Dirty and mean, like the pug aiming to put you to sleep. Dirty and mean, like these boys in the playground.

So, like the confused, dumbass I am, I keep searching for the desperado in me, the bare-knuckled, brawling hobo in a freight train boxcar. Like James Dean in *Rebel Without a Cause*, needing to drive closest to the edge so that he can prove some meaningless lesson to himself—scratch the itch that won't go away no matter how much you cover it with lotion.

The 'red badge of courage' that may get you killed but will let you tell yourself that you're no pussy-assed coward.

Some might even call it a death wish. Ever notice how many of the gang colors you see have an image of the grim reaper? What normal person aspires to be dead?

THE BRONX

You ever try and figure out how they came up with the term pigeon-holed? Pigeons are not a country-type wing flapper, and though my trips to rural settings are on an extremely limited basis, I've never seen one other than in the city. Pigeons are just rats with wings. So, I ask, where are all the holes to corner the pigeons in? If you chase them into a sewer then they're pretty safe from capture. You'll lose your patience and then they'll come waddling out unscathed. Outside of sewers, I don't see too many holes unless they're tearing up the street to fix a water main break. Well, despite not being a pigeon and not standing near any holes, I still managed to get pigeon-holed.

It happened like this. I was in bed the other day, sleeping as late as a Puerto Rican, when I heard my mom talking to a couple of men outside my room. Wonderful invention these doors, we never had them at the old place, so I just stayed put and pulled a pillow over my head. I'm a working man and I'm entitled to a little catch-up naptime. This luxury will be gone when I add a day job to my routine so I might as well milk it while I can.

The pair of male voices outside my chambers turned out to be old faithful, Brother Brian, and my ma's pal, Duke, from the racetrack. Formerly Brother Brian opened the bedroom door and approached my bed. I did my damndest to feign unconsciousness, but the bastard wasn't buying it and pulled the pillow off of my head and . . . and . . . placed his foot on my ribs and started shaking me back and forth.

Pissed me off for sure but he's not a guy I can stay mad at for long. The first thing that crossed my mind was that he was there to rip me for not showing up to his wedding. My mind was already forming excuses when my mom stuck her head in and yelled, not that politely, "Jack get your ass out of bed, now!" Smartass me responded, "You shouldn't curse in front of a former man of the cloth," but she didn't laugh and no one else did either.

Ma went into the kitchen while the other two present escorted me to the living room. My siblings were all at school, including the college boy, Mickey. Turns out Brian (it remains difficult for me to call him that) and Duke were there for an 'intervention,' whatever the hell that is. My mother had been informing them of my various exploits which mostly focused on my coming home legless drunk, often with marks on my face and bruised knuckles. She apparently told them that she actually felt relief to hear me unlocking the door in the middle of the night because she lived in fear that I'd eventually end up on a slab at the local morgue. She's at the end of her wits and with no adult male presence in the household, she imported some.

Duke and Brian proceeded to launch a tutorial on the detriments of alcohol. Duke, it turns out, was a problem drinker for years before he quit fifteen years ago. He told me that his alcoholism had stolen everything valuable in his life, a life he had almost given up on and that he was on the verge of icing himself when, with the grace of God, he discovered AA and a path to a new life.

Told me he had given way too many years to being a drunk, and that he hoped he could help me avoid the same. Sitting there I questioned, in my head, how this polished man with the silky Barry White voice could possibly have been the equivalent of a Bowery bum. I knew what a Bowery bum looked like—my grandpa, my mother's father, had been a real live one, who mom took us to visit on the streets of lower Manhattan, but always failed to coax him to come back with her. He eventually conceded, months later, but was so ravaged by the devil's fermentation, that his diseased liver put him in the grave not many years later.

Typical me, I went on the defensive. 'I've got two jobs and had three in the summer. I have five thousand dollars in the bank and I'm seventeen years old. I'm in better shape than almost anyone I know, and I can prove it to you by dropping to the floor right now and ripping off 60 or 70 fully legit push-ups. I'm only seventeen years old for Christ's sake and I live indoors. These cats weren't buying any of it.

Then Brian (gulp) piped in with his own rendition of the hopeless sot down on his luck with no place to turn. Oh man, did he spill his guts. He was depressed each and every day when he was drinking and praying for an early death. He was selfish and uncaring, didn't give a shit about mankind, had no ambition or plan for the future. I sat there listening, but I truly couldn't soak it in. Duke, a bum? Brother Brian, a selfish prick? These two guys are sitting in front of me. Men, that I had come to idolize for their approach to life? Telling a friggin' 17-year-old kid that he was an alcoholic?

Then Duke, smooth as ever, segued into a different bit. He told me he wasn't here to judge me, that he'd never judge me. Said calling me an alcoholic at any age wasn't something he was qualified to do. The reason he was there, he told me, was because my mom was beyond worried about me and as someone who was once a kid in trouble himself, he just wanted to share his personal experience, maybe say something to me that might help.

And, of course, the usual refrain about how smart I was and all the potential that I had. Don't try to think your way into good actions, he said, act your way into good thinking. *Holy Dalai fucking Lama!* I'm thinking to myself, *where does he come up with this shit?* Then he finished by telling me that he'd always have an open ear for me, and to never even think about inconveniencing him if I needed to talk to someone, about anything under the stars. Well, he kind of finished there. Don't the brilliant also close with some kind of kicker that blows your mind? Get this, he said that I could help him too, just by allowing him to help. Go figga— Man oh man, the tough guy holding back tears again.

Then it was Brother Brian's turn. It almost struck me as a strategy where Duke pulled the tears up into my sockets and then Brian opened the fire hydrant to let them gush out. I managed to avoid embarrassment and not cry like a baby, but it wasn't easy. But that wasn't their strategy anyway, not these fellas, they weren't there to shame me or embarrass me.

And just like Duke, Brian flipped the script, telling me how much I've helped him! How I allowed him to see things about himself that he spent years and years barely recognizing. He too had a ferocious drinking problem—the booze, like a prison guard outside his cell, making sure he never escaped the captivity his misery created. Eloquent words he spoke, but amazingly all of it went into my head, not over it. He went on about everyday being the same thing, how tomorrow it will be different. Hating life was one thing, he said, but doing nothing to change your circumstances was another thing altogether.

"Look at me now," he said, "free as a damn bird, I am, not stuck in that hellhole that was my life. I hated being an

Irish Christian Brother! Screw this idiotic concept that we're meant to suffer for some goddamned reason none of us can even understand. I want to live my life, no, I'm damned sure going to live my life. Jack, you've got a beautiful life waiting for you out there, if only you'd get out of your own way. Like Duke said, Jack, we're not here to judge, just to maybe share things about ourselves that you can relate to and maybe keep in mind. Maybe they can help, or maybe they can't, but they still need to be said. We're here for you, pal, now and always."

When they were done speaking each of them gave me a hug and reiterated their promise to be available anytime I needed them. Mom was standing off to the side trying to be inconspicuous, but I could see she was crying. What kind of son of a bitch puts his mother in a position where she's gotta go and ask her friends to help with her own son? It's not like that's something that comes easy to her. The tears in her eyes right now are telling me that she's at a point of desperation. Here I am feeling sorry for myself when she's the one getting pigeon-holed. So, I ask myself, am I going to be the old Duke and the old Brian or am I finally going to do something with myself that can make these people proud of me, with my mother being at the front of that list.

Chapter 29

Love to Love You Baby

I got a letter from Mary! A sweet, beautiful letter from Mary. She loves me, she loves me not, she loves me! That girl says the nicest things in the most pleasant of ways!

When my mother handed me the envelope and I saw the return address I almost jumped through the roof with glee. I guess I never truly believed she'd write, here it was, barely two weeks from her departure and she'd taken the time to write to ol' Jack McGee!

My first instinct was to tear the envelope open to get at this sacred note, but I managed to calm myself down and open it gently—I wanted to keep as close as possible to this item that had touched her glorious hand as she dropped into a mail slot. Slowly and deliberately, I removed the letter and brought it to my nose and took a long, deep whiff, hoping to catch a scent of my beloved. Her handwriting is like art, pretty as a picture, pretty as my Bronx Irish Mona Lisa. I fell into a magical swoon, the swoon to the moon.

Before I started reading it, I pressed it against my heart and then took another attempt at summoning my beloved's fragrance. Oh God, I wished she was with me at that moment. Then I finally read the letter. School was fine she said, and she liked her roommate. She said she missed me and looked forward to seeing me when she came home from school. What she didn't say was that I should come and visit her and that she never stopped thinking about me and how she wished I was there with her, the same way I was longing to be with her at this very moment. She signed off with a lousy, 'hope all is well and don't forget to write back.'

I read the letter over and over again trying to make sense of what it said. Why was it so Goddamned bland? Where was the emotion? Why hadn't she taken a stab at the 'L' word? Then, I went the other way for a while. She did take the time to jot me a note, even if it was more of a note than a full-blown letter. Mary wrote to me before I wrote to her, and she used terms like 'miss you.' It wasn't all bad and the girl is first and foremost focusing on her studies like she should be. As for using the "L' word that was beyond ridiculous. I'd never use that expression with her even though there was this thing going on in my heart that was damn close to it.

Unfortunately, that's not how my personal breed of insanity works. My messed-up bean went right to extremes. She was just being nice to me by sending the note—she already had a new boyfriend up there. I'm not even her boyfriend to begin with—she's too damn good for me. In another couple of months, she'll forget I even exist. Maybe, I thought to myself, the truth lies somewhere in the middle. I'll write her and she'll write me back and so on, and she'll focus on school and not have time for guys and partying.

Besides, none of the preppy propeller heads could be as good looking and cool as Jack MeGee, Mary is a Bronx girl and has street savvy; she'll be able to see right through these goofballs. But who's kidding who? I'll start giving up hope in a day or two, assuming I haven't already. Rollin' with the punches again, staying in that crouch peek-a-boo style. What's a boy to do when that's the only thing he can do? Only the good die young, they say, and being good isn't much fun anyway. Keep telling yourself that clichéd crap from the little minds of the excuse makers. "If you can't be with the one you love, love the one you're with," and other hymns of comfort for a heart in despair.

CHAPTER 30

Small Secrets Kept Long

Terry, Alibi's owner, wants me to start checking IDs now. I, of course, will ignore him, in order to save about twenty percent of the usual Saturday night crowd; I am also not going to remind him that his most popular bartender, that being me, is underage. Apparently, there have been a few raids by some government do-gooders, New York State Bar and Liquor Authority, or some such organization of high esteem that have resulted in one or two of the local gin mills losing their licenses. I get Terry's concerns, as a lost license means a lost livelihood, and that's some scary shit for any bar owner to have to deal with.

I view the whole thing as a humanitarian crisis. Where else do these young punks have to go on a weekend night? Driving them out into the streets on a cold winter's night, or even a slightly chilly September eve, could have rash health implications, Besides, the bar can also serve as a sanctuary against a harsh, harsh world by surrounding the otherwise wayward with a stable environment in the midst of similar-minded friends. Think of it as a community center for drunks and hoodlums where unity brings a common benefit.

What's good for the goose is good for the gander, and if you take a gander at the lot of them, you'll concede that their goose is cooked if they're left to navigate the world on their lonesome. Being a clean and upstanding establishment, we strongly condemn the use of drugs, though we do turn a blind eye on occasion, particularly to the bathrooms, where the lowlifes generally get their kicks, unconcerned as to the puddles of piss at their feet. If I have my say in the matter, any underaged kid that wants to kill himself in the Alibi will have to do it with alcohol.

I'm half inclined to enforce Terry's wishes anyway as most of the sixteen and seventeen-year-old pricks are lousy tippers. In a typical crowd of five or so of them, there will be one guy who has money and the other four mooching off him. If any of them were to come into a windfall, the dumb fucker would incinerate his cash pile in no time, on an hour's worth of cocaine or a similar sound investment for the future.

To supplement myself for their lack of contribution to my personal wealth, I'll overcharge them once or twice or three times during the course of a night and feed the difference into my tip cup. Experience tells me that very few of these nitwits can add numbers in their heads even when stone cold sober. If one of them was to question a tab, I'd just throw a multiplication equation at them and paralyze them on the spot. They'll have a dumb look on their face as if they're running numbers in their head and then say, 'oh,' and walk away.

As for continuing to harbor the underaged imbibers, from my perspective it makes sense to roll the dice and take our chances. These raids don't happen without the local police being notified in advance and those very same cops, our cops, would blow the whistle long before Eliot Ness and his boys showed. We'd clear the place out fire drill style and have it looking like a library before the first black car pulled up outside. So, we'll keep operating as per usual with small reason to fuck with a winning formula. Maybe, we'll even get recognized for all the positives we do by keeping drug addicts off the street and safely sequestered in an environment where all they can do is get drunk and maybe throw up a few times. Jack McGee, peacekeeper and potential Nobel Prize winner. Just call me Ghandi, why don't ya?

Knucks got busted with a bag of weed, a lousy nickels' worth. The cops, a mick and a ginzo who were new to the precinct, wanted him to roll over and give them the name of his dealer who is, of course, my boy, my black boy at that, Jamaican Al. They threatened Knucks with getting locked up and all if he didn't squeal. The men in blue, who were actually plainclothes, wanted to take down the kingpin, and offered the Knucklehead a free ride in exchange for a name. It was obvious they knew who it was and figured a good little white boy would have no problem ratting out some spook dealer. Shit, by most counts, it wouldn't even be considered 'ratting.' More like civic duty.

Knucks didn't budge. He told me later that I'd vouched for him with Al and that he'd also told Al personally that he could be trusted. The narcos didn't get the drop on the Jamaican Nicky Barnes and Knucks kept straight with his little honor code. He walked away with a slap on the head and a confiscated bag of weed. Made me damn proud to know him.

THE BRONX

I was talking to Mahoney, light pole climber supreme, about this and that, when the ever-present topic of sex came up. He told me he'd been walking around with a constant hard-on for what seemed like weeks. Said he wished he could find something to do with it other than beatin' off but admitted his chances of a romantic conquest were slim indeed. We both agreed that, based on the high ratios of progeny, that Irishmen were likely among the horniest species on earth, even up there with the primal, feral types like hyenas, rabbits, and Puerto Ricans.

Mahoney mentioned that our maternal ancestors have endured hell for centuries, reminding me of the joke describing Irish foreplay, i.e., 'brace yourself, Bridget.'

Our little dialogue brought back memories of horniness past with Mahoney recalling that he got his first hard-on in the second grade in concert with falling in love with his teacher, the buxom Miss Andrews. I called bullshit immediately but conceded quickly that maybe he wasn't imagining it after remembering what I believed to be my first boner, which occurred in the fourth-grade courtesy of the beguiling charms of the lovely Miss Conley, the prettiest teacher in the entire school. Deducing that Mahoney had a year on me chronologically, it pinpointed, all puns intended, our puny ramrods within striking distance of each other's origin. Both of us were on the trail of our sexual yesteryears now, searching for other early signs of our Irish driven instincts.

Before Mahoney got too far ahead and started mentioning family pets, I jumped in with the time a bunch of us, including Mahoney, went to see the movie, *Jenny*, starring Marlo Thomas at the Bainbridge theater as part of a double feature. The Bainbridge lets you stay as long as you want after you buy a ticket, and you can almost move in for the day. I couldn't tell you what the hell the movie was about, only that it was God fucking awful, but it had a single moment that caught the attention of us all as if we were on the same radio frequency. For a split section our gal, Marlo, flashed some tit during a breast-feeding scene, a small portion mind you, but enough to send us into a frenzy.

"Mahoney," I said, "we couldn't have been more than ten years old! Which gives your boner in the second-grade story more than enough credibility." Mahoney was now laughing his ass off but not as much as he would be a couple of minutes later when I relayed the rest of the story. The handful of us little horn dogs suffered through the other movie, which I couldn't even remember the name of, and then through *Jenny* 'round two' just to see that nipple scene again. "And it was you, my pal, Mahoney, who wanted to stay a third time!" If we had gone along with my boy, our parents would have had the police out looking for us. Mahoney had tears flowing out of his eyes from hysteria and was clearly damn proud of the fortitude he'd shown at such a tender age.

The basic conclusion of the whole thing is that this is just another area where the Irishman displays his dominance; we can make babies like you read about. The offsetting side effects being that we're in a constant state of agitation, and that our eyesight is below average.

Mahoney stirred up the dog in me and got me thinking about Mary in a completely different context. Man, I better censor my thoughts and leave it right here. That girl deserves a whole lot better.

I think it was Brother Brian who told me that I was only as sick as my secrets. If so, that means I'll be eternally ill because some of the cats simply need to stay in the bag.

Chapter 31

Nights in the Bronx Are
Longer and Darker

This night owl stuff is wearing me out. It's lit a fuse to my biological clock and my whatchamacallit rhythm. Seems I don't know when to sleep and when not to. I can't imagine that I'm averaging more than four hours of shut-eye a night, or day, or whatever time period I finally pass out in. My life exists in a time zone all my own and sometimes it feels like I'm part of a different universe, only mine seems to be going on a completely different spin, like fucking backwards.

If I work the bar, I can pretty much call it a day when I close the place. We're talking hours of the night when the only things left out on the street are rats, human form and otherwise. That also gives me an excuse to sleep in. But when I lock up the gas station at ten, I know I have a snowball's chance in hell of rolling myself into unconsciousness. What's a boy to do?

My first instincts take me to the places I know best like Creston Avenue, the formative street corner of my life, hoping there's some straggler from the neighborhood to have a beer with or smoke a joint with. I'll know even before I ride my ass over that no one I want to spend a minute with will be there, but I'll do it anyway. Besides, the newcomers to the neighborhood, the dancing tribes of the Caribbean, keep later hours and could only stir up my fury by occupying the fucking side of the street that belongs to me. I give it until next summer and it'll be all theirs anyway, the nasty motherfuckers.

Other times, I just ride my motorcycle through the streets aimlessly not giving two shits who my pounding exhaust pipes annoy. Inevitably, I'll shift into a joyous rage as I head in a southern direction, through the streets of these people that are not my own.

The more I rev the throttle creating an ear-splitting commotion with the intention of pissing off every last one of them, the more elated I feel. I tend to link them all into one concentrated object of my hate, as if there wasn't a decent kid or man or woman among them. These are the people that killed my father, and Jimmy Welsh, and messed with my life in so many different ways.

The deeper I go into the bowels of the Bronx, the more desolate and fucked up it becomes. Burnt out building after burnt out building. A virtual ghost town save the junkies and gang members congregating around burning trash cans to keep warm and prolong their evenings. If my bike ever broke down here, I'd be dead, I'd end up in one of those trash fires and have to be identified by my dental records, assuming they even exist. I feel like James Caan in that movie *The Gambler* tempting fate, taking the ultimate gamble. Seven, eleven, or snake eyes. Nothing to win but some idiotic pride at defeating death at its own game.

Shorter days and longer, darker nights, always too far from that somewhere I'd like to be. Sometimes, my instincts pull me in a different direction like it did this past Tuesday night when they led me north to places that maintain their whiteness even in the dead of night. I spun my wheels northbound on Marion Avenue towards Mosholu Park when I spotted a chopper and a few bodies sitting on the fence rails of the park outside the playground. It turned out to be Brendan Burns, Skinny Billy, and the ex-con Richie. I pulled up, hopped off my bike, and booted the kickstand into place. The boys actually seemed excited to see me and immediately offered me a beer. Despite the cold, the most insulation among them was a dungaree jacket—Lee brand of course, just like the one I was presently wearing.

It struck me as odd that they would be here on a quasi-frosty Tuesday night and I imagine they thought the same thing as to my sudden appearance under similar circumstances. Brendan Burns kidded me about cruising fags which got a fine chuckle all around, including from me. I wasn't gonna let him get in the last word, so I informed him that if I was out cruising fags I'd come to the right place. As I've said a thousand times, if you're not getting your balls busted then you're not among friends. It's always comforting to be called a fuckhead or a douchebag in the right circles.

When I inquired as to their reason for hanging out in the park on such a dreary night, what they told me was interesting indeed. Neighborhood security and a thirst for revenge was the answer. It would turn into a night I'd never possibly be able to forget. Forever and a day, from here to eternity, stuck in my head like King Authur's sword in the stone.

Apparently, Brendan Burns's old man had been walking along this same spot a week or so previous in what was mostly darkness. He's a foreman at UPS and works in their west side office down in Manhattan, He keeps a crazy schedule, with lots of overtime, so his hours shift all the time, and it was around ten o'clock in the evening when he was walking along deserted Mosholu Parkway, in pretty much this same spot, on his way to Marion Avenue, after getting off the D train up on the Grand Concourse.

The long and short of it is that he was mugged and beaten by a group of three or four niggers, he couldn't remember exactly how many. This wasn't your average roll where they take the money and run. Brendan's old man, a tough, thick-headed Mick from the other side, wasn't going to lay down for anyone, less so for a pack of spooks. He refused to hand over a cent even with a knife staring him down menacingly. Clearly at a huge disadvantage, he was preyed upon savagely and beaten to a pulp, battered enough to have a collapsed eye socket and a couple of broken ribs from being kicked countless times as he lay indefensible on the floor. Not content with just a beatdown, they spit all over him and showered him with racist rants as to his white skin, like honky, white motherfucker, and you name it. The conclusion, at that point, was a multiple day trip to the hospital for Mr. Burns, a lost wallet with his driver's license and about forty bucks in it, and an enraged son who was fully capable of killing the perpetrators for real should he ever find them.

When the crime was reported to the police, the cops informed Brendan, and his mom and pop, that there had been a series of robberies in the same vicinity, fitting the pattern of this thievery and violent assault. They told them that a band of teenagers, whom the fuzz openly referred to as nigger punks, were assumed to be from the South

Bronx, and were likely hopping a train up north where they hoped to find easy prey with a dramatically lighter shade of pigmentation.

When the Great Bronx spins these days, it mostly swivels around years of deep-rooted loathing between the classes. It's always assumed that the honkies hate the jigaboos more than vice versa, but only from those observers who haven't lived it. Those motherfuckers hate us just as much, maybe more so.

Now to give you a clearer picture, this young man, Mr. Burns, has been pulled further into the depths of a war, the same war that's existed in his head for quite some time now, only now the stakes had been raised. To his mind, a severe beatdown would be the most compassionate response. His ruminations, however, go well beyond that to things like torture, disfigurement and even murder.

Brendan Burns is the closest living form to a superhero I know, at least among my age group. He's incredibly smart, and more so in ways that are difficult to explain and has the uncanny ability to draw people into his world, a world where he is lord and master. Cunning and calculated, with a cultish command and more than a touch of psychosis. He's built like a brick shithouse, scrappy and fearless. When he engages in a fight his intention is not just to win, but to completely dominate his opponent, and inflict maximum pain. Brendan wants to ensure that you walk away, or crawl away for that matter, with a lasting memory of your demise at his hand. I may consider myself as tough, but not in any shape or form that would prompt me to even consider fucking with my boy. Best to pretend, not defend.

Burns has just recently turned eighteen, not more than a few weeks ago. He's already got himself a tricked-out

Harley with a long, ominous fork and all the accoutrements, like German Spike tire lugs and a Grim Reaper saddlebag. His helmet, if and when he wears one, is one of those hard metal ones like the Nazis wore in WWII. I know he rides and hangs out often with his pal, Stu the Jew, and sometimes Stu's badass brother, Ralph, the killer cop, so I view it more like biker chic than anti-Semitism, though I sincerely doubt he's all warm and fuzzy in relation to Jews in general. I'd say he's not much different than me in that regard. I can hate every last one of them until I meet one of them, I don't hate, and maybe even like a little. Like little Mark the muscle-bound kike from our football team. Hell, I think I even almost hugged the guy once when we were standing on the sidelines after he had just finished nailing one of the bad guys from the opposing side, and smiled at me with blood dripping down his head and a newly dislodged tooth front and center in his mouth.

I've seen Brendan B zooming on his cycle at speeds that would scare the shit out of the average rider. To boot, he does so with that long, long fork that could twist and turn if it hits a larger than average pebble. I mean you're playing with fucking fire with that shit, almost daring Lucifer to pry open the ground below you and suck you in. I guess when you're a living, breathing badass motherfucker you need to play the game 100% of the time, even in your sleep.

So, I think I've given you a stark enough picture here of this developing blockbuster movie that could end up making *Death Wish* and Charles Bronson look like a Donald Duck cartoon. Think *Twelve Angry Men* times ten with the sum of that collective fury compressed into the heart of my dear, rageful friend.

No monopoly on anger here, however. Skinny Billy is no rank amateur in this department, not by a long shot. He wakes up every morning with his main purpose, even his sole purpose, being to exact revenge on the hit and run monster that erased his little sister from his life. Billy has spent the years since his sister was killed doing his own detective work, to no avail. In our current Bronx world, the NYPD has more hot cases than they can handle so cold cases, which can be defined as no more than a few months old, are already trash bin history.

The cops will never find him; Billy has reconciled himself to this fact, and he's now at the point where his vengeance will need to be of the class action variety. Add this mixture to the dual cancer deaths of his parents and what you get is what he got—a plateful of misery. A simmering affliction, barely contained in a glass bottle holding a Molotov cocktail with a short, flimsy wick. Don't fuck with a man who's got nothing to lose, they say. Skinny's indifference to shuffle the cards of life is at a stage where he'll take a hit on eighteen in a Blackjack game, and he's not playing with a full deck to begin with.

Another thing, one shouldn't underestimate Skinny's small frame and lack of height to equate to a lack of physical force. Barely a hundred and thirty-five pounds but he's got those tightly coiled muscles that react like a spring. Sinewy, is what they call it, I think. Like a cobra, only he'll bite more than once.

Then there's Richie. He has a few crazy coins to toss into the pot. Remember, this is a guy who did a five-plus stint in the state pen for beating some junkie to death with a hammer. That's not an accomplishment many men can brag about. Scuttlebutt also tells us that his old man was an abusive prick whom a teenage Richie once bludgeoned with a baseball bat, not quite adept at that stage of his life to rely solely on a hammer for his handiwork. The old man survived but Richie was shipped off to a reformatory, probably Spofford, where bad boys become even badder boys. By the time he was sixteen, he was done with school and for all intents and purposes, he was living on the streets.

Half Irish, half Rican, and one-hundred-percent certi-fied. He managed to take the best traits of both tribes and was teen-idol handsome with curly locks and striking green eyes. Chicks loved him and more than a couple would rescue him from the streets from time to time and give him a roof over his head and a bed to sleep in, which also happened to be the same one they snatched their forty winks in. His skin was olive, but he was as white as can be in his heart. I guess hating his old man, the Puerto Rican side, made him hate that part of himself. If you asked him flat out, which would be a mistake for some, what he was, he'd tell you 'Irish' and leave it at that. I chose to leave it at that.

Richie was prison fit and then some. If he had any fat on his body, he was doing a helluva job at hiding it. Push-ups, pull-ups and dips—the locked down man's gymnasium. Motherfucker was flat out ripped to shreds. Great athlete too, or at least he was. You get to a certain age, and you move on to more practical things. Though older than Burns by at least seven years, he still seemed beholden to him. On this fine autumn eve, he appeared to genuinely share every ounce of anger Brendan had for his father's assailants. Maybe he had less skin in the game, but maybe, in some convoluted way, at least inside his own head, he had more.

Which leaves me, Jack McGee, to round out the Four Horseman. A little reminder here that I am a bit of a badass

313

myself. That's why I'm here; it's why I keep getting pulled back. Test yourself boy. Show some balls, why don't you? Keep telling yourself that you're something you're not and really don't want to be.

I remember some shits and giggles and taking a few sips from my can of Bud. The rest is dreamlike, as if I wasn't really there, just hanging at the periphery like a ghost in the night.

I've discovered over the years that you can be jovial on the outside, even laughing so hard that you have tears in your eyes and mean and seething on the inside at the same precise time.

That's my personal view, or really my actual experience, because more than once, or more like a hundred times, I've had that switch flipped in my brain in a nanosecond. Singing and dancing one moment, and then zero to sixty trying to strangle someone to death the next, eyes bulging out of my skull. No pause button can get activated where none exists. I'm no shrink, but it felt to me like that exact phenomenon was occupying the air around my three confederates. Each of them laughing and busting balls without ever losing, even for a wisp, the bonafide emotions that brought them to this park rail on a chilly weekday night in the first place. There was no talk of the Yankees and their pursuit of another World Series. These boys had their minds on a different style of sport, one with a lot more contact. But the game isn't on if the other team doesn't show, so you bide your time and hope that things clear up so the ground crew can pull the tarp off the playing field and the ump can give the 'let's play ball' signal. If I knew what was about to transpire, I'd have prayed for rain and run to the showers. What life gives you in clues it takes back in lead time.

Some lives bring gradual change over many years; some barely change at all in time with a landscape that avoids dramatic events. Some change is somewhat better or somewhat worse; some change is quick and dramatic but still manageable. Some change happens in the blink of an eye and your vision is never the same from that moment on.

Chapter 32

Unwilling Accessory

I heard some clatter coming towards us and as the noise moved closer it became evident that it was human voices. The ears of all four of us perked up and we were now in unison, looking towards the direction from which the fuss came. From beneath the glow of a streetlamp, the shapes of three bodies came into view. The voices were louder now, but outside of some laughing it was hard to decipher much. My first instinct was that it was just some neighborhood kids, the types that keep their noses clean and do things like homework, headed home before it got too late, this being a school night and all.

Skinny Billy, however, picked up on something the rest of us missed and proclaimed, "They're talking like fucking niggers." That didn't alarm me so much because these days a lot of these little jackass, punk, white boys think it's cool to talk like they're from somewhere far down in the ghetto. My instincts were not shared by the others. I could see their facial qualities altering, eyes intently squinting to narrow their sights, lips pursed and slightly trembling.

Brendan Burns hopped off the rail where he'd been sitting and now all of us were standing erect with our shoulders pulled back. It almost felt like I was in a Comanche camp and the tribe was putting the finishing touch on their war paint and preparing to jump on their horses with the first glimpse of Custer and his boys coming over the hill.

By the time the approaching threesome made it to the next streetlight, it was obvious they were dark-skinned. They appeared at ease and their laughter amplified with each step closer to us they took. Joshing and kidding each other just like the four of us on the other side of the street had been doing barely five minutes earlier. Nothing about them seemed menacing to me but nonetheless my anger was building that they were even here, in our neighborhood. Again, it's our neighborhood!

Now, my demeanor was taking on a wholly different air. Who the fuck were they to have the balls to nonchalantly stroll into our world? I felt challenged as if someone had just spit in my face. The motherfuckers were testing us, expecting us to be the type of white pussies they could intimidate. If so, bad, bad assumption on their part.

I'm sure Brendan Burn's foremost conviction was that these were the same nigger bastards that had rolled and severely beaten his old man. He certainly was not inclined to pause for any clarification or deductive reason—he had all he needed in the form of three foreign bodies, all fitting the loose description of 'them,' walking in the same place, and around the same time of night that his father had been attacked. Like myself, actually like all four of us on this side of the street, Burns lacked the ability to overrule the warp speed rage onrush that saturated his brain, with a stop and take a deep breath pause button. Forget zero to sixty, we're talking zero to the speed of light in a single nerve twitch.

Once again, I'll tell you that none of this feels real in retrospect, more like a hallucination. I can't remember what I was thinking or how I felt. When I think back, I'm not even sure if I was still even angry. What I do recall is that every inch of me knew, absolutely knew, that something grim and awful was about to happen.

One of my recurring dreams, to this day, is being in an alley chased by a pair of snarling Dobermans as I latch onto a chain link fence and try to climb high and fast enough to elude their fangs. The nightmare always concludes at that point but, more often than not, I wake up in a pool of sweat. This much is certain in my mind, if those dogs managed to pull me down from the fence, I'm gonna be dragged into a world of no return. Now, I was in a bad dream of a different essence but with the same pending result if I didn't wake up in time. If this thing pulled me in, it was pulling me all the way in. The Dobermans will have gotten me.

The strategy, which happened without any verbal communication from any of us, was to run across the street and get in front of these guys before they had a chance to run. My feet didn't get the message and remained firmly rooted to the concrete below them. Burns, Richie, and Skinny Billy sprinted across fifteen feet or so of asphalt and formed a blockade of menace, foaming from the mouth with anticipation, much like the Dobermans from my nightmares.

Their path now blocked, these strangers of a different shade, were now forced to acknowledge the foreboding obstacle that had confronted them, in the form of Brendan Burns, Richie, and Skinny Billy. I, for my part, stood back a few feet and off to the side a bit. Richie was the first to speak, maybe thinking it was his role as senior statesman. He skipped the diplomacy and got right to the heart of the matter or, more appropriately, the matter seething in his heart. "What are you doing in our neighborhood, you fucking niggers?"

The tension in my body electrified, a third rail of trepidation shot through me with a sickening sensation. I can't remember if I was trembling or not, but I do vividly recall a complete sense of bewilderment. Is this actually happening? Am I really here? Now, I'd been in situations similar to this my whole life. It's the way things happened in the Bronx when natural enemies crossed paths. Always, a lot of this guy and that guy talking shit and then maybe a fistfight. More often it was just both sides calling each other's bluff and moving on. Saying and doing enough to prove you weren't intimidated, walking away with your manhood intact. This set of circumstances was different by miles. The players were different, and the script was different. Here you had the very angry son of a man who'd just recently been hospitalized after a nasty mugging, along with his two friends who were carrying their own powder kegs of dynamite formed from the misery of their pasts. Between the three of them there was enough distorted passion to decimate a small city. I was no longer the fourth in the party, as each second that passed pulled me further into the background. These boys were on a mission that neither included me or needed me. It confused me that I didn't feel a similar sense of anger.

After all, weren't these the same types of motherfuckers that put a bullet into my own father?

Brendan Burn's dad was still alive, for Christ's sake! Here I had an opportunity to wreak revenge on my lifelong enemies and the only thing I felt was sadness for these poor bastards. I almost can't bring myself to admit it, but I wanted to slide over to their side of the divide and protect them, maybe talk my friends out of beating them mercilessly into a pulp. But maybe in just a few minutes I'd be feeling completely different? They'd turn out to be the lowlifes I first expected them to be, and my own lethal brand of rage would find me straddling over one of them and smashing his head into the concrete. No matter how street hardened these fuckers were, I didn't see even a remote chance of them getting the best of this scrap. We were the beast, and they were the prey, be it easy prey or the type that drags on longer and leaves a trail of blood before it eventually succumbs.

And it wasn't just the venom that coursed through their veins that made them dangerous. All three were tough sons of bitches from the get-go. The way their minds worked made this a necessity. They know that you can't take on a world you despise without being equipped to do so. Whether building muscle, or becoming adept with weapons, or building a complete and total resistance to fear, the endeavor was to make yourself ready for when the day comes, for the very instances like this one, front and center, right fucking now. *Me, too, man*, I'm kinda thinking to myself. I've been preparing for this shit as well, for a damned long time—yes, I have. I want to prove to my three friends, be they my closest buds or not, that I can mix it up when the bell rings. I can scrap just as well as they can. I'm no pussy and I can prove it.

Time stood still for me as Richie launched his opening salvo. I finally took closer notice of the dark-skinned trio in front of us. My immediate interpretation was that they were not what I'd expected to see from ghetto hardened thugs. They were better dressed. A couple of them were holding books. They weren't particularly big, and all lacked that Black Nation swagger.

Nothing about them struck me as menacing. Both instinctually and logically, I couldn't reconcile these visitors into the night with the gritty muggers who had hunted through these parts in the recent weeks. In fact, I was one-hundred-percent convinced that these three were not the bad guys we presumed them to be. Even if they turned out to be up to no good, their intentions would be of a much milder scale. But they were black, afros and all, and they were still in a place where we had conclusively decided they absolutely should not be.

Skinny Billy spoke next, "You think these are the same motherfuckers, Brendan?" Burns didn't answer right away, almost as if he was thinking exactly what I was thinking. Then Skinny said, "Answer the question, motherfuckers, what the fuck are you doing here?"

The three of them stood there speechless, kind of looking around to each other. The best thing they could do, from my perspective, was to meekly surrender to the impending threat, and talk their way out of a beating, and move on to wherever they were headed in the first place.

Maybe that option existed or maybe it didn't. I so wish to God that they'd at least attempted to take it. Why test fate? Why does any dumbass Bronx kid always think that the world is going to collapse on him unless he proves his metal? Don't ask Jack McGee because I'm that dumbass kid in spades. When it comes to the riches of reasonable thinking, "I'm a man of means by no means, king of the road." Riding in a boxcar to wherever the hell it takes me.

I have this theory about kids from the Bronx—no matter how much of a pussy you might be, like those kids who stay home after school and barely come out on the weekends, you still get some oomph just from living here. Even the Jews with their glasses and *yamakas*. Even the goody two shoes Catholic girls who'd never lower themselves to hang out on the corner. Hell, even the old guys feeding the pigeons in the park have a tad of the badass in them. Makes you too stupid to run or just keep your mouth shut. Maybe Jack McGee, growing up in Westchester with a father and a house, would be a bit of a pussy, instead of this half grown-up clown with a chip on his shoulder standing on the train tracks daring the iron horse to run his ass over. In the Bronx, you survive by keeping at least a little bit of a jump in your step. Doesn't matter who you are, but it sure as shit matters.

Like I keep saying, I keep thinking back about how this whole thing could somehow have been reversed. What if they'd simply been kids from anywhere in the world but the Bronx? What if they'd had the good sense to keep their mouths shut and take off in a sprint that would have left the whiteboys gasping for air after a fruitless chase?

The tallest and widest of the three, who wasn't all that tall and wide himself, suddenly took a step forward between his friends and answered the question, or at least replied to it. It was obvious that he was the big man in this small pack. "Get the fuck out of my way, whitey, we ain't bothering nobody."

His response definitely ebbed my sympathy for him and, in fact, reignited my disdain. Okay, tough guy, you just dug your own grave. Whatever happens from here is on you, you imbecile cocksucker.

Well, 'Whatever happens from here . . .' happened in a big, ugly way. In what seemed like a nanosecond after the last syllable left the Black kid's tongue, Richie lurched forward and hit him with a sledgehammer of a right hand. I mean he fucking clobbered him. The guy went down like a ton of bricks. It happened in an instant. Here I was on what certainly appeared to be the winning team, but there was no elation on my end, none whatsoever. What I had instead was a sickening feeling that the wheels were off the cart and that there would be no turning back.

But with all the dread I was feeling, it paled in comparison to how sorry I felt for that poor son of a bitch lying on his back on the cold concrete. I wanted to figure out a way to make it stop, limit the damage, protect these poor fuckers. But I didn't. I didn't do a damn thing. I stayed locked in my bad dream, unable to move.

If these kids were ghetto hardened hoodlums, they would have fought back like motherfuckers. They would have pulled out weapons and been attempting to do twice back whatever was done to them. The wild streets of the South Bronx simply don't breed any other kind. Yet, that didn't happen, they barely did anything. That is other than trying to protect themselves by wrapping their arms around their heads. Richie now stood menacingly over their leader, waiting to see if he'd show a reaction so that he could resume pummeling him. Brendan Burns pounced on the second guy, and Skinny went towards the third. Once again, I'm recalling this as best as I can from inside that glazy-eyed stupor I was in.

The first guy who was hit was conscious now and he was muttering something to the effect of, "what the fuck, man," as he tried to climb up with one arm under his side and the other shielding his head. It sounded like he was actually crying. Yeah crying. I zeroed in on him and lost sight of everything else that was going on around me, as if Burns and Skinny Billy were no longer in the movie. I just couldn't let this kid get beaten anymore, bad guy or not, and I finally did something, grabbing Richie's right arm in my two hands and screaming at him to stop. "You're gonna fucking kill him, man, and get your ass locked up again. C'mon man, no more." Richie glared at me with such disdain that I thought his next swing would be at my head.

Then, out of nowhere, I heard Skinny Billy yell out, "Let's go. Get the fuck outta here!" I saw him start to trot away towards the park, and then I saw Brendan Burns and Richie pick up the pace behind him. I had no choice but to run away with them.

As I ran, I heard noises behind me that I still can't get out of my head. A dreadful moaning and a horrifying voice saying over and over, "Oh no, please God, no, oh God, please no, please, no, no, no, no, no . . ."

Those sounds that would become etched in my head for a long, long time to come, probably forever, but a sight that would equally become chiseled into my brain was of Skinny trotting away with a knife in his right hand. Yeah, I know it was dark and people will say I was probably imagining it, but I swear I saw drops of blood trickling off the blade as he moved away.

I fled the scene feeling like I was running from one life that I wasn't comfortable with right into another one that was a whole lot worse. All I knew was that I had to get the hell out of there as fast as possible, far away from that awful moaning in the background. It was all adrenaline and animal instincts now because my brain was numb. I was sprinting so fast I passed Burns, Richie and Skinny like they were standing still. I know it wasn't God reaching down to help, but my bike turned over on the first kick.

No, God wasn't involved here, not in any way, shape, or form. Nor, for that matter, was it good luck, because it was not possible that anything good could come from what had just happened. In what seemed like an instant, I was off like that bat out of hell I knew so well. I lost sight of the others and thankfully, for that moment in time anyway, the only sounds I could hear now were the engine of my motorcycle and Burns's bike rumbling to life in my wake. That other awful sound was drowned out, but it would come back again and again and again, to haunt every ounce of my being.

Like a frenzied maniac I shot up 203rd, which is a one-way street, almost hoping some car would come speeding down the opposite way and take me out of my misery. When I got to the Grand Concourse, I rode right over the divider between north and south and swerved my bike into a sharp left and headed south towards Minerva Place, like a homing pigeon, until I suddenly realized I no longer lived there.

So, back across the divider I went, reversing from south to north this time. By the time I pulled up in front of our house, I was soaked with sweat even though the temperature had dropped quite a few degrees. My hands were shaking, and I felt like vomiting. Then it struck me; I was barely a few blocks from where it had all just happened. In my head, it felt like I'd traveled halfway across the earth just to get back to where I started from. Like the saying goes, you can run but you can't hide, but I needed to at least try. I needed a hole really bad.

This was gonna be just the first of many near sleepless nights to come. Even when I do pass out from sheer exhaustion, it doesn't last all that long and there's nothing restful about it. Every time I reawaken, I have the same hopes and prayers that all of this never really happened, and that this nightmare is just a bad dream.

Over and over, I recall the events as I remember them. And what I do remember, I question. How accurately do I recall each detail? I think of my first impression of these black kids as a pretty mild version of the ghetto niggers I've hated and fought with for what seems to be my entire life, and then I try to convince myself that they were the real kind of bad, the types out looking for trouble. Didn't they bring it upon themselves just by walking past us like they didn't give a shit who we were? What were they doing there in the first place if they weren't up to something? Did they mutter shit under their breath? Did they stare us down to egg us on?

Why test fate you motherfuckers? If they'd just decided to turn a corner and change direction so they didn't have to walk past us, none of this would have happened.

In order to get on with my life, I'm gonna have to justify what happened here from my perspective. Hey, I didn't do a damned, fucking thing! Never threw a punch, never kicked anyone in the head, never even called them a single name. I was kind of minding my own business and got pulled into a windstorm. Yeah, that's how I see it. That's the truth, you can't tell me different.

As for my friends, I can justify their point of view as well. For the most part, I think. Take it from their perspective—all three—Burns, Richie, and Skinny Billy have a right to their anger. Of course, they should protect their neighborhood given all the crap that has happened around here lately. It'd been way worse if they just sat there and let it go. Shit, I'd had a right to my anger too, if I'd actually felt any. You have to consider everything before you jump to conclusions.

Maybe even make those conclusions stick.

The thing I can't come to grips with is the bloody knife and the crying and moaning from down on the sidewalk. That's what tortures my mind the most. Who knows, maybe there was more than one knife? Skinny Billy could have been acting in self-defense. I was watching Richie almost the whole time, so I never really saw what Burns and Billy were up to. So, basically, I don't know the whole story. If the cops were to ask me what exactly happened, I'd hardly be able to tell them a thing.

So, I'm lying here in my bed, Mickey in the bunk above me, and my little brother, Danny, pushed over into the corner of the room sleeping like a log. I'm asking God for help with all my might. I'm pleading with him to keep that poor fucker alive, please don't let him die, assuming he's not dead already.

Again and again, I go over the events of the night, my mind twitching incessantly like a mouse running around in a shoe box, like a hamster on black beauties. Think, Jack, think, maybe you're forgetting something, some detail that changes everything. Of course, maybe the kid isn't hurt that seriously, I'm just exaggerating it all in my head. Could be Skinny just stabbed him in the thigh—that would explain the bloody knife and our need to get the fuck out of there ASAP. Yeah, it could definitely just be something like that. His friend could have just thought his soul brother was stabbed somewhere else when he saw and felt the blood and overreacted.

As I lie here, I realize I'm still sweating like a pig out to slaughter, and my sheets are drenched. I kinda feel like that pig myself, like what's waiting for me is gonna be pretty goddamned nasty. A shute's gonna open and a sledgehammer is gonna come down on my head and the whole world will become dark. That mouse keeps jumping around inside the box and as much as I keep telling myself that it'll all turn out okay, something else goes right on insisting that this shit is for real, and that I'm living in a genuine nightmare. Sometimes you just know.

There are instincts that exist to protect you, that started with the cavemen and then ran the route through Darwin's evolution and are as natural as a newborn baby. Then there are instincts that live to tell the truth, and those instincts are what's with me now and that truth will be harder to swallow than Squid's shot of gasoline. Not so natural, maybe more supernatural. There's the heaven kind and then there's the ones created by Lucifer himself.

Then suddenly, there's light from the sun creeping into the sky, making its way into our bedroom through our flimsy curtains. I guess I must have dozed off a bit, but I still feel like it was only five minutes ago that I was in the park. My brothers are still sound asleep, and I envy every peaceful breath they exhale. It feels like someone woke me up by tossing me headfirst into a tub of ice water. My eyes have a feeling of being held open with toothpicks. My heart feels like it's about to explode through my chest. The cold sweats are resuming, and the claws of dread once again have me firmly in their grasp.

THE BRONX

It's been a couple of days since it happened. I've been walking around in a catatonic state, not knowing where, how or even who I am. My mother keeps asking me what the hell is wrong with me. I've snapped back at her a few times, telling her to get off my back. That's so unlike me and she knows it. I bet it's worrying the hell out of her. I can get mad at almost anything and anyone in the world but never ma. She senses something's up—my mom is far from a fool—she knows me better than I know myself, and it's not a close race.

Word is out. Everyone has heard by now. *The Daily News* ran a full-page story on page five. Mostly what I hear people saying, adults included, is that 'the niggers deserved it,' and 'they started the whole thing.' Yeah, I guess I keep forgetting to mention that the kid is dead—sixteen years old. According to the *Daily News*, he was a star basketball player and an honor student. My friends joked that they call all these murdered kids honor students and that it's all a bunch of bullshit. 'Honor student my ass' is what they say, laughing along with what they think is a joke.

The street is simultaneously the longest and shortest of grapevines. News travels fast and it travels far. The narrative gets knocked around a bit, but it always defaults to what the like-minded decide it should be. 'The whole truth and nothing but the truth,' is really nothing more than, 'This is what we believe, and we're gonna keep on believing it.'

Nobody I know, from my family members to my Creston Avenue buds know that I was actually there when this big news story happened. Scuttlebutt is that it was the P.S. 20 schoolyard boys from over by Mosholu Park, but everyone is keeping tight with the names that are getting kicked around. Sure, there's some names you can throw out there, but why create a scent for the police bloodhounds to sniff after? Our team won the game but there's lots of times they lose.

That's life and shit happens. Ain't that big a deal in the scheme of things.

To most of my friends, it's just some nigger who got killed by some white boys who were defending the neighborhood. Hey, this is what happens when they come looking for trouble. It's usually the other way around.

Bobby pipes in with "Hey, Jack, remember your friend, Jimmy Welsh, left in the gutter to bleed to death?"

"Yeah, I sure do," is all I can mutter in response.

"Payback's a bitch," says Bobby.

Payback, I'm thinking, what a stupid word. Who's getting paid back for what? Not a soul is getting compensated for anything, everybody's just shelling out money they don't have. What they don't have in money they have in misery times ten. Yeah, you paid them back and now you both have nothing.

Keeping this stuff inside is so hard. I've got an explanation, after all. Well, a justification anyway. I want to tell someone, someone I can trust like my mom, but then I'd be putting the burden on her or them. My ma is too damn decent anyway, she'd want to hold someone accountable. I'm sure she'd say something to the tune of, 'well, if it was self-defense then why don't they just come out and say it, prove their innocence.' She's not one to default to the 'white is right' dictum.

"I don't believe in coincidences," is one of the phrases that Brother Brian repeats all the time. I tell him over and over, and right to his face, that that is a dumbass statement if I ever heard one. Why call it a coincidence in the first place if it isn't one? These heavenly types have their halos shoved up their asses sometimes. Well, there is a bit of a freak coincidence in this evolving drama, and it actually involves my mom. Man, I can't shake that lady no how. Maybe, more ominously, some would call it a twist of fate. I don't like the sound of that but I can sure feel my fate getting all twisted up and it scares me to hell . . .

As for my mom, she came home from the track last night with some interesting news indeed. I was up watching TV when she walked in at close to midnight. Normally, I'm in bed by that time if I'm not working, so she was rightfully suspicious. Just more proof to her that something's up with her second oldest son. Well, I can work the radar on my mom almost as well as she can work it on me, and I can tell she's a bit shook-up. Actually, more than a bit. She takes off her shoes and plops down on the couch next to me. If I could buy my mother anything, I'd get her a new pair of feet, Poor old gal wears those things out every night and every day, Mom proceeds to tell me about her friend, Julie, at work. Says her heart is breaking for the poor woman. Turns out she knew this dead Black kid, knew him well, like family. "James," my mother says, giving this dead kid a name for the first time, at least to me. I hadn't wanted to know his name. I'd have rather just keep on treating him like a fictional being, not an actual person in the flesh.

Ma told me that after they'd hung up their aprons tonight, Julie had cried on her shoulder, wrapped in her arms, for what seemed like an eternity. Now, mom had the Nile River running down her cheeks as she spoke to me. She had to pause for quite awhile before she could compose herself and go on with the rest. I wanted to scream at my mother to stop, to go tell someone else if she needed to spill it so bad, but at the same time I wanted her to hold me in her arms and let me cry just like she had allowed Julie to do. One thing was for sure, I had to keep my cool.

My mother continued on and filled in a lot of blanks I'd have rather left empty. James, all sixteen years of him, had recently moved up to Webster Avenue, a block or so north of Bedford Park. He had a little brother and sister, and his mom was raising them on her lonesome, the same as my mom was doing with us.

People had been saying that there were 'niggers moving into' a building there that was alongside of the Metro North train tracks. It was a huge building, two sides of eight stories each, with a massive court space in the middle of them, that faced out to the tracks, keeping the comings and goings hard to keep up with. Webster Avenue is mostly store fronts and factory buildings, so, to us, it's a no-man's land that we rarely find ourselves in.

The only times I find myself on Webster Avenue are the scarce times I'm going to the Gutter Bowl, the aptly named bowling alley where junkies shoot up in the bathrooms, or to that dive bar, the Drunken Sailor, establishment names that could only float in the Bronx, NY. My point being that people of any shape or form could move into that building without causing much of a stir. If people had known, in fact, I'm sure there would have been a mob with torches outside trying to prevent it.

According to Julie, as relayed by my favorite gal, James's mother had moved as far north as she could afford, to escape the constant crime and burning buildings that made civil existence in points due south near impossible. James was an outlier, a teenage kid who stayed off the streets, stayed in school and stayed alive as a result. Julie had taken him in for a couple of years when he was about 14 years old and was showing signs of getting pulled into 'the life.'

He'd turned the corner and was only recently back with his mother because of their move north.

He had a 'head on his shoulders' and was a starting guard on DeWitt Clinton's basketball team. I know for a cold, hard fact that you don't start for Clinton unless you're an outright stud.

NYC B-Ball is the best there is anywhere on God's earth and Clinton is one of the best of the best in the high school arena.

The two kids with him, both from the old neighborhood, and with cleaner necks than most, were also going to Clinton, and all three were headed down to James' apartment after basketball practice and were gonna spend the night together in the new apartment. They were also on their way to a greatly anticipated Jamaican dinner courtesy of James's mother. In other words, the only thing they did wrong that fateful night was walk down the wrong block. The afros on their heads preaching Black power just made them bigger targets in a white-tinted telescope.

White people prefer their darkies to have straight hair like James Brown—makes them whiter somehow. Like they're trying to conform to what we think they should be. Not that straighter hair would have made a fuck of a difference. Twist of fate for certain, a coincidence or maybe not. I'll leave that up to the man upstairs. It sure as shit won't get sorted out in the crowded freeway that's my head.

So now I know a name and a history. I also know that most of the nonsense I'd been telling myself was utter bullshit. More than anything though, I knew that this secret

I was keeping from my poor, beloved mother, now had arms and legs and a heart. My secret was a human. Not a them-human or an us-human, just a human. We all bleed alike and what hurts us hurts them just the same.

Mary called the house when I wasn't home. My little sister gave me the message in a sing-song lilt that teased me about being in love. Normally, I would have laughed along and given her a big smile and a light punch on her arm, but I kinda just ignored her. I don't like the person I'm turning into, and I barely liked the one before him. A week ago, I'd be jumping for joy on this same news, and I can barely feel anything other than that creeping sadness that won't leave me the fuck alone. I didn't call her back. Man, I love that girl. I love her so much that I'm not gonna drag her into my miserable life. Yup, sleep in the bed you made tough guy. My bed is right there at the bottom of the grave I dug for myself.

THE BRONX

"Yo, Al. Whatcha got that can blast me into another universe and get me as far away as fucking possible from this here spot I'm standing on?"

"Lil Jackie Poo, I miss you, my man! Hey, what up with you whities killing Jamaicans? My brethren, yo! That's some bad voodoo, Jack. You bring it on the Jamaicans, they bring it back. Know what I'm saying, Jack? I know you ain't involved but watch your sweet, little, white ass just the same. You my man and I love you, bro. Yeah, I got what you come lookin' for little brother.

"This shit gonna shoot your ass into another realm. You gonna kiss the sky and walk on water at the same motherfucking time. A-motherfucking-men!"

I hope to high heaven Al, I'm thinking to myself as I walk away. Another realm would be really nice right now. But you can only make reservations for a round trip so the flight back to reality comes with the package. And, oh yeah, my Jamaican friend, I wasn't involved—not at all.

Every day that goes by pushes the story further back in most people's agendas. By now there's new topics of interest, mostly involving themes like the impending encroachment of 'the niggers and spics' on our sacred grounds, an incidence of a fight on the subway, or someone getting ripped off or mugged. When I hear my friends talking about this stuff, I listen tightly so I can carve out some more justification for what had happened right in front of me just a couple of weeks ago. Yeah, I keep repeating to myself, they had it coming. Maybe not this kid in general, but all of them in general. What do you expect to happen when all this other shit is happening around us? Are we supposed to just punk out and let them take over? Used to be we'd stay away from them and vice versa. It was them that changed the rules.

Well, needless to say, my agenda hasn't changed. That night is front and center of every event in my day, small or large, including brushing my teeth and pulling up my socks. To my boys on the corner, it's just about over and done with. Sure, they're still curious about who may have done the stabbing, and they still swap theories and share inside scoops, but it stopped being an obsession (to everyone but me) after just a few days.

Mary, Mary quite contrary, how does your garden grow? With silver knives and baseball bats, and a pretty girl I may never get to know.

It's been too tempting to scratch the itch that tempts me to the schoolyard. I need to be among these guys to get a feel for what they've been up to. I've heard that the cops have been around there asking questions. Detectives including one black one. Any old Irish maid who may have had her nose out the window, pulling on a clothesline or the filter of a cigarette, and got a glimpse of what had transpired, would certainly just keep her mouth shut around the police. The Irish cops and detectives wouldn't be trying too hard to coax it out of her anyway.

The Black sleuth would have a different spin. He'd have the mindset of a man investigating the murder of a human being, as opposed to the perspective of a game warden.

Saturday afternoon on a sunny day that's warm for this time of year. I'm walking instead of riding, letting the labored stroll soothe my fears and tame my guts. They're there, a whole pack of them, taking advantage of the 'Indian Summer' to hang alongside the park across the street from P.S. 20, right smack in the geography from my nightmares. Burns, Billy, and Richie are all present, sitting together on a rail, surrounded by the rest. I get greeted by the guys I know with pleasantries like "Hey McGee, you fucking fag" and "look what the cat dragged in, a little pussy."

Then there's the punches on the arm and the mussing of the hair. The generosity continues with a can of Bud and a Marlboro. I am among friends, second-tier friends, but friends all the same. It's gonna take some doing to edge me towards the center of the hierarchy. I'm gonna have to play the game until I can ease my way in. There's no doubt that the big three are more than a little bit curious with how my ass has been occupied these last few weeks. I'm betting they think there's a tiny sliver of a chance I could squeal, and that's a big enough piece of prospect for them to want to do some poking of their own as it pertains to Jack McGee, their fair or foul comrade in arms.

Nobody wants to be too conspicuous, myself included, but there's some things that need to be said, and there's four of us in this crowd that are itching to drop all pretenses and proceed with the whisperings. So, bide my time I must. Playing the game once more. My life is just one long stream of playing the game. Richie and Skinny are trying to be discreet but I can feel the burn of their eyes moving up and down me. Burns is acting like he could give a flying fuck but I know that's not remotely the case. He cares, man, oh, does he care. Him sitting up there on that park rail in the center of everyone gives Burns the aura of Marlon Brando in *Apocalypse Now*.

At least to me it does. Follow someone into a jungle and you get what the jungle gives. Jack McGee plays the part of Martin Sheen in today's performance.

Maybe I'm being coy or maybe not but after wiggling my way through the pack with few interruptions, I find myself in the midst of my co-conspirators.

Burns, acting like he's just noticed I'm among the adoring, says "Well, if it isn't the indomitable Jack McGee." Like myself, he fashions himself a connoisseur of the English language. He then turns to his girl, whose name I don't remember, and asks her to "give us a few moments here, darling." I immediately wonder if she knows the reason why. Not spilling the beans is hard when you're lying in bed between sessions with time to kill before reengagement.

As if by some dash of black magic everyone other than Richie, Skinny, Burns and me has faded into the background. Now, it's a sci-fi movie I find myself in, surrounded by a force field that excludes all but the four of us. It's not like it's a big surprise as to what they want to hear from me, so I immediately blurt out, albeit it in a hush-hush tone, "I haven't said a word to anyone and I don't plan on telling anyone a fucking thing. No need to worry about me, I'm not saying a word to a fucking soul including my mother. I'm no rat." Anyway, that's God's honest truth. I haven't even told my dog, Charlie.

My statement gets slight nods of approval from Skinny and Burns but doesn't seem to mollify Richie. He's a scary motherfucker and I'm more than a little shook up when he gets right in my face with, "You were barely even there, you pussy motherfucker. What the fuck could you say anyway? You were sitting in the fucking bleachers, and I don't remember seeing you with a pair of binoculars. Besides, you say a fucking word and your dead; that's a motherfucking promise."

"Whoa, whoa, whoa boys," says Burns. "No reason for hostilities. We're all on the same team here. Jack's no pussy."

Dr. Frankenstein has spoken, and the monster shrinks back into his cage. It continues to amaze me that Burns can keep a guy five years older than him in his spell. Richie has said all he's gonna say from this point on. Burns is in charge and the floor is his. I may have been intimidated by Richie at first but now I'm pissed off all to hell. I'm glaring right back at him now and if I have to throw down, I'm ready. In fact, I feel like taking the initiative myself. The prick has hit some bone raw nerves that I've been smothering for weeks.

I've been carrying this shit around like a sack of bricks so even talking to people who actually know is a relief. I do feel like talking some more but I'm not sure what to add to what I've just said. The main points have been addressed, namely that mum's the word and 'I'm no rat,' Now I want to hear what they have to say. They being Burns mostly, whom no doubt will be their lead spokesman. They've been privy to more than I have with the cops snooping around and all.

All the same, to them I'm just a cat that needs to be herded in. *Have no illusions,' Jackie boy, I tell myself, these boys will toss you under the bus to save their own necks if and when push comes to shove—you're not dealing with Bobby, Luke, Sal or Mahoney here. Those guys are the best friends you have in the world—these other guys here are just the best friends I can find at this moment in time.*

It's no surprise when Burns takes the lead. What he's gonna deliver, I'm sure, will be a combination of a lecture and an interrogation, concluding with a set of directions that he'll insist I abide by.

Burns: "This whole thing is pretty simple, Jack. Some nigger who shouldn't have been where he didn't belong got what he deserved. Fact. It happened fast and it'll go away fast. No one needs to say a fucking word to anyone. Keep your mouth shut just like you've been doing and everything will be fine."

Burns is far from finished when Richie pipes in again with, "Yeah, just watch your fucking mouth," but Burns shuts him down immediately with an angry, "Richie, back the fuck off and close your mouth!" The boy talks down to the man, but the boy is hardly a boy, and the man is barely a man when in the company of this boy. The Socrates in me. I'd like to get my hands on a fortune cookie that promises that 'good fortune is coming your way.' I can philosophize about all kinds of things but there's no Zen waiting for me on my motorcycle or any other fucking place under God's blue sky, no time soon, that's for shit sure.

Burns: "The man has been poking around inquiring. They know we hang out here and they're looking for witnesses. They've been knocking on doors and asking around. Best I can tell, nobody knows anything. Other than the four of us that is, and we've got our own asses to protect so you'd have to be a moron to say anything to anyone. Like I said, before we even realize, they'll go away, and it'll be over and done with. The people in this neighborhood don't give a shit about some nigger. Most of them are pretty happy about it, if you ask me. The white cops are the same. They see these animals destroying the city on a daily basis. It's the spook cop we have to worry about. But he's out of his league around here. No one is gonna bend over backwards to help that Black cocksucker."

The whole time, Skinny Billy just stands there not saying a word. As a matter of fact, I don't think he's heard a word Burns has said. I also realize that he never even raised his eyes towards me. Just floating in some detached existence, wrestling with the demons in his noggin. *The poor bastard*, I'm thinking. He killed someone before my eyes and yet I don't see him as this monstrous guy. He's one tortured soul. Two dead parents within a year of each other and his little sister killed by a hit-and-run driver. Living minute to minute in a white rage at the world. It was just a matter of time before a match got lit and he exploded Hiroshima-style.

Burns has paused his speech, and I sit there dumbfounded. I'm not sure what I truly expected when I saw these guys but if there's any remorse I sure as shit don't spot it. Some tension from Richie but that cat is always wired. Burns doesn't seem rattled at all. Billy? Who knows? I guess I'm searching for answers that don't have any questions. Nothing's cleared up here, no resolutions for my heart and mind to be had. Back to square one. Back to that awful night, back to my deep, dark hole.

Burns back on the podium: "So, Jack, this is the deal. Take some wisdom from the Emerald Isle—whatever you say, say nothing. Even if they suspected us, they have no proof. No confession, no crime. Keep your mouth tight as a clam and we'll do the same. Then, like I said, it all goes away. You good?"

"Yeah, man, of course I'm good. Don't give it a second thought."

"I never doubted you for a second, Jackie boy."

Burns is a master manipulator. He's making sure that I know I'm in as big as he is, that I have as much to lose as the rest of them. We're never going to share the same narrative but that matters little to him. As far as he's concerned, there's only one account and it's his to own and distribute.

The rap session is over, and I fade back into the crowd. The Stones are playing in a boombox in the background. "Sympathy for the Devil," as one would expect for such an occasion. 'Pleased to meet you, hope you guess my name,' I think I have it figured out, Mick. I even know where the devil lives. A few quick good-byes and I skedaddle. Shuffling off to Buffalo. Green grass and high tides forever.

THE BRONX

There's no escaping my mother. She knows something's up. Word travels and whispers echo and therein they multiply. People have heard things and they're talking; they may even be talking about mom's little boy. That cute little wiseass who can make anyone laugh, but who now seems bound to wipe the smile from his ma's Irish eyes.

My mother's not the only one who's catching the smell of a dead fish off of me. Mickey sleeps four feet above me and he's as savvy as any Bronxman tends to be. He can hear me tossing and turning and getting up constantly to take a leak that I don't need to take. I'm not sure if he's connected the dots or what he suspects or doesn't suspect. According to Burns, nobody knows nothing. Mickey doesn't seem to be taking any chances, so he's got my group of friends, the tier one crew, playing coy and checking in on him. Not washing my hair and wearing the same clothes day in and day out can check a lot of boxes in an insanity test.

Bobby and Lukie, Mahoney and TC, Roger Dodger and Blind Baby, all poking without pressing in too far. Even Sal and Knucks and a few others. All of them just making sure if I'm alright and reminding me that they have my back. Always. I still haven't uttered a single word to any of them about what transpired that night. Oh man, let me tell you, it's goddamned hard not to. It would be such a relief. But you know what they say about that genie in the bottle.

The party of well-wishers extends beyond my closest pals. Mary has continued to call despite my inability, or decency, to ring her back. Only a madman would let that gal fade away. Ma has called up Brother Brian once again and is talking to my Uncle Joe and Duke as well about coming to talk to me. I will make sure I'm not available. What the hell would I say to them?

It's hardly a jovial time in my life but I'm still around some of the funniest fuckers to ever grace mankind. So, it's still possible for me to travel back into the light, remove my mask, and have a few chuckles. Thank God for the idiotic genius that constitutes my boy, Sal. He seemingly has accomplished the most amazing feat of his young life by memorizing the words to the Stones's masterpiece "Star Star." If the lad could sing, I'd be fighting to get him on the *Tonight Show with Johnny Carson*. He's so proud of his master stroke that he barely comes up for air when reciting the tune. He repeated the lyrics to me twice in a row to make sure I didn't think the first time was a fluke.

Sal: "Yeah, Ali McGraw got mad with you, for given' head to Steve McQueen, yeah, you and me, we make a pretty pair, fallin' through the silver screen. Honey, I'm open to anything, I don't know where to draw the line, yeah, I'll make bets that you're gonna get John Wayne before he dies . . ."

At this point, on his second go, I finally interrupted, knowing the rest of the song is just a bunch of 'starfuckers,' etc. Sal is no Rico Caruso, and his Ginny infused Bronx accent has the local rats running for cover, so it's a personal act of mercy when I cut him off.

Me: "Holy shit, Sal! I swear to the almighty that I didn't think it was possible. For Christ's sake, I wouldn't have bet that you could memorize the average nursery rhyme. I'd even bet that there's no fucking way you can say the Our Father of Hail Mary beginning to end. And assuming you even have one, I'm 100% sure you don't know your Social Security number, or even the name of your kindergarten teacher. Forget the Yankees starting line-up. If I had the scientific talent, I'd freeze your brain at this moment in time and give your future a fighting chance."

THE BRONX

I'm so torn by what's going through my mind, like my nut's about as stable as a schizophrenic squirrel's. That poor son of a bitch lying in a box under six feet of dirt, and his

343

mother's life shattered to pieces. I think of my own mother's grief if the same thing happened to one of her kids. Sure, my mom also has my dad's death in her past, but I'd wager that the kid's mother has her own trail of agony dating way back. We're all just humans, man, dead or alive. We're all just on the same minute by minute struggle to get through life. Then, in the flash of a second, all those hardships are wiped from the slate because you're no longer getting through life because you're stone fucking dead, whether you're still breathing or not.

Even weirder, I kinda feel the same way about Billy, which is stupid, I know. What a life he's had, and his struggles just got added to. He was never gonna be the same kid he was just a few years back, and now he's even going to be a worse version of that messed up, broken shell, with the tormented soul. The way I've described him is like he doesn't have a conscience, but that's nonsense. I know in my heart that he's not walking around feeling good about what he did. The sweet taste of revenge can leave a bitter after taste. One of my favorite books of all time is the *Count of Monte Cristo*, but it probably teaches one of the worst lessons you can ever be taught. Basically, the Count gets fucked over royally but eventually manages to spring himself and begin the process of exacting revenge. In the end, every last bastard that did him wrong is skewered like a fat pig with an apple in its mouth, and the count basks in the most gratifying of glory. Hey kids watching from home, give it a try. Whack your sister over the head with a hammer. It'll feel so nice, and she'll get taught the lesson she so desperately needs. She won't be touching your stuff ever again.

My only defense against insanity these miserable fucking days is to pray to God. In what shape, manner or form I can't tell you, but I do believe there's someone or something on the other end of the line. Maybe my dad's working the switchboard for God sometimes when I dial in. So, I'm making yet another pact with God. I'm not saying God has spoken to me but I'm the one begging for penance, not him. I also think it's something my old man would sign off on. An eye for an eye works more ways than one. I may have an eye to donate. We'll have to wait and see. It won't be too long of a period of suspense.

The deal I've come up with is this. I'm gonna give God a chance to set things straight by serving myself up for reconciliation. It's his choice to make. All I'm asking in return is for him to cut me loose one way or the other. If he decides to keep me around, he's gotta free my conscience and pull the dagger from my heart. Then I'll know afterwards if I can continue on, knowing I did the best I could have under the circumstances.

So, this is what I've come up with. Later tonight, when the streets are mostly vacant and the devil has the upper hand, I'm heading southbound on the heels of my Chuck Taylor's. I will walk straight into that lion's den where the pale of skin is neither plentiful or wanted. South of Tremont Avenue, or even deeper into the jungle where burnt out buildings outnumber the ones still standing two to one. Where after ten o'clock on a weeknight the only people on the streets are the ones who are up to bad things. I'm too young looking to be taken for an undercover cop so no force field there. I'll be the three-legged gazelle on the tundra who's separated from the pack.

If they take me down the score will be even. One of ours for one of theirs. I won't even put up a fight. Like I said, God will be filling in the scoresheet. Misery multiplied but the scale of justice firmly balanced. An eye for an eye, a honky for a nigger, and so on and so on the band plays "Waltzing Matilda." After the game's been played, God can jot down the final stats and call it a draw. I'm pretty sure God doesn't differentiate between black and white so he can scratch out the details that don't matter.

I'm sure all of this sounds like an asinine proposition to the levelheaded, but to me it's the only choice I have right now. Those other potential options, like ratting to the cops, or putting a bullet in my head just ain't gonna happen. I'm paving my own road to perdition.

Off I go into the wild, dark yonder. Gotta make the trip on foot because if I was to try and make it part of the way on my bike, I'd quickly run out of roads that would protect my unattended black and gold Triumph for more than a few minutes. Might as well leave it to Mickey or one of my pals if this thing goes down in an ugly kind of way. The warmth of the past few evenings is gone and I'm freezing my ass off. It doesn't help that all I have on is a T-shirt, part of my penance I tell myself. A nice crisp white one fresh from the laundromat that'll look good in the crime scene photos, assuming any of the white fabric survives the drenching.

Down the Grand Concourse, Kingsbridge Road, Fordham Road, Tremont Road and so on.

I keep heading south with my ultimate destination being in the 160s where the shit really gets crazy. Then I'll hang a few blocks east or west into the netherlands where the landscape changes dramatically from the mostly intact boulevard of the Grand Concourse. The buildings I pass are actually pretty nice for the Bronx with courtyards and fancy figures, like gargoyles and such, carved into the upper regions of the apartment buildings. Babe Ruth and some of the other Yankees used to call these places home back in the days when the Bronx was the envy of the five boroughs. Fuckers are flipping over in their graves now, I bet.

The streets are mostly empty this time of day and the few passersby I encounter give me that sideways glance that asks, *what the hell you doing down here, Whitey*? Something about the number 169 nudges me to pull a right and head west, I think, down towards Jerome Avenue, or whatever streets await me over there. I don't have to go more than a block before the chill starts running up my spine. 'These har,' are some bad parts, the urban cowboy might say. I know these streets a bit from going to Yankee games all these years. Little punks, me and my crew, testing ourselves by venturing into them just for a thrill.

Now the buildings start to disappear and the empty lots increase. I can see and smell garbage cans burning in the night to keep the junkies and the badass motherfuckers warm. No love for the uptowners here, no sir, none at all. It shouldn't take long for me to get sniffed out as 'one of these is not like the others,' a la Big Bird and his pals on Sesame Street. I try to figure out if it makes sense to jumpstart the procedure by yelling "niggers!" into the biggest pack I can find. Get the shit over with and take a trip up to visit my dad. Sorry, St. Pete, I won't be bringing along any Irish whiskey.

I'm close enough now to the glow of a fire blazing from an ashcan with seven or eight of the Zulu Nation, or whatever whiteboy killing, gangster party they belong to. I keep walking in a beeline toward the mess of them. Oh yeah, here comes the sacrificial lamb. I imagine I appear like an apparition, like Moses coming down the mountain with the Ten Commandments. Thou shalt not kill, and that other stuff no one seems to pay attention to these days.

The noise from behind the fire quiets down, the shitty ghetto music from the boombox gets lowered. A beer bottle crashes at my feet but still I walk on. I'm within twenty feet or so now and I can glimpse the looks of bewilderment on their faces. Yeah, maybe I'm just some solitary body but the whole situation is just too fucking weird for them not to be spooked. Scary ass motherfuckers who are motherfucking scared. Man, even at my point of reckoning I am still one clever individual. Get this, I don't feel spooked at all, not even nervous. Maybe I get lucky and it's over with fast. Then the score is even with one bad guy for one good guy, or one good guy for one bad guy, or even two good guys for no good reason at all.

Then, out of nowhere, God makes his call. Jack McGee shall live. A dark-colored sedan which has just had a flashing cherry slapped on top of it, skids onto the scene. The headlights are beyond blinding, Doors open and slam and it's not Spock and Kirk that get out of this spaceship but two undercover cops. These two aren't in uniform, and don't have the customary mustaches that dominate the faces of the patrol men in blue.

Rather, they're scraggly and beat-up looking, with long, wild hair and patchy beards, and clothes that the Salvation Army would reject if you tried donating them. Part-time badass police and part-time movie actors in a cowboys and Indians flick. John Wayne and his right-hand man scoping out the Comanches, waiting to pounce.

In the meantime, the crowd at the fire has scattered like rats. If they weren't dealing drugs, it's still a better than 50/50 chance that there's a warrant out for their arrest. These dudes are as streetwise as they come and they know that the fuzz ain't up for a game of hide-and-seek, so scooting off is an easy decision to make. They'll be back at the fire doing what they were doing when the dust clears, and the three whiteboys have moved on.

The bigger of the two cops grabs my shirt just below my neck and pulls me towards him like I'm filled with feathers. Strong as an ox, this motherfucker, and his hand seems big enough to cover my whole chest. I can smell alcohol on his breath as he pulls my face in close to his.

They say booze is liquid courage, but I bet this guy has plenty of courage without it. He screams in my mug, "What the hell are you thinking? You realize that these fucks would have ate you fucking alive? We would have found your bones in that can over there tomorrow after the stink of your melted body started to piss off the natives. You fucking out of your mind, you stupid little prick? Please beg tell me who the hell are you and what in god's name you're doing in this shithole of a neighborhood at this time of the day?"

I looked at him with what I suspect was a bewildered, glassy-eyed stare, and proceeded to give him my name, age, and address. The other plainclothes had drifted into the background. But I wasn't able to come up with answers to his questions. What was I doing here? Oh, I witnessed some Black kid get murdered, and I figured this was a good way to get it off my chest without having to squeal on anyone. To answer his questions, I was gonna have to come up with some stupid shit that was even crazier than the real reason he found me where he did. I mumbled some nonsense about having a fight with my mother and then taking a walk to clear my head and not paying attention to how far I walked and where I had walked to. Even after only a few minutes back from the dead, Jack McGee can still rattle off a bullshit story like nobody you know.

Mr. Badass was obviously not buying it, nor did he seem to want to know anyway. He let me keep it at that. His partner, the other longhair, then yelled over, "Hey George, you never gave me a chance to win the bet. I said he'd be dead in five minutes, but you barely waited a minute."

It seems I have a penchant for getting cops in patrol cars, marked or unmarked, to bet dinner on my demise, or not.

I didn't have to walk home. The pair of lifesavers took pity on me and gave me a lift. By this point the lack of a jacket in the brisk night air had gotten the better of me. I was shivering like an alley cat in a snowstorm.

On the ride home up the Concourse, Officer George Sullivan, (he informed me as to his last name), quizzed me on where I went to school and what I wanted to do with my life. He told me that I needed to make good on my tenth life being that the other nine had probably been used up in that one fell swoop. I thanked both of them for basically saving my life and asked them what I could do to repay them. The other cop, whose name I still did not know, told me I could settle up by, 'getting your ass out of the car and keeping your nose clean.' Easy enough, mission accomplished. But George had a bit more to say. These big, burly types can surprise you with their soft sides.

So, yet another chapter in the ongoing saga of my life where a wise male, many years my senior, distills solid, well-meant advice which I will more than likely choose to ignore. The most recent of my angels gives me the vibe of James Cagney in *Angels with Dirty Faces* but with facial hair.

Street hardened but with a touch or two of genuine heartfelt kindness. Except, if you really think about it, he's really more like Pat O'Brien, the kid who got over the same fence that Rocky Sullivan did not. There's God in my head again, tossing the Sullivan connection into the mix like I'd thought about it beforehand, which I did not. I'm the Bowery Bum kid who asks, 'say it ain't so "fodder," Rocky didn't die yella?' 'I'm afraid so boys, he did . . . ,' replies Pat O'Brien the priest. So Rocky Sullivan had a heart of gold after all which makes two Sullivans with the same. Officer Sullivan begins to speak, much to the irritation of his partner what's-his-name, who gets out of the patrol car to smoke a cancer stick, making sure to slam the door for emphasis.

Sullivan doesn't seem to even notice, and the look in his eyes keeps me in the movie realm, only now he's Paul Newman in *Cool Hand Luke*. I realize I'm going a bit overboard with all these movie references, but it does seem like I'm living in a movie lately with no control of the script. His coolness has the effect of calming me down considerably and I'm no longer shaking like a leaf. I'm ready, at least in the present, to soak up his wisdom.

"Listen Jack," he goes on, "I didn't mean to come at you like that, it just drove me crazy that you could do something so insane. Look, I'm gonna let you slide on your reasons for doing it, but I know I'm not taking a flier here when I think something is seriously fucking with your mind. That was a suicide mission, no doubt about it. Whatever it is, you need to do something about it before you end up dead. And I'm no dummy, I can tell right off the bat that you're no idiot. So, I can guess, guess, guess what it is that's eating you alive, whether it's some girl or a D-minus on your last history test, but whatever it is won't matter, What will matter is what you do about it. Go to confession for Christ sake or go see a therapist. Do something is all I'm asking. You're running out of wildcards, kid. If I did toss out a guess, I'd say it's something serious, something you really need to get off your chest. I'm asking you to do me a favor here, Jack. Please talk to someone you can trust, and don't do anything stupid in the meantime. I'm gonna leave you with my phone numbers, both at home and at the precinct house. The very next time something screwy gets into your head, you call me, and I'll drop whatever I'm doing and come help. You remind me of my little brother, a really smart kid who did something really stupid and paid a big price.

"Have you ever watched that movie, *Angels with Dirty Faces*? I'm the one who got over the fence. Never mind, that's a different story for another time. Maybe I could have done something for my brother, but I didn't. At least, I can feel like I did something this time. Just get home in your warm, safe bed and move your brain out of crazy town, thank fucking God that you're still here you dumb stubborn mick. I still can hardly believe what my eyes were seeing on that street a half an hour ago. See ya, kid, get some rest. I mean it about you calling me whenever. It's weird, kid but I feel like I know you."

A lot of coincidences just now with the *Angels with Dirty Faces* crisscross, and that stuff about his kid brother. Yeah, okay Brother Brian, there are no coincidences, blah, blah, blah. One has to wonder, how many saints does it take to save one Jack McGee? I didn't call for help, but God still sent the cavalry. Only an ingrate wouldn't recognize that, 'What matters is what you do about it.' Okay, my boy, do something then. Something different than what you've already been doing, which is clearly not fucking working.

The next morning, I woke up feeling better than I had for weeks. Maybe that test I put myself through really solved the problem. God was going to let me off the hook. I didn't kill that kid, and I couldn't have done anything to stop it. Me and the man upstairs are square, and now I can finally get back to living. Like Dylan says, "if you ain't busy living, you're busy dying." Man, I was pretty busy in the latter category for a damn long stretch.

I went to bed with a few inches of city grime starched on me, so I go to town in the shower, washing my hair and my entire body, every crack and crevice, three times or more. Behold the beauty of modern plumbing and real water pressure, unlike our old dump of an apartment where a trickle was more than you could hope for. A new set of clean clothes, the duplicate style of dungarees and a white T-shirt, and I'm ready to take on the world. Free at last, free at last, God Almighty, I'm free at last. Mom is none the wiser to my recent adventures, so all is copacetic there.

Right after breakfast I worked out like a madman. Weights, push-ups, pull-ups and even a three-mile run which really did me in. Gotta get back in killer shape. I have some big plans with this new lease on life, so I gotta keep moving. I'm even going to lob a call into Mary today.

Getting that girl back in my life will be a game changer. Then I'll get back on the scholarly path and swap some of the garbage in my head for bonafide smarts. Finally, get serious about the boxing gym and enter the Golden Gloves. Maybe even stop cursing so much. The sky's the limit and I'm gonna get a pilot's license to the clouds. You know, the figurative kind, like the ones Jimi Hendrix excuses himself to touch.

My boys from the corner take me back with open arms, no questions asked. There basically is no corner left so the meeting house and social center has pretty much relocated to the Alibi.

Crazy how quick I get back to being pissed off at the Ricans for invading and taking over our corner. Yeah, again, OUR corner. Just came down to numbers and theirs just kept rising while ours have been on a steady decline. That doesn't keep me from wanting to go down there and light the fucking place on fire. My transformation into Ghandi or MLK is definitely going to encounter some major hurdles. My path to Zen, of the motorcycle version, or any other for that matter, will be bumpy as all get out.

Back to the home base, surrounded by my best friends in the galaxy, laughing and busting balls. When I'm behind the stick the giggles are that much better. Things are just getting better and better for the kid, the kid being *moi*, Jack fucking McGee. Sorry Dad, eliminating the cursing is going to take time but I'll keep working at it.

Just when you think it's safe to go back in the water . . .

Chapter 33

A Death Too Alive to Go
Quietly into the Night

Alas, my stay in Eden was short lived. That damn snake has fooled me again. It's no more than a couple of days and the horde of ghosts are back in my nightmares. There are different versions of that awful night on Mosholu Parkway, and they all result in me screaming in my sleep and waking up drenched in sweat. My little brother pulls his pillow over his head in terror, but Mickey is either too irritated or too alarmed to keep quiet. He'll start with a, 'will you shut the fuck up, Jack,' but follow it up with a 'you okay, Jack.' I couldn't ask for a better big brother; I also can't figure out how to respond so I tell him I'm alright and it was just some stupid dream. Keep dreaming boy. Please God, take these friggin' nightmares away before they completely do me in. I thought we had a deal but clearly, I misunderstood. Can we revisit this?

Walk on, one foot in front of the other, one moment in time to the next. It's no stroll in the park, more like climbing up the Empire State building with a one-hundred-pound pack on my back. I'm a walking powder keg, but one that explodes on my insides, over and over and over again. I think the rest of the world is safe. Most of my life has been filled with the rage of getting even with 'them,' 'those,' and everyone in between. Now, I Ping-Pong from not wanting to hurt a fly to being enraged at the world for landing me in this hell of an existence. Offing myself doesn't seem like a bad idea at all but I could never do that to my mother. Be a man, I keep repeating to myself. Stop being a crybaby and feeling sorry for yourself. I may pass on swatting the next fly that buzzes by my head, but I doubt I'll be as kind to the next roach or water bug that ambles near the sole of my Converses. Some things do need to be stepped on.

Like figuring out who and what is the dilemma challenging this boy. Yeah, "boy." I was getting to a point in my life where I was ready to start using the word 'man' instead. One step forward . . .

I need to talk to someone. I can't stand it anymore. Someone I can trust. Someone wise enough to show me the way. Someone to cut the chains and release me. Someone to tell me it's gonna be alright. Someone to tell me what I should or shouldn't do. Someone tough and strong and smart. Someone like my mom.

As for the matter of the dead Black kid, things have quieted down considerably. It doesn't seem like the heat is on. The trail is as cold as an apartment in a building with an Albanian landlord. My friends have stopped talking about it. I haven't even heard my mother mention her friend, Julie, from work in days. The only place the story is getting traction is on the inside of my head.

I've made up my mind and I'm fully committed to spilling the beans to mom. How and when are what I need to figure out. But it has to be soon, as in ASAP. The way I see it is that I'm getting a chance to appeal the sentence that sent me to this swell resort on the banks of the river Hades. I'll state my case and prove my innocence and get a free pass to sanity, courtesy of my mother. That's the plan anyway, 'The best laid plans of mice and men,' and so on. I've hatched a plan or two in my life that has actually worked, so there's better than a zero chance this one will too.

"Hey, Ma, can we talk?"

"Sure, Jack, what's up?"

"I mean really talk, Ma."

"Okay, so really talk then, I'm all ears."

"Somewhere private. Like where nobody can hear us."

"Well then, let's take a walk. Even your little brother and sisters won't hear us until we're at least a few blocks away."

"I love you, Ma."

"I love you too, Jack. Always have, always will."

"Just one thing Ma. You have to promise, solemnly swear in fact, not to ever tell a soul what I'm about to tell you."

"When have you known me to do otherwise?"

Out of paranoia, I waited until we were well out of earshot of every living being imaginable before uttering a word. Well, my words at first were just ers and ums anyway. People from the Bronx seem to have a supernatural ability to overhear tidbits of conversations from distances that you wouldn't think possible, so 'well out of earshot' is a relative term. Then they spin their own version of what they think they heard and turn it into something drastically different. One would think that a conversation between a mother and her son as they strolled the streets of the Bronx would be of little interest to the average passerby but never underestimate the desire of some people to nose into your business.

My mom was patient and allowed me plenty of time to find my footings. She knew, without question, that I wouldn't have dragged her along for something insignificant. I imagine she was thinking I banged up some chick or had enlisted in the Marine Corp or had dug myself a hole elsewhere. Maybe, I was into the local bookie for a couple of grand? This was not to be some idle bullshit or an easily repaired problem. Money or a wedding ring wouldn't be much assistance here.

We walked a couple of blocks without me saying anything. Yeah, I had second thoughts. Third and fourth as well. Maybe just bag the whole thing? Tell her I changed my mind, and I'd tell her some other time. Tell her it was really nothing earth shattering, and I'd deal with it on my own. But, no man, this needed to come out and I needed to find the balls to get it out. I had the best audience in the world to tell it to.

Before I even realized it, we were zeroed in on an empty park bench that was sitting all by itself at the far end of Mosholu Parkway. Not only was it empty but it was the only one there. It's not like it's a park-ish location, sitting on a triangle of mangy grass in the middle of two intersecting roads, and close enough to the overhead el train to hit it with a rock on a half-ass toss.

I courteously allowed my mother to sit first. Had I not she probably would have smacked me in the back of the head. My ma may be new age in some regards, but she's a stickler on tradition and proper etiquette. She was pleased that I acted accordingly. I may not be a budding Dale

Carnegie, but the gal has certainly taught me a thing or two about common decency along the way.

Then I spilled my guts and spilled them some more. I kept spilling them until I spilled every last detail I remembered from that night. It was like I was lying on a hospital bed and attached tubes were draining the poison from my veins.

My ma soaked up every word without interrupting me. I could tell that it wasn't easy for her to do. She did, however, need to pull some tissues from her pocketbook to stem the stream of the tears that flowed down her cheeks. If a devil had appeared on my shoulder during my confession, Ma would have produced an angel that would have kicked its ass upside and down. You can bet that she hated what she was hearing but never once during my exorcism did her heart know anything but forgiveness and love for her little boy. I believe that with all certainty.

When we rose from the bench and stood facing each other she hugged me fiercely, tears still flowing like a flooded river over a broken dam, down her magnificent face.

"I love you, Jack. I'm sorry this happened to you."

"I love you too, Ma, but remember, mums the word."

"Sure, honey, I gave you my promise. I won't tell anyone anything unless you give me permission otherwise. I'm just happy that you told me at all."

Permission otherwise? What the hell was she talking about? I left it at that but I also knew we weren't done talking about this. No one and done here. No, sir. One's not done, and don't you run until we've finished all the fun. The Irish poet in me searching for wittiness to save his soul. Well, this was no laughing matter, but it was a joke to think it would end here.

So, the big blue and green globe continues to twirl, but unlike *As the World Turns*, this is no soap opera. There won't be any knight in shining armor to save my ass. No lucky spin of the wheel or a white horse to catch a ride on. A lucky seven will be hard to come by and there are no aces in the deck, never mind in the hole. So, what's a boy to do?

Sure, I feel relieved having talked about it but that feeling of dread that has nagged at me won't be taking the midnight train to Georgia any time soon, I keep asking myself if what I shared with my mother was a 'confession?' Each time the quick answer is, 'what do I have to confess to?' I wasn't the one doing the stabbing. But if you do call it a confession then that's even worse because then I'm admitting I did something wrong. Keeping my clam shut can't be wrong because if I started singing that would violate everything I thought I knew about myself and how wrong is that? As wrong as wrong can be, I'll tell ya that. Oh yeah, and then some.

There's a kid dead, a Black kid. No, just a kid. A kid who won't go away and leave me in peace. I feel him looking down at me, watching and waiting for me to right his wrong; I try to tell him that there's nothing I can do but he just ignores me. He just keeps coming back. 'The Tell-Tale Heart' keeps beating. Almighty God-no-no! They heard! They suspected! They knew! They were making a mockery of my horror!

Okay enough! Change the subject! Did you know that Edgar Allen Poe once lived in the Bronx? You don't believe me? Well, his old house is right there in the middle of Poe Park on the Grand Concourse and Kingsbridge Road. Right in the middle of hundreds of half naked, drunk and high, Puerto Ricans come a hot Saturday night in the summer. If they weren't comfortable fornicating in the great outdoors, they'd probably break in and use old EAP's former bed for that very same purpose. Not something I haven't thought about myself, to be honest.

You can't hold off the inevitable just by wishing it away, no more than you can whitewash your conscience.

Chapter 34

A Truth Too Short

My interactions with my mom are really weird and uncomfortable; I can tell she wants something more from me. Something else that can convince her that her son is the man his dead father would want him to be. Everything is different between us. No casual la-di-dahs. Not a single exchange that somehow begs for something more. "Something" is the key word here, but that 'something' remains undefined and elusive, and not available to me.

Brother Brian surprised me at the bar. Came in by himself, so I joked that he was aspiring to be the perfect Bronx Irish husband who does his best thinking in gin mills, well out of the grasp of his wife. The guy has this beautiful, hearty laugh that makes people like him on the spot. He passed the Alibi membership interview without having to say a word.

It was pretty busy, and the former man of cloth engaged in conversation with those around him while I tended to my business. I poked my head into the assemblage once or twice to warn a couple of the gals that the handsome Irishman was spoken for and that they should have grabbed him a year ago when they still had a chance. That Irish lilt can get a woman naked without taking her clothes off, in her own mind anyway. Then, you start to notice things like an extra-opened button on a blouse or a mysteriously unclasped snap on a pair of jeans.

It was only a matter of time before Brother Brian got me to his lonesome. He told me that he'd spoken to my mother, and she thought that maybe there was something I'd like to talk to him about. He said he had no idea what it might be but that whatever it was he'd love to help. I believed him, my mom had kept her word. Well, kinda anyway. Before he left, breaking the hearts of the lasses, I agreed to swing by the Community Center sometime in the next couple of days. Both of us, I'm sure, had strong doubts about that actually happening.

Another couple of days of the weirdness with my mom has drawn me to the edge. The questions just keep swirling in my head. I don't know much other than that I can't keep going on like this. If you keep doing what you did, you'll keep getting what you got. I can't remember if it was Brother Brian or Duke or my Uncle Joe who told me that but that saying makes a genius out of one of them. My strategy is to do nothing about my problems and just hope they go away. They don't go away though, they multiply.

Well, I certainly surprised myself by showing up at the Bedford Park Community Center on a fine, sunny, Tuesday morning, but I bet it was even more astounding to my Irish mentor. To add to the surreal nature of the experience it wasn't Brother Brian (look, at this point I'm not gonna refer to him as anything other than that no matter how many times he insists I do—he simply has to be Brother Brian to me. I just can't explain it and won't try to), who greeted me when I walked in but that super smooth man of ebony, Duke from the racetrack.

My first instinct was that it was an ambush, but I knew that Duke had no idea I was coming there that day, so it made zero sense that he'd been waiting in the wings for me. I was certainly taken aback by his presence, but he acted like my showing up was as natural as the morning mist. "Hey kiddo," he said, "nice to see you." Then he put up his two hands in the boxer's stance and took a couple of playful jabs at me. My nervousness left me, and a smile beamed across my mug. Then Duke grabbed me in a hug and mussed my head like I was his very own kid. To be perfectly honest, at that moment I wished I was.

The deal was this. Duke and Brother Brian had become pals. Mostly because of my mother but also because of me. They say kindred souls can magically come together just by being of the same vibe. Coincidence? Don't get me started on that shit again.

What Brother Brian and Duke have most in common is that they're givers. They like people and want to help them, plain and simple. Duke had told Brother Brian how much he admired what he was doing to serve his community. He also threw in one of those, 'let me know if there's anything I can do to help.' You see, Duke is a man of tremendous energy and a heart of pure gold who has some free time during the day. Brother Brian thought about it for maybe half a second and replied, ". . . there just may be at that."

Brother Brian explained to Duke that the people coming into the center for assistance with rent relief, landlord complaints, or just questions about how they could properly feed their kids, were of all stripes and colors. Most of the staff was white, hence the conflict. Brother Brian told Duke that it would be reassuring for the Black people to have an actual Black man they could confide in. Mistrust of the opposite race is natural when you consider the history.

Yeah, this is Jack McGee talking, The same kid who would have told you that blacks (and I wouldn't have used that term) were dumb and lazy, not a helluva long time ago.

So, Duke was signed up for a rate of zero dollars an hour for fifteen hours or so a week. That's how he came to be here and that's why he was standing in front of me at this exact moment in time. From the corner of my eye, I saw Brother Brian watching our interaction with an ear-to-ear grin.

When Duke volunteers he bounces around lending a hand wherever help is needed.

Brother Brian was in the middle of a consultation, so he asked me to hang loose for a bit and maybe follow Duke around while he did whatever he did. The Center provides a daily lunch for the neighborhood's seniors and before I knew it, I was buttering roll after roll for the expected guests. There was a lot of hustle and bustle in the cafeteria-style kitchen and a ton of work to do to get ready, but everyone seemed pleasant and happy. They were also volunteers. Not the dog-eat-dog world I was used to. Maybe God was telling me that if I volunteered here once a week, I could square away the last bit of the tab that was outstanding. Yeah, why not? It was just like the man upstairs was whispering to me that there was just a little bit more from me that needed to be done and then all would be copacetic between us, and that I could get on with my life without the ghosts following me. If you put that contract in front of me, I'll sign it right here and now and with my best penmanship.

I snagged a free lunch out of the deal and sat next to a one-legged veteran of World War I. The old guy's name was Dempsey, and he was a hoot. He kept telling me that when lunch was over, and if I'd be kind enough to push his wheelchair, he'd take me over to Madden's pub for a couple of beers. Duke, who was sitting right across from us, couldn't stifle his laughs. Here I was with a bunch of old people having the time of my life.

Brother Brian was busy as hell and kept pleading for my patience to stick around. If I started to lose my nerve, I'd have plenty of excuses to bolt, that's for sure, but I think I almost wanted to talk to him more than he wanted to talk to me. Besides, hanging with Duke was medicine. The man has a certain magic about him that had me as calm and peaceful as I'd been for months. I called back upstairs for confirmation that me and God were square because it certainly was feeling that way. Maybe he'd shoot me some sign like a butterfly in an alleyway or a flower growing in the cracks of a sidewalk. As usual he just kept me on hold, as per his habit.

Towards the end of the day when things calmed down, Brother Brian came out of his office to call me in. He asked me if I minded Duke sitting in and I told him that of course I didn't mind. Two geniuses are better than one was my way of thinking.

The three of us sat down. I was feeling pretty comfortable in fact, not jittery or apprehensive at all. I can't really explain it other than that it just felt right. I wasn't even sure exactly why I was there or what I expected from our meeting. Something had gotten me here and I wasn't going to question it. No doubt my mother had told them something significant was going on with me, but I remained sure that she'd kept the details to herself.

Brother Brian took the lead by starting with why he thought it made sense for Duke to be there with us. He said that he could identify with me as if he was an older brother or cousin, but that he'd never been a father and couldn't provide the same wisdom that came with being one. Not only was Duke a parent, he said, but he was a damn good one, and one of the wisest men he knew to exist on Mother Earth.

"So, what's up, Jack? What is it that's got your mother worrying so much about you? You know you're in a room with two men who you can trust. Two men who want to help. Share what you're comfortable sharing, not a word more." Duke stayed quiet. Cooler than cool, keeping the pressure off me. Letting me ease into whatever it was I wanted or needed to say.

The thing was, I'm not sure what it was I wanted or needed to say. That is, until I said it. Then I said it some more, and some more, and then I just kept going until I'd said it all. It was like I was Linda Blair in *The Exorcist* and someone else was doing the talking for me. Like a burst pipe needing to gush until it ran out of water. The whole time these two men listened without interceding. There were no interruptions to judge, or condemn, to preach, or to correct. Just two solemn faces displaying little emotion. I was going to have my say and they were going to make sure I did. They hadn't forced a word out of me. They weren't the forcing type.

Then the three-way conversation began. One I never imagined I'd be part and parcel too. So far, it was a day of small miracles but even the Good Lord has limits on how much magic he'll spin.

Brother B: "That's quite the story, Jack. I'm immensely proud of you for sharing it. I certainly understand your hesitation. I know it wasn't easy."

Duke: "God bless you, son, you did the right thing. A burden shared is a burden halved. From this point on, we're in this together. But let me make one thing absolutely clear—we do nothing from this point on without your say so. Got it, kid?"

Me: "Yes, sir, I do. Thank you both for letting me get that off my chest. I'm not sure what to do next. I need some time to think about it. You guys cool with that?"

Duke: "100 percent, Jack."

Brother B: "I don't think I'm quite at your mother's stature, but I'm pretty damn good at keeping things in confidence. It stays between us. Like I said, Jack, I'm damn proud of you."

Another quick consultation with the man upstairs. We even now? C'mon, we have to be square? Can I please get an answer? Hello? Damn guy never answers his phone.

Yeah, it sure felt nice to unburden myself yet again. What a relief. Whew, time to move on. But I can't. I still feel sick to my stomach. This shit is never going to end, and I'll never ever be good ol' Jack McGee again. I'm tired, man, I'm just so fucking tired.

A day goes by, and I find myself back at the Community Center talking to Brother Brian.

He can tell just by looking at me that all is not right in my world. I'm the same kid he saw yesterday. Hell, he didn't even need to look at me to know that. He knew it even as I was walking out of his office a couple of days ago. Duke knew it too. My story was too short, it needed another chapter.

I've gone from calling God exclusively from fox holes to simply asking him for the strength to do what's right.

Chapter 38

Bronx Boy Gets Life

This time I'm here to ask for advice. Hopefully, use that advice to unlock the vice, so to speak. Desperate times call for desperate measures and I'm as desperate as a dog in heat locked in a kennel. I'm not sure what kind of advice they could possibly offer, but if they suggest jumping off a bridge I might do it. Short of telling me to go rat, which is completely out of the question, I'm doubtful there's much they can tell me. I say 'they' because Duke happened to show up shortly after I did, and Brother Brian, once again, has asked my permission to include him in part two of our discussion. Of course, I consented, I'd be both a fool and a coward not to.

After the "how are you doing, Jack?" and "what brings you here today, son," I cut right to the chase. I'm going crazy, I tell them, I can't stand it anymore. I can't sleep, I can't eat, I can barely put a sentence together half the time. I thought I'd feel better after talking to my mother and you guys, but I don't. I feel the same way that I have for the last couple of months. Shit, excuse my language, but my life is torturous. I know you won't believe me but sometimes when I'm on my motorcycle driving on the Grand Concourse, I get this insane, but very real, desire to jump the island and crash straight into the path of an oncoming bus.

Duke spoke first.

"We believe you, son. That's a painful way to live. It'd be an awful thing for everyone involved so I'm begging you to straighten this out before you leave this room. You'd not only kill yourself, but you'd also kill your mother as well."

Then Brother Brian.

"You wouldn't have come here today, Jack, unless you were searching for answers. Answers you can't find by yourself. Hopefully we can help. Duke is right, if you ever did something like that, and I am also of the opinion that you're not exaggerating what's going through your mind, you'd leave a trail of sorrow ten miles long. Add me to the list of those that would be altered for life. Time is running out to fix this and I'm not leaving your side until we do."

My turn again.

"What the hell am I supposed to do?"

"Think of that boy's mother," said Duke.

"Think of your own mother," added Brother Brian.

Thus ensued a small mountain of listening to advice coupled with a much greater summit of soul searching. We discussed the difference between right and wrong in all kinds of contexts. They peppered in the usual nuggets of wisdom like, 'doing the right thing can be really difficult, and feel awful while doing it. Your conscience is yours alone and can only be fixed by you. Dad even piped in from heaven, 'You know what's right, son, make me proud and do it. There's nothing worse than running from the truth.'

I knew what my plan was before coming to the Community Center. Maybe not consciously, but I still knew.

I'd like to think it was an innate goodness that brought me here. I wanted it to be mine to own but I also know that benevolence can be contagious. I'd caught their bug. The right thing needed to be done, and I needed to do the doing. A kid was dead, and his mother needed answers. My mother did as well. There's a risk factor in every equation that involves choices made. The tough guy in me dreaded the stigma of being labeled a squealer, maybe for the rest of my life. Stoolie and rat would be the nicest things they'd call me. Brother Brian and Duke would tell me afterwards that the 'real tough guy' was the one that did what I eventually did. What I finally did. It wasn't God who reneged on the original pact.

Thus was how things proceeded. I asked my two mentors to contact Detective Sullivan, the most recent angel in my life. Fortunately, I had kept his phone numbers. I told them I knew I could trust him. Like I keep saying, some things you just know.

The four of us met in an office at the 52nd Precinct. It wasn't Detective Sullivan's homebase, but it was the location that made the most sense. Once again, I went over the details from that night as I remembered them. I tried to leave nothing out and I'm pretty sure I didn't. My memory was crystal clear. It had been preserved in my nightmares from day one.

"You'll have to testify in a courtroom, you know that kid, don't you?" asked Detective Sullivan.

"I do, sir," I replied.

"It won't be easy, Jack," he added.

"Doing the right thing often isn't," I retorted. Brother Brian and Duke beamed at this comment. The boy was learning. Jack McGee was coming back to life.

The heat came down on Burns, Richie, and Billy. It didn't require a brain surgeon to figure out who had brought it on. All three were arrested and let out on bail. They'd have the full support of the community. They were the defenders, not the defendants. To most, there'd be only one bad guy in this drama.

Well, what would happen to them? Burns would no doubt skate through. The boy is bullet-proof, he's teflon. I don't know how I know this, but I do. He's him and that's all there is to it. Another easy prediction—I'd have some sworn enemies for life.

Richie? He'd be cited for parole violations and sent back to jail. Some kind of accessory to a crime charge. It wasn't his hand that did the stabbing. Every push-up and pull-up he does in the joint will be done with me in mind.

Billy? Well, that answer is easy. Billy is dead. He killed himself.

Hopefully he's home with his mom, pop and little sister, wherever that might be. I can't picture the guy in hell. His hell was on earth, he did his penance. That may sound callous to some, but I don't care. I just can't peg the guy as a monster.

Even in death his family came first. He did it on a park bench where no remaining family member would find him before someone else did. He did it with a naked upper torso, giving away the 'shirt off his back,' you might say. I think of that line from the Irish song about the man at the graveside of a war veteran he had chanced upon. "I hope you died quick, and I hoped you died clean, or Willie McBride was it cold and obscene?"

Billy used a dagger to kill himself. One of those decorative types that you might hang on a wall, with fake jewels and an ornate haft. It wasn't done for symbolism though. He used that dagger because it was made of strong, sharp steel. Kind of like the boy himself. He used it because it was the best tool for the job. It could be held with two hands instead of one, thus maximizing the force. In a sitting position, he took that dagger in both his hands and plunged it into his chest.

He was discovered still in a sitting position, his back pressed against the bench, his head tilted to one side. In death, as in life, he was expressionless.

Two dead. One from each side. Tie score, no overtime. No sudden death. As quick as they seemed, those deaths were years in the making.

They were proud of me, they all said. Brother Brian, Duke, Detective 'Rocky' Sullivan and, most importantly, my very own, blessed mother. The people that count the most you might say. Maybe there will be others, we'll have to wait and see, I guess. There will, no doubt, be plenty of others chiming in who will be considerably louder and appreciably less kind. I'll deal with them as they come. With the team I have at my back, I should be able to handle them, But again, maybe not.

Therein lies the legacy of young Jack McGee—rat or saint, boy or man?

Epilogue

I'll go with this for the time being—well, I sure as shit ain't no saint but it seems God may have finally returned my call. I think he might even have conferenced in my old man. My theory being that if the heavenly beings sprinkle down some pixie dust, even a punk kid can transform into a saint, if just for a while. And even a punk kid can become a man, maybe even forever.

But, I'll have a hell of a time shaking the rat from my brain. My life code was violated. Pretty funny, huh? Life code. Like Willie the Rogue, I brought my submarine to the desert. One dumb idea begets a dumber one in response. I've lived with dumb ideas most of my life. Contempt prior to investigation (look, one of them said it, I just can't remember which one. These guys have my head spinning non-stop). When you're judge and jury, the facts don't matter so I never considered them. Humbly down on my knees has always meant submission to me. I hear people pray like that. My verdicts have almost all come before the case was laid out. A red badge of courage in ignorance.

Brother Brian won't shut up with the 'grace of God' stuff.

Duke told me, 'Hey kid, I heard rats have tails and I'm sure as hell not seeing one on you. Besides, you can't be hiding with your tail between your legs if you don't have one to begin with. No sir, you're no rat. But I also heard that saints have halos and there's sure as hell a glow all around that handsome head of yours right this second. That son is the Gospel truth.'

The Gospel from the lips of a black man, I'll be damned.

Then the old gal told me, 'I've never loved you more than right this second.' If being a rat gets me all of this, I'll take it.

www.ingramcontent.com/pod-product-compliance
Lightning Source LLC
Chambersburg PA
CBHW070551100426
42744CB00006B/256